Racial Taxation

Racial Taxation

Schools, Segregation, and Taxpayer Citizenship, 1869–1973

Camille Walsh

The University of North Carolina Press CHAPEL HILL

This book was published with the assistance of the Authors Fund of the University of North Carolina Press.

Set in Espinosa Nova by Westchester Publishing Services

The University of North Carolina Press has been a member of the Green Press Initiative since 2003.

Library of Congress Cataloging-in-Publication Data
Names: Walsh, Camille, author.
Title: Racial taxation : schools, segregation, and taxpayer citizenship,
    1869–1973 / Camille Walsh.
Description: Chapel Hill : University of North Carolina Press, [2018] |
    Includes bibliographical references and index.
Identifiers: LCCN 2017021190 | ISBN 9781469638935 (cloth : alk. paper) |
    ISBN 9781469638942 (pbk : alk. paper) | ISBN 9781469638959 (ebook)
Subjects: LCSH: Educational equalization—United States. | African
    Americans—Education—United States—History. | Segregation in
    education—United States. | Taxation—United States. |
    Education—United States—Finance—History.
Classification: LCC LC213.2 .W26 2018 | DDC 379.2/6—dc23
    LC record available at https://lccn.loc.gov/2017021190

Cover illustration: *Clinton, TN. School integration conflicts* (1956) by Thomas J. O'Halloran (courtesy of the U.S. News & World Report Magazine Photograph Collection, Library of Congress Prints and Photographs Division, LG–DIG–ppmsca-03089).

Portions of chapter 5 were previously published as "White Backlash, the 'Taxpaying' Public, and Educational Citizenship," *Critical Sociology* 43, no. 2 (2017): 237–47. Portions of chapter 7 were previously published as "Erasing Race, Dismissing Class: *San Antonio Independent School District v. Rodriguez*," *La Raza Law Journal* 21 (2011): 133–71; in "Rodriguez in the Court: Contingency and Context," in *The Enduring Legacy of "Rodriguez": Creating New Pathways to Equal Educational Opportunity*, ed. Charles J. Ogletree Jr. and Kimberly Jenkins Robinson (Cambridge, MA: Harvard Education Press, 2015); and in "'The Poor People Have Lost Again': *San Antonio Independent School District v. Rodriguez* (1973)," in *Poverty Law Canon: Exploring the Major Cases*, ed. Marie Failinger and Ezra Rosse (Ann Arbor: University of Michigan Press, 2016). All material used here with permission.

For Peggy,
for all my teachers and my students,
and for all those who fight for public education and justice

Contents

Acknowledgments

I am a proud product of a public school education, and my ability to engage and be inspired by my teachers was the direct result of the public tax funds that paid their salaries, built my classrooms, and bought the textbooks that opened up the world for me outside my small rural town. I am also the result of the taxpayer money that fed, sheltered, and clothed me through much of my childhood from programs like Aid to Families with Dependent Children, as well as the federal grants and loans that allowed me to pursue higher education at public and private universities I couldn't have imagined existed as a child. Having spent much of my life as a "taxeater," I am compelled to first acknowledge the many people whose participation in a faceless system of public taxation gave me the capacity to grow, learn, and become who I am. This book is one small dividend from that investment.

My adviser, Peggy Pascoe, passed away shortly after she chaired my dissertation defense, and her wisdom and guidance on everything from research to revising to teaching to mentoring still reverberate with me every single day. She was an astonishingly generous and thoughtful scholar, mentor, and teacher, and this book is dedicated to her memory. I also owe an enormous debt of gratitude to my many graduate school teachers, mentors, and colleagues, including Ellen Herman, Joe Lowndes, and James Mohr, who each supervised me with grace and insight, and Chris Brooks, Matthew Dennis, Margaret Hallock, Torrie Hester, Elizabeth Medford, Daniel Pope, Elizabeth Reis, Veta Schlimgen, Martin Summers, and many others. Thanks to the Mellon Foundation, the Spencer Foundation, the University Club of Portland, the Risa Palm Fellowship, the University of Oregon History Department, and the Wayne Morse Center at the University of Oregon Law School for the community, research support, and camaraderie they provided.

I was fortunate to be a Jerome Hall Postdoctoral Fellow in Law, Society, and Culture at Indiana University's Maurer School of Law under the mentorship of Ajay K. Mehrotra and Michael Grossberg. Between them, they were experts in just about every field covered in my book, and their warmth, encouragement, and support cannot be overstated. Sadia Saeed and Jen Erickson were wonderful comrades in arms as we explored Indiana that year and worked to develop our book manuscripts and research agendas as scholars, and Jeannine Bell and Kevin Brown provided insight into the process.

My colleagues at the University of Washington–Bothell have been a constant source of companionship, camaraderie, and support for many years, and I feel fortunate to work at an institution where hard questions and critical thinking are our guiding light, and empathy and justice our foundations. Janelle Silva and Johanna Crane, thank you for toasting and cheering me on at every step, as well as for all the adventures, the commiseration, and the new things you always brought to the table for me to learn about research, teaching, and life. I also appreciate the incredibly generous camaraderie, support, and wisdom of too many colleagues to name, among them Wayne Au, Nancy Beadie, Dan Berger, Bruce Burgett, Charu Charusheela, Martha Groom, Dan Jacoby, Ron Krabill, Alka Kurian, George Lovell, Keith Nitta, Wadiya Udell, and so many others. The Royalty Research Fund at the University of Washington generously provided me with a summer free of teaching to focus on my research. Finally, thank you to the Interdisciplinary Arts and Sciences staff for endless support in navigating academic life; and to Joren Clowers for a terrific index.

I am very grateful for the guidance, patience, and support of the editorial team at the University of North Carolina Press, in particular Brandon Proia. Parts of this book have been presented in a number of forums, invited talks, and conferences, including Institutes for Constitutional History at Stanford Law School and George Washington University School of Law; Centre for Citizenship, Civil Society, and Rule of Law at the University of Aberdeen, Scotland; Workshop on Vulnerability and Education; Conference on Civil Rights and Education at Pennsylvania State University; Organization of American Historians Annual Meeting; American Historical Association Annual Meeting; Policy History Conference; History of Education Society Conference; Class Crits Conference; Social Science History Association; American Society for Legal History Conference; Lat Crit Conference; Critical Tax Theory Conference; Poverty Law Conference; Fiscal Sociology Workshop; Law and Society Association Annual Meeting; and numerous others. I would like to thank the organizers and participants of each of these events and panels for including me and discussing this work at various stages of development. Thank you in particular to Dorothy Brown, Mary Dudziak, Martha Fineman, Risa Goluboff, Kenneth Mack, Isaac Martin, Serena Mayeri, Monica Prasad, and many others for their insightful comments on my work at different stages.

I believed Harvard Law School to be a mythical place when I first arrived. In many ways, the institution bore out those assumptions, with everything from free ice-skating rinks set up in winter to boost our happiness, to quarters preplaced in the lockers of the library so that no one in those elite halls would have to search for change to use the lockers. I was lucky to meet Ramya Ravindran on my first day of orientation, and to share a house with her for the last two years of law school, when she regularly brought me down to earth and helped me clarify my ideas. Ann Blaylock has been a wonderful and generous friend since that first year and, along with Ramya, provided me with a home away from home, along with nourishing meals and company for countless research trips to archives in Washington, D.C., as a poor graduate student. Saru Matambanadzo has not only been my intellectual twin and confidante since the first year of law school, she has also unceasingly encouraged me to do things I might have never considered otherwise—starting with studying for a PhD. Thank you for dreaming big and seeing me as I am.

This book would not have been possible without my family and friends, starting with daily visits from Arya, who came in and sat next to my computer as I wrote, occasionally giving me subtle hints to stretch and pause for a head scratch. Momo and Leo reminded me that sometimes a walk outside in the sunshine could clarify a challenging idea. Mom, you inspired in me a commitment to empathy and justice that has given me a sustaining passion. My grandfather Albert fought against inequality his entire life and planted the seed for my life's work. Luke, you moved me into college, and again from college to law school; you told me I could go anywhere and be anything, and I owe so much in my life to your love, steadfastness, and support. Gareth, I pass the torch to you—it's in impeccable hands. Charles and Mary Walsh, and the huge and fabulous Walsh clan, thank you for so many holiday reprieves throughout my (seemingly endless) years of schooling— you showed me whole worlds I couldn't have imagined before. Thank you to all my wonderful friends, including Charlotte Garden and Owen Davies, for their unwavering support, loyalty, and willingness to show up with pizza and wine when needed or help me with random formatting questions. Erin McGladrey, Jake Spavins, and the entire, extended McGladrey family, thank you for the example of your commitment to public schools and students and your inclusivity to random outsiders. Robin (Bill) McGladrey was lost far too early, but I am grateful for the time I was able to spend talking to him about my research and teaching, as well as trees, animals, and justice, during graduate school. And for my dear Tim, who gave me a home, a garden in which to play, and the best corner of the office for me to do my work, I love you. Thank you for understanding all the times I had to turn down a hiking trip or a glass of wine to work on this project. Like all things, this has been a collective labor of love that would not exist without my community's support. Any mistakes are mine alone, but any insights are owed to a wide web of friends and intellectual mentors, past and present.

Racial Taxation

Introduction

Taxpayer Citizenship and the Right to Education

"But what on earth is whiteness that one should so desire it?"
Then always, somehow, some way, silently but clearly, I am given
to understand that whiteness is the ownership of the earth forever
and ever, Amen!

—W. E. B. DUBOIS, "The Souls of White Folk," in *Darkwater*

Legal interpretation takes place in a field of pain and death.

—ROBERT COVER, "Violence and the Word"

In the 2016 U.S. presidential election, the question of whether the Republican candidate, Donald J. Trump, had paid U.S. income tax became regular fodder for the news media. Based on pages from his tax records in 1995 that were leaked to the *New York Times*, there was speculation late in the campaign that Trump had very likely not paid federal taxes for many years.[1] Yet the unapologetic, winking response from the candidate was, as he said to reporters before and after the election, that "people don't care" about his tax returns, and, therefore, about his "taxpayer" status.[2] Trump spokesperson Kellyanne Conway announced immediately after his inauguration that he would not release his tax returns, despite a petition that had gathered several hundred thousand signatures calling on him to do so.[3]

New York Times op-ed author David Brooks took on the question of Trump's taxes a few days after the 1995 tax records were released, arguing that "you can be a taxpayer or you can be a citizen."[4] In Brooks's view, the two mentalities are mutually exclusive, the first defined by its individual self-interest and economic position, the second by a "larger desire to be part of a lovely world" in which "we all pull our fair share." While Brooks's description of citizenship is compelling as an idealized notion, this book will illustrate that the historical reality has been very different. Indeed, far from being mutually exclusive, the categories of "taxpayer" and "citizen" have been mutually constitutive, and together they have reinforced inequality through the hidden currency of whiteness that undergirds each term.

In the 2016 campaign, that currency of whiteness was on public parade. White supremacist groups were strengthened and legitimated by their embrace of the campaign of Trump and his "alt-right" advisers, and the groups' messages spread via social networking platforms and elsewhere online. A popular meme that circulated in the closing months of the election was taken from a series of 2012 voter maps drawing on electoral data from that year that reflected how different categories of voters would have impacted the presidential election in various states if *only* they could vote—the maps broke down groups by race, gender, and age and were originally intended to show the significance of universal suffrage in history.[5] The initial set of maps drew only on those categories that CNN asked about in exit polls in 2012, and extrapolated from the other state data to predict voting patterns in the twenty states that did not do exit polls.

But the meme was quickly taken one step further in the 2016 election, and the map showing only white voters began to circulate on white nationalist websites under the headline "What if Only Taxpayers Voted?"[6] The website Daily Pepe, named for the iconic image of the white nationalist right, republished the map under the title "What if Only Taxpayers (or White People) Could Vote?"[7] After claiming falsely that "90%" of taxpayers are white, the website then mused about the poll tax and asked, "Racial issues aside, perhaps we should be asking why non-meaningful taxpayers are even allowed to vote in the first place?" With increasing attacks on voting rights in recent years, it's notable that the romance between white supremacists and the Trump campaign played out in part through a fantasy of excluding presumed nontaxpaying people of color from one of the foundational elements of citizenship. And yet, Trump's own potential nontaxpaying status raised few concerns among his base of supporters, precisely because his whiteness already did the necessary work of symbolic citizenship. The story presented in this book suggests that Trump's presumptive status as a "taxpaying citizen" candidate was deeply rooted in the historical elisions between "taxpayer," "citizen," and "white" that have been deployed to help justify and alibi racial inequality.

The legal definition of "taxpayer" shifts depending on the jurisdiction and the claim asserted, but the popular and political usage of the term is vastly more fluid, to the point that the term has been emptied of almost any literal meaning and is often code for something else. So what do we mean when we say someone is a "taxpayer"? Does it mean the individual pays income tax at the state or federal level or both? Or Social Security taxes? What if the person paid Social Security taxes under a different name, such as with many undocumented folks who will never receive those payments back? Does it mean that the person has paid sales tax at some point on a soda from a deli or a cup of coffee at a café—and if so, can children be taxpayers? Are you a taxpayer if you have paid a premium on a good whose price was reflective of taxes along the production process (indirect taxes)? Does it require homeownership and the payment of property tax? What if a renter pays a higher rent because the landlord has transferred the burden of property taxes into the rental price—is the renter then a "property taxpayer"? Is the implication that "taxpayers" have paid more in (direct) taxes than they have withdrawn from public funds through services and support, and if so, how could such a ratio be calculated on a per-person basis? Or does the term simply suggest that the individual is part of a group (men, white people, adults, workers, documented residents, the wealthy) that is implicitly or symbolically somewhere closer to the center of an assumed social contract? And by always reiterating some group's centrality, what groups are left outside the circle of safety that the "taxpayer" label creates? In this book, I suggest that the deployment and popularity of the "taxpayer" identity category has helped coconstitute whiteness through its symbolic exercise in defense of exclusionary ideas. This identity has been tightly linked to the racialized entitlements to educational access and resources from the late nineteenth century onward and has helped to entrench a school finance system with differential levels of citizenship and rights.

"Taxpayer" sounds like a firm word. A word that is definitive, clarifying. You either are one, or you are not. You can either claim the identity or you are outside it. It's premised in numbers, surely, so it must be one of those comfortingly measurable identities, not like the fuzzy ones that many people claim vaguely, like "middle class" or "rich." And because the term sounds so simplifying, it calls to mind other definitive terms that can be used and deployed to claim rights—words like "citizen." I hope to show that the word "taxpayer" is anything but definitive, and in fact that it is a slippery term that is ultimately a rhetorical symbol rather than a substantive factual description. Sometimes the claims of taxpaying status can seem progressive—a dignitarian claim for taxpayer identity is very appealing on behalf of those who have been historically disenfranchised, and a communitarian approach might suggest that a community's symbolic entry into any taxpaying system, through members' work or property ownership, should suffice to protect the rights and privileges of all community members. Yet "taxpayer" has more often worked as a barely hidden code in service of white supremacy, patriarchy, and racial capitalism to define out the "nontaxpaying other," who is implicitly less entitled to protections and rights.

Taxes are the way we tangibly show our connection to strangers. They link us in a far-reaching social and political network of obligations to people distant from our personal communities. It is perhaps to be expected, then, that taxes have also been a contentious space in which the most fundamental debates have taken place about civil rights, justice, exclusion, and inequality. *Racial Taxation* explores the complicated and intersecting connections between race, education, and taxation in post–Civil War U.S. history. As such, it takes part in one of the central intellectual debates of the twentieth century, how we define our role as citizens and our duties to one another in a large and complex society. This book argues that the claim of "taxpayer" almost always has a hidden symbolic meaning premised in whiteness and has served as a currency of exclusion and inequality (whether supporting it or combatting it), particularly when that identity is deployed in discussions of the right to public education.

Public schools are a foundational institution in creating both rights and obligations as citizens and in solidifying an ideal of meritocracy and democracy. They have also been the site of a constant battle over race, rights, and taxes. After the Civil War, separate and racialized tax structures were set up to enable segregated schooling in the South and North. Astonishingly, nearly 150 years later, despite a few superficial adjustments—"separate" tax systems gave way to "color-blind" systems—those same systems of property-tax funding continue in most U.S. school districts, allowing and even facilitating the continuation of de facto segregated schools on the basis of resource inequality and access. In making this connection between taxpayer legal consciousness and equal education claims, courts both contributed to and reflected the disconnection between race and class categories in school finance cases. *Racial Taxation*'s argument engages with the work of critical legal histories both inside and outside the courtroom by locating many of these "taxpaying citizen" identities in personal letters, transcripts, and other sources produced by the people who were most affected, as well as by acknowledging the role of power—in particular the power of judicial pronouncements—to shape arguments, activism, and rhetoric.[8]

Taxpayer Citizenship and Equality

Both people of color and whites in the late nineteenth and twentieth centuries frequently described their right to educational equality (or inequality that favored one group) in terms of their identity as "taxpayers." For people of color, this right was usually to access education equal to that provided to white students. For whites, it was often the perceived right to access superior education, or "unequal" education, in comparison to the education provided to black and other minority students. This legal consciousness of "taxpayer citizenship" contributed to the erasure of the connections between race discrimination and class discrimination that would ultimately lead the Supreme Court to uphold separate and unequal education maintained through local taxation structures in *San Antonio Independent School District v. Rodriguez*.

The paradigmatic example of taxpayer identity and tax revolt today has become a white fiscal conservative opposed to federal income taxes, but this project traces the earlier entitlements by people of color as well as whites to taxpayer rights around schooling and education. The antitax backlash that this racialized framework generated among many whites would later be channeled by the Republican Party into racially coded opposition to federal programs such as welfare, but its roots can be seen in a broad sense of proprietary rights to public school funds.[9] Indeed, in tax politics, the embrace of "taxpayer rights" and suspicion of "taxeaters" is not a partisan position—as Molly Michelmore has persuasively shown, liberals instrumentally embraced the same conservative taxpayer rights rhetoric as the Republican right in the post–New Deal era.[10] The specific sense of white racial entitlement to school tax funds was also in evidence decades earlier, as illustrated by the late nineteenth-century Louisiana political slogan, "The whites pay the taxes and the Negroes go to school." It would ultimately come to the forefront as a way to defend segregation after *Brown v. Board of Education*.[11]

Many cases brought by African American activists and families from the late nineteenth and early twentieth centuries highlight the double taxation structures African Americans were subject to in mandatory segregation states, whether what I call separate taxation or "color-blind" taxation. This claim to taxpayer identity continued in the NAACP cases pressing for equal graduate school education from the 1930s until *Brown*, and then returned to the court and the political sphere through the rhetoric of segregationists after *Brown*. The claim for "equality" as taxpayers by segregationists was a claim for the right to access *better*-resourced schools, while those fighting segregation typically had a much more egalitarian conception of how taxpaying status "bought" entry into the marketplace of rights and citizenship. I describe the taxpayer citizenship approach of desegregation advocates as a "threshold" approach, in which reaching the basic threshold of minimum participation in taxation entitles an individual, family, or community to equal rights and resources. In contrast, the taxpayer citizenship rhetoric of segregationists—and the rhetoric so widespread today—is a "consumer" approach to taxation, in which public goods and services should be distributed and quantified specifically according to the level of tax contribution from the individual, family, or community. In the end, I illustrate how this claim to rights as a taxpayer would ultimately be reflected by a court that interpreted it through the lens of local control, fiscal conservatism, and racial invisibility, which served to maintain an unequal financing system.

As many historians have recently illustrated about race in the twentieth century, "taxpayer" identity was a category permanently in danger of losing hold of its own definition. Though status as a taxpayer is easily claimed for rhetorical and political purposes, it is deeply problematic and difficult to delineate as a legal category. This is a key reason why courts have overwhelmingly tried to avoid the question of taxpayer "rights" or "standing" in twentieth-century litigation.[12] Even a cursory exploration illustrates that "taxpayer" as a robust legal category could be both overinclusive (granting rights and standing to foreign corporations or travelers who pay some nominal tax) and underinclusive (potentially excluding those who pay hidden or indirect taxes in the form of higher prices or rents). Despite the consistent refusal of courts to recognize a strong form of taxpayer standing, the law helped produce this identity by first enabling the language of taxpayer rights in equity litigation brought on behalf of African Americans during Reconstruction, then shifting away from taxpayer litigation in the early twentieth century. In some ways, this made invisible the contributions that the black community was making at a time when the rights of African Americans were consistently under attack.

The idea that a child's right to educational quality, and equality, was closely tied to the parent's status as a taxpayer, and therefore class status, is clear throughout these sources, despite the questions raised by the unique position of children in any discussion of citizenship and rights. The notion that educational equality was a commodity that citizens were entitled to in proportion to their ability to pay for it both predated the New Deal and was particularly resonant in the area of educational access in the twentieth century.[13] The idea of education rights was particularly linked to taxpaying status in part because education was historically rooted in local tax levies and community decision-making processes and was thus tightly linked to the idea of individual and local "pay-in."[14]

While a legal consciousness of rights as deriving from taxes may seem practical, the construction of citizenship premised on the relative amount of taxation also strongly implies a concept of citizenship based on degree of wealth.[15] On the other hand, we could imagine a construction of citizenship in which the proportion of income devoted to taxation was the determining factor, which would generally tend to recognize lower-income, working-class people as "larger" taxpayers.[16] The "marketplace" notion of taxpayer citizenship, then, is connected to race- and class-based claims of citizenship, political authority, and rights. "Taxpayer" identity in the letters from segregationists to the Supreme Court was defined as white and middle class, while a "welfare recipient" was defined as black and poor.[17]

In part, this concept of racialized rights as directly responsive to the amount of taxes paid to the state correlates to the special position of market and exchange relationships in American history and life. In this "marketplace of citizenship," the amount an individual (or racial identity group) contributes in taxes should correspond to the amount and quality of rights and privileges he or she obtains from the state.[18] This view of taxation as corresponding to rights is also tied to an understanding of rights as an isolated reciprocal bargain between the individual and the state, rather than as a combination of entitlements and obligations connecting individuals to one another in a community. As legal scholars Stephen Holmes and Cass Sunstein point out, however, if rights are dependent on the rate of taxation, "then does not the rule of law hinge upon the vagaries of political choice?"[19] One of the contributions of my research is identifying the consistency between legal actors on both sides of the famous battles over segregation in asserting this ultimately exclusionary conception of rights, and articulating the ways this concept contributed to the failure of educational equality in courts.

While, from a broad perspective, virtually anyone who purchases anything, pays rent or the cost of utilities, or engages in a variety of other economic transactions "pays taxes" either directly or indirectly, it is precisely the way in which taxpayer citizenship was utilized as an argument for education rights by those who claimed it in the post-*Brown* era that made it a category of exclusion. Taxpayer status was and is an identity that can be deployed to both reflect and contribute to economic inequality. It is a structure that coheres class categories by sorting people based on wealth, perpetually implying an "other" who does not pay taxes and therefore has not earned rights. Property-tax-based financing or the separate funding of education has been historically constructed by the demands of separate, segregated school systems and later, in turn, residential segregation.[20] But it has also facilitated the continuation of educational and residential segregation at points in time when these systems were under moral or legal attack.

Particularly in the postwar era, taxation systems mediated segregation for white parents, especially in the North, providing an attractive rationale for moving out of more financially insecure school districts in order to send children to "better" schools. A rapid increase in the number of white home-owners thanks to the GI Bill and the Federal Housing Administration's home lending policies was now coupled with a growing sense that overt, statutory racial segregation was not entirely socially acceptable.[21] The assumed parental obligation to provide the "best" school possible via the property-tax-financed public school marketplace enabled parents to send their children to virtually all-white suburban schools without feeling directly implicated in a system of legal racial segregation. Because state and local tax structures, especially those used to fund public schools, were not modified or overhauled when federal taxation was reinvented during the New Deal, they were among the remnants of previously widespread systems of segregation to remain largely intact from the nineteenth century to the twentieth century. Indeed, local tax structures around education remain in many states comparable to their origins in the mid-nineteenth century, with votes on school taxes serving as "annual tests of legitimacy for the schools," tests to which other public services, such as the police and fire departments, are not subjected.[22] Property-tax financing has also served to solidify educational inequality based on wealth on a district-by-district basis and to construct a definition of "equality" that has been sharply at odds with what many children and families have experienced.

Historiography, Methods, and Theory

This work examines racial and economic inequalities as they were articulated and understood by those who fought for educational equality and those who defended the status quo of inequality, both rooted in an idea of taxpayer citizenship. In doing so, I rely on letters sent to courts, judges, and legal advocacy organizations to illustrate taxpayer identity and the legal consciousness of the "right to education"; newspaper articles and political documents to provide context and commentary; and briefs, depositions, and trial and appellate court opinions to trace how courts, lawyers, and legal discursive frameworks divided race from class and supported an ideal of equality and integration that in practice often became its opposite. This book combines and builds on insights from citizenship scholarship, civil rights movement historiography, political science, legal history, histories of educational policy, and critical race and class studies.

Citizenship studies have grown robustly in recent years. This project contributes to the connections between economic and social citizenship theory by tying educational equality litigation to taxpayer citizenship claims. In discussions of class and the economic basis for citizenship identity, Lizabeth Cohen and Meg Jacobs have persuasively argued that the twentieth-century United States has been a fertile ground for the identification of rights by and as consumers, an economic identity category that partially overlaps with taxpaying status.[23] The right to work in particular is connected with my discussion in this book of the identification of citizenship rights based on taxpaying status and an identity of "productive" citizen through property ownership, paid employment, or both.[24]

The linkage between the "obligatory" aspects of citizenship and the rights consciousness that is connected to them has been relatively understudied in the literature on citizenship.[25] Linda Kerber describes the connections nineteenth-century women drew between the obligation of taxation and access to the right to vote in "no taxation without representation" campaigns.[26] In a similar vein, Alice Kessler-Harris has argued that in the gendered contest for economic citizenship in the twentieth century, lines drawn between men's and women's ability to pay income taxes became important in delineating claims for access to rights.[27] The invocation of taxpayer status that I describe in the following chapters ties strongly felt rights of individuals and groups to the foundational obligation to pay taxes and traces the way in which the taxation duty was successfully racialized in the twentieth century. Indeed, political scientists and historians have both noted the development of a white, middle-class "tax revolt" in the late 1960s rooted in suburban homeowner identification, welfare resentment, and Nixonian party politics.[28] This book expands on the connections between earlier ideas of taxpayer legal consciousness and educational inequality in building the foundation for the political development of postwar conservatism and suburban politics.

Examinations of *Brown* are numerous, and this project engages with and builds on the critical scholarship that identifies some of the ways in which *Brown* failed to live up to its promise of desegregation and the right to equal education.[29] Litigation and equality claims in the North and West in the post-*Brown* period have now become especially important, as the resegregation of recent decades has been linked to the racialized poverty inherent in patterns of residential and employment discrimination. While these regions have traditionally been treated as less significant to the story of segregation, the major states in them—California, New York, New Jersey, Michigan, and Illinois—are in fact the modern sites of the heaviest incidence of school segregation, when measured by the number of schools with 99 percent or higher nonwhite student populations.[30] Focal cases in this book include key moments in the legal development of educational equality and taxpayer claims in Virginia, Missouri, California, Texas, New York, and many states in between.

Legal historians have also done valuable work examining the civil rights litigation strategies of the NAACP and its general organizational history and personalities.[31] There has been little examination, however, of the intersecting legal history of economic litigation and racial litigation in the realm of education. Here I will build on recent work on the importance of class in other areas of civil rights litigation in this period. Risa L. Goluboff's argument about the lost potential of the NAACP's labor litigation for combining claims of economic equality and civil rights provides a useful starting point for a further examination of the history of education litigation through the lenses of simultaneously race- and class-based arguments.[32] Kenneth Mack's work on the complexities of civil rights lawyering strategies in the decades prior to *Brown* also acknowledges the meaningfulness of economic equality arguments for many civil rights lawyers in the era of openness in the 1940s labor movement that Goluboff discusses.[33]

I have used a broad geographic and temporal scope in this book in order to trace the ways in which legal discourse and precedents have developed and built on one another. Courts are not isolated in their rulings by either time or space, and cases from the North in one decade often have their strongest ripple effect in the South decades later, and vice versa.[34] While following the argument of modern legal historians that law and society are interconnected, I focus specifically on the connections between the growth of legal rights to equal education, legal categorizations of race and poverty as separate, and the development and articulation of a legal consciousness as "taxpayer citizens" by people dealing with courts.

Taxation history and the history of public finance have been relatively understudied by historians, likely because of the ever-changing complexities of tax codes at the federal, state, and local levels.[35] The majority of tax histories focus on the emergence of the federal income tax in the twentieth century and its expansion during the 1960s.[36] The property tax as a tool of local funding has been even less discussed, though one historian has written an examination of the political and administrative history of this "worst tax" through the nineteenth century.[37]

Historians and political scientists have broadened our understanding in recent years about the way in which white pro-segregation conservatives and moderates deployed the language of federalism, privacy rights, "natural" ideas of race, economic conservatism, and location-based policies of exclusion.[38] Yet the way in which the specific identity of "taxpayer" was invested with legally imagined power and privilege by these same groups has been comparatively underexamined. While other work examining the threat of a "taxpayer revolt" from the 1960s on has focused mainly on the links between party politics and suburban taxpayers' anxiety as homeowners, this book argues that taxpayer identity was linked prior to the 1970s to a white legal consciousness that obscured class while hiding behind an imagined marketplace of citizenship.[39] And very few rights are as pivotal a marker of citizenship as the right to education. Thanks in part to its complicated entry language, tax rhetoric and politics has thus served as a color-blind alibi for racial inequality in public education, and elsewhere.

Ultimately, taxpayer rights language has concrete effects on the lives of those judged to be outside the taxpaying community. The word is useful precisely because it can serve multiple purposes—affirming the dignity or superiority of those to whom it is attached while simultaneously acting out discriminatory goals in seemingly neutral and even legal-sounding language. In 1960, Douglass Township, Pennsylvania, refused five African American foster children admission to elementary school, arguing that because the foster families were being paid for their board, the children were not legal residents of the district. According to a statement issued in the decision, though the board was "sympathetic" to the situation of the children, "it feels that its prime obligation is to the bonafide residents and taxpayers of the district."[40] While exclusion explicitly on the basis of race was no longer legally permitted, the language of exclusion is a slippery and powerful thing. It can easily take on the rhetorical cloak of freedom, rights, citizenship, dignity, or neutrality—and often the only way we can see who is being excluded is if we can trace where this language came from, and with what purpose and power it took hold of our imagination.

Chapter Overview

Chapter 1 introduces the early history of taxpayer litigation against segregated and unequal education from the post–Civil War era until the turn of the twentieth century. In these cases and opinions, there was a continual assertion of a legal identity as taxpayers by families of color, and I trace the way taxpayer citizenship became linked to the idea of a right to education in these families' arguments and claims, and even occasionally in the judges' opinions. Nonetheless, even the victories in many of these cases were in name only, as plaintiffs of color continued to struggle without adequate remedy after courts granted a superficial nod to their taxpayer claims yet continued to ignore white appropriation of virtually all school funding.

Chapter 2 examines a handful of pivotal Supreme Court cases brought against school desegregation at the turn of the century and the first few decades of the twentieth century. The *Cumming v. Board of Education of Richmond County* case in 1899 indicated a demand for equality on the basis of taxpayer status that was understood by the plaintiffs to be intertwined with race, a demand that was interpreted by the Supreme Court only in the language of taxation and federalism. This chapter also highlights regional variations and a number of cases brought at the height of Jim Crow segregation by people of color who fell outside the black-white paradigm, even if courts then imposed it on them.

Chapter 3 shifts to state and local court cases in the early twentieth century, many of which highlight the different unequal tax structures imposed in mandatory segregation states in the South. Whether separate taxation or supposedly "color-blind" taxation, I argue that these systems were deployed by all-white school boards and excise boards to ensure that black schools received a tiny fraction of the resources due them and that in many cases African Americans were doubly taxed for the support of white schooling. Finally, I examine the letters written to the NAACP in the 1920s and 1930s, as well as news articles and speeches illustrating the importance of the taxpayer claim made by many African Americans in this period.

Chapter 4 looks at the NAACP's strategies in fighting for desegregated graduate school education leading up to the *Brown* decision. The organization's legal strategy changed to center on integrated schools in the mid-1930s, but the early cases indicate the ongoing struggle to obtain equality from schools and the legal system through the legal articulation of taxpayer identity. In examining the cases that the organization brought from the 1930s to the 1950s, such as *Murray v. Maryland* and *Missouri ex rel. Gaines*, this chapter traces how the organization's legal strategy often centered on taxpayer status and taxpayer rights. Finally, I look at the way in which the *Brown* decision was rooted in legal theories that ignored or discounted economic and funding disparities and served to immunize white educational privilege against charges of inequality.

Chapter 5 examines how the responses to *Brown* in defense of segregation were consistently framed in terms of taxpayer citizenship and the rights of whites to unequal and better-funded schooling. In addition, this chapter identifies the tax-centric debate in Virginia in the era of massive resistance and the private school–state action questions raised in the wake of *Brown*, including its impact on tax-exempt institutions like Girard College in Philadelphia. This chapter builds on and combines the recently expanded historiography of the white backlash to the "long civil rights movement" by tracing the continuous assertion by segregationists of a legal identity as "taxpaying citizens." This rights claim drew deeply on the debate over whether taxation and education should facilitate equity or facilitate privilege, and the use of the taxpayer identity by segregationists anticipated the justification for unequal schools in the decades to come.

In Chapter 6, I focus on how demands for racial integration in education after *Brown* also frequently deployed citizenship-based activism to achieve their ends, from busing cases to the important, though brief, extension of civil rights litigation logic from education to poverty and welfare rights. In this decade the effects of the War on Poverty and welfare activism worked together to generate the first combined race- and class-based equal protection claims. Response to the poverty jurisprudence of the court was largely filtered through the language of whiteness and taxpayers' rights. Finally, I examine the *Swann v. Charlotte-Mecklenburg Board of Education* case in 1971 and the response of many angry "taxpaying citizens" to the thought of desegregation and busing. *Swann* was the high point for the judicial attempt at equalizing educational opportunities, even as the de jure/de facto distinction was beginning to break down.

Chapter 7 describes the culmination of the tendencies toward combining demands for recognition of class- and race-based discrimination in the early 1970s. Among a series of other similar cases, *San Antonio Independent School District v. Rodriguez* was a pivotal "taxpayer" case that shut the door on meaningful legal remedies for school inequality. The *Rodriguez* claimants were low-income children and families of color whose school district was dramatically unequal in comparison to the local, wealthy, white school district in the city. The court, however, treated the claims of race and class discrimination that the claimants put forward as separate and ignored the race claim in order to focus on class alone, which they dismissed as a category not entitled to constitutional protection. This chapter argues that the result of *Rodriguez* was directly tied to the idea that tax status—and therefore taxable wealth—was legitimately connected to educational rights and equality. The court's decision provided an anticommunist rationale for school tax funding inequality by defending capitalism, economic privacy, and local fiscal control against the intersectional claims of race and class inequality.

Finally, the conclusion briefly traces the repercussions of the project of taxpayer identity, whiteness, and legal racial liberalism in the post-*Rodriguez* era, looking at school financing cases at the state court level in the 1980s and 1990s, as well as partial victories for educational access, such as *Plyler v. Doe* in 1982. Recent taxpayer rights claims to "take back" school districts (and school funding) are a significant continuation of the same articulations of whiteness that pervade the history of property-tax-based school funding. In the end, I argue, the remaining high level of racial segregation and inadequate, unequal educational funding can only be remedied through a more integrated legal understanding of the historical connections between race and class, taxation, and inequality.

CHAPTER ONE

A Shabby Meanness
Origins of Unequal Taxation

In the decades after the Civil War, black education was frequently deployed as a political tool by white elites to rally poor and working-class whites away from potential coalitions by implying that tax funding for education was really "white" funding for black schooling, and that it would only encourage black resistance and rebellion. In her famous analysis of Southern lynch law in 1892, Ida B. Wells traced the classic excuses offered by the *Memphis Evening Scimitar* newspaper to justify lynchings, beginning with the narrative about protecting white women and moving very quickly to "the chief cause of trouble between the races," which the paper described as "the Negro's lack of manners." The *Scimitar* defended the violence in the city's history by blaming it on the black population and calling it "a remarkable and discouraging fact that the majority of such scoundrels are Negroes who have received educational advantages at the hands of the white taxpayers."[1] This belief in white taxpayer "generosity" and the "ingratitude" exhibited through African American resistance to structures of inequality and oppression helped crystallize a deeply entrenched sense of white entitlement to public school funding and spaces that would span generations to come.

This chapter introduces the origins of property-tax-based school financing and identifies the racialized nature of this funding system during the late nineteenth century. In addition, it traces the history of litigation against segregated and unequal education from the post–Civil War era until the turn of the twentieth century. Many of the cases on segregated and unequal education, which set the stage for the struggles of the NAACP and other organizations in the next century, were fought in Northern and midwestern local and state courts. One analysis has found eighty-two cases concerned with racial discrimination in schools filed from 1834 to 1903 in twenty states—almost all outside the South—and has concluded that blacks won in 55 percent of the cases in which a decision was rendered.[2] In examining the judicial reasoning employed in these decisions, the long-term effects of these cases, and the concrete remedies offered to litigants, my research indicates that the formal victory that appears in many of these lawsuits was in fact largely illusory and failed to either desegregate schools or, of more direct relevance to the nature of many of the lawsuits, obtain equitable tax funding through practical remedies.

One predominant aspect of litigation in this period was the assertion of a legal identity as taxpayers by families of color; taxpayer citizenship consequently became linked to the idea of a right to education, a trend that would continue to have ramifications in the next century. As taxpayers, these individuals and groups were asserting an identity that precariously balanced democratic and antidemocratic potential. Though there were more formal victories in taxpayer lawsuits than direct segregation attacks, the middle-class aspirational rights framework this legal strategy envisioned is illustrated by the cases discussed in the next chapter that were brought at the height of the Jim Crow era, invariably on behalf of wealthy, propertied people of color. Ultimately, this framework of taxpayer citizenship would redound to the detriment of low-income people of color seeking educational equality. But in this era, even in the cases in which parents and families won small victories against school authorities, courts were unwilling to grant broad forms of relief or effective remedies, thereby enabling local authorities to find additional or marginally varied avenues toward protecting inequality and a white supremacist educational funding structure.

The Origins of Local School Taxation

Tax support for education has been cobbled together somewhat haphazardly since the earliest days of the common school movement. Connecticut used proceeds from liquor licenses to fund schools starting in 1774. New Orleans licensed theaters in 1826 on the condition that they pay an annual amount toward school support. And New York began using state lotteries to raise large amounts for its schools in 1799, as did Kentucky, Delaware, North Carolina, Mississippi, Michigan, Louisiana, and Maryland in the ensuing decades.[3] Bank taxes were also used as a popular means to finance schools, which had the added bonus of helping to accustom people to the concept of public schools "without appearing to tax them for their support."[4]

This late eighteenth- and early nineteenth-century idea that a system of common schools could be maintained through license fees and other funds from land sales and lotteries was abandoned when it was seen how little they actually produced and how rapidly the population of most states was increasing.[5] This funding challenge led Northern states to begin to fight for direct local and county taxation for schools by 1830, carrying out "campaigns of education" to win over those who thought tax-supported schools might be dangerous and undemocratic.[6] A national system of educational financing was even briefly considered, and then abandoned, after the Panic of 1837.[7] One ongoing battle throughout the nineteenth century was over the elimination of pauper schools and the opening of public schools as free to all.[8] Even then, however, most schools in the North were segregated. The South was far behind the North in developing common schools—by the time of the Civil War, North Carolina alone had a stable system of public education—but the schools that did exist were solely for white students.[9] Southern educational exclusion would begin to change only during Reconstruction.

During the early period of Radical Reconstruction, Charles Sumner and other Republican allies founded the Department of Education in 1867, sought to enact a civil rights bill to outlaw school segregation, proposed massive federal aid to eliminate illiteracy, and attempted to amend the first Reconstruction Act to require Confederate states to create free and open public schools as a precondition to readmission to statehood.[10] Sumner argued that "you cannot give the colored child any equivalent for equality."[11] Though the Radical Republicans were ultimately unsuccessful on most of these fronts, they did add their voices to pressure for educational equality. Their main victory was in the establishment of the Department of Education, which was demoted and then promoted again in the coming decades to stand for a federal interest in education. In the language proposing and supporting the department's creation, the "natural right" to education for all the nation's children was invoked by many supporters.[12] In the end, however, it was in courts that much of the tension between white supremacy and black pursuit of educational equality and funding would receive a hearing, though with similarly mixed results.

The struggle over education in the late nineteenth century was primarily focused on the basic needs of building and obtaining any funding for schools for black children, after their categorical exclusion from education in the South for much of the century. One strategy used to circumvent straightforward equal funding by Kentucky, Maryland, Delaware, and Washington, D.C., after the Civil War was to apportion the school fund according to the real estate or poll taxes paid by blacks and whites. This creation of a racially distinct tax base was then emulated by other states and funds were assigned to white local officials to allocate as they wished, leading to large disparities in the funding of white and black schools.[13] By constructing a school financing system dependent on both property ownership and race that was centered in the hands of local officials, these Northern and

Southern states set up a structure that continues today in which educational services are treated as something that could and should be directly indexed to the amount of taxes paid, and therefore property and (at this time) race. This created what one historian has called "a double irony: expecting education to provide a meaningful substitute for power and then putting that education in the hands of the enemies of the powerless."[14] The system that directly linked taxation with education rights also, however, generated a legal consciousness that would manifest in the litigation discussed in the rest of this chapter, emerging out of the "resentment" felt by many African Americans toward the unequal distribution of school taxes.[15]

Some states did formally require equal expenditures for black and white schools for a time. Only in the South, however, where blacks were a significant voting bloc during Reconstruction, was anything close to formally equal expenditure ever achieved. Even then, this partial equality lasted only briefly during the 1870s and was often the combined result of Northern aid and "self-taxation" by the African American community.[16] South Carolina, for example, spent nearly three times as much per pupil in white schools as it did in black schools by 1895.[17] Similarly, Alabama went from spending $3.14 for a white pupil and $3.10 for a black pupil in 1890 to spending $10.07 per white pupil and $2.69 per black pupil on teacher salaries in 1910.[18] These statistics show how states chose to classify the expenditures, but they do not capture the entire picture of racially distributed school funds and the inequalities they represented.

Even within a framework of facially "equal" state expenditure, funding was regularly diverted to white schools by school board and county officials, who were almost uniformly white. Historians of school finance in the nineteenth century have argued that one of the key educational funding developments after Reconstruction was the appropriation by white schools of local black taxes and state funds formally earmarked for black schools.[19] Both of these techniques, Robert A. Margo argues, had the effect of increasing white school expenditures and lowering white school taxes, creating a particularly strong incentive to minimize spending on black schools where the black population was especially large in comparison.[20] Margo also suggests that whites may have felt an entitlement to appropriate these funds based on their perception of racial tax differentials, as exemplified by the popular antitax slogan at the time, "The whites pay the taxes and the Negroes go to school."[21]

Additionally, however, the history of the slave tax in many antebellum Southern states may have created a legacy of entitlement even among nonslaveholding whites, who had benefited from a system in which property taxes were very low thanks to the heavy subsidies provided from the slave taxes paid by the wealthiest third of the white population.[22]

As we will see in more detail in the next chapter, however, many wealthy blacks viewed their property and tax payments as linked to the right to education at least as much as whites did. Leslie Brown's examination of Durham, North Carolina, indicates that for many middle-class African Americans with property, they felt *more* entitled to education than whites since they were essentially under a double tax burden to disproportionately subsidize white schools while still providing resources for black schools.[23] Entitlement to education and to adequate funding was therefore cast in both racial and economic terms from the earliest public school taxation structures, and it was treated, sometimes on both sides, as a commodity that should be allocated on the basis of the amount of taxes paid.

Several attempts at federal aid to education were made after the Civil War. The Freedmen's Bureau was the first national organization that focused on the education of former slaves. Between 1866 and 1870 the bureau spent two-thirds of its funds on education, and it came under criticism from many in Congress for its "racial exclusivity" at a time when illiteracy among poor whites was also high. Supporters responded that the education provided by the bureau was, in a sense, compensation for the wages lost to African Americans through slavery, indicating the beginnings of a combined racial and economic right to education.[24] In fact, demand for education outpaced the ability of the bureau to build schools, locate teachers, and provide Northern aid—many freedmen in Virginia and Maryland were raising their own private funds even while paying taxes for white schools and in some cases were "building schoolhouses before teachers were available."[25]

In 1870, as the bureau ran out of funds, Representative George Hoar of Massachusetts introduced the Hoar Bill, which would have created a national system of education for white and black children alike, something that Hoar believed was an essential component of Reconstruction policy.[26] The system was to be funded by a federal tax and distributed according to population. After the Hoar Bill died, Mississippi representative Legrand Perce in 1872 introduced another bill for federal funding of education, this time from the proceeds of public land sales.[27] Though the Perce Bill passed the House and had the president's support, it failed to reach a vote in the Senate. Even after Democrats had regained control of much of the South by the 1880s, the Blair Bill to provide federal aid for education directly from the government treasury by taxing wealthier states to help support poorer states won passage in the Senate repeatedly before being defeated in 1890.[28] Legal scholar Goodwin Liu has argued that these bills illustrate a view of education among legislators as an inherent right of national citizenship that was at odds with the Supreme Court's unwillingness to interpret the Fourteenth Amendment's citizenship clause more broadly.[29] The uneasy tension between a popular assumption of education as a right of citizens and the reality of the constrained judicial interpretation of the Fourteenth Amendment would frame educational lawsuits throughout the next century.

"Fraud on the Taxpayers"

In the early 1870s a group of four Illinois taxpayers filed an injunction against the directors of their school district in order to prevent the directors from carrying on a separate school for children of color.[30] According to the Supreme Court of Illinois, the bill was originally filed to prevent school authorities from building a twelve-foot-wide and fourteen-foot-long schoolhouse exclusively to educate four children of color in the district. Before the injunction could be served, however, the building was finished, so the injunction was altered to prevent the directors from continuing to employ the teacher they had hired to teach the (now two) children of color. A schoolhouse had been built for the district three years previously on the same lot as the new building, and the appellees argued that there was enough room in the older building to accommodate all the children. The bill was filed by four people only described as "tax-payers of the district" who sought to prevent the directors from "a misappropriation of the public funds, in which, in common with the public, they have a direct interest."[31]

In January 1874, the Supreme Court of Illinois affirmed the trial court decision in *Chase*, finding in favor of the taxpayers. In the opinion, however, the court pointedly did not address segregation as a policy and anticipated the language that would be used by the Supreme Court in the decades of "separate but equal" established by *Plessy v. Ferguson* in 1896, stating that if there had been sufficient numbers of white and nonwhite students to provide separate and "entirely equal" facilities, that would have raised a different legal question.

The court went on to state that the conduct of the directors in this case, in keeping and maintaining a school for "three or four" children of color when they could easily be accommodated at the schoolhouse with other students of the district, "can only be regarded as a fraud upon the tax-payers of the district." Though the plaintiffs won their suit, the court made a point of establishing that, if it were economically feasible, separate but equal schools would not have raised the same legal problems. The dissenting justice wrote briefly that he found the directors' action within their discretion and that he did not believe their action "amounted to such an abuse of power as called for the interposition of a court of equity."[32]

For litigants, education as a right of citizenship was a common starting point, but the preferred mechanism to claim this right was through an assertion of taxpayer identity. Partly this was a result of the tradition inherited from the British legal system in which courts of equity—the courts commonly turned to in cases demanding intervention to restore justice—were locations in which taxpayers could press claims against their towns and municipalities. While the tradition of taxpayer litigation in courts of equity faded away with the modernization of the U.S. legal system by the early twentieth century, its legacy of "taxpaying citizen" identity has lingered much longer.

The role of courts of equity, and their distinctiveness from courts of law, is an important aspect of many cases brought regarding school segregation in this period. Equity courts, traditionally, were not bound by precedent in the way common law courts were. Equity courts were intended to serve the ends of fairness, which meant they had power to create practical remedies—for example, in a breach of contract case, the role of an equity court was to actually attempt to put the parties in the positions they would have been in had the contract never been breached. In the case of school segregation and inequality, equity courts were most often used for injunctions, which was another practical remedy intended to prevent an unfair action from continuing until a common law court could decide on the constitutional or statutory legality of the matter. Particularly for a citizen who felt treated unfairly by her government, equity provided an opportunity to claim a right to be heard. Equity would regain importance for remedies in the post-*Brown* decades, as discussed in the last two chapters, when courts granted injunctive relief to plaintiffs seeking affirmative desegregation of schools.

Indiana and White Parents' Rights

The cases of the 1870s were not uniformly supportive of either taxpayers' claims or goals of integrated schooling. In an Indiana case the same year as *Chase*, a man named only as Carter, an African American father of two and grandfather of two (all of whom lived with him), petitioned the court to issue a mandate compelling the directors and teacher of the local school for white children to admit the four school-aged children in his household.[33] The Supreme Court of Indiana in 1874 overturned the lower-court ruling, which would have enabled Carter to go forward with his complaint. In his lengthy opinion in favor of the school authorities, Chief Justice Samuel Buskirk elaborated his theory of constitutional interpretation in detail.

In an 1850 Indiana case that Buskirk utilized heavily in his opinion, a white taxpayer had brought suit against the trustees of the local school district for allowing African American children to attend school with white children. The African American children paid their own tuition and received no public money. The trustees fought the mandamus and won in lower court. In this case, *Lewis v. Henley*, the state Supreme Court agreed with the lower court's decision that the petition had not explicitly stated necessary facts, such as that the African American children were attending the school at the time of the application, and that the trustees had been notified and had refused to comply with the parent's wishes.[34]

By dismissing the mandamus petition on technical grounds, however, the main question presented by it was left unanswered, and the court decided to avoid "the labor of again presenting it" by going out of its way to rule on "whether colored children may be permitted to attend our public schools, paying their own tuition, where the resident parents of white children attending, or desiring to attend said schools, object."[35] In contemplating this question, the court asked itself why the legislature had excluded black children from attending public schools and concluded that "this has not been done because they did not need education, nor because their wealth was such as to render aid undesirable, but because black children were deemed unfit associates of white, as school companions."[36] This case was especially important in affirming legally that if a white parent objected to a child of color sharing a classroom with a white child—even if *no public funds at all* were expended on the child of color—white parental choice or preference would supersede black children's access to education. This premium placed on white access to class uplift through education and the "white veto" of black educational access continued to lurk behind judicial reasoning and school board claims in education segregation and inequality cases throughout the next century.

Indiana had also taken a complicated road in its support for public schools more broadly. The state passed a general school law in 1826, followed by an 1836 law that provided for compulsory township taxation of schools. The second law then became the chief election issue in the state in 1837, leading to its repeal.[37] Illiteracy after the repeal skyrocketed to among the highest in the nation, and the state constitution of 1851 again provided for school funding.[38] After the ratification of the Fourteenth Amendment, the state passed an act for taxation for schools in 1869. Prior to that act, assessment of school taxes was confined to the property of whites; afterward, all property was "taxed for the support of common schools without regard to the race or color of the owner of the property."[39] In part, this was a response to the petitions of black conventions in Indiana, such as the one in 1865 that resolved to ask the legislature for access to the public school fund.[40] In a supplementary provision to the 1869 act, the legislature specified that school authorities would use the funds to provide separate schools for white children and children of color. The Supreme Court of Indiana therefore asked itself whether that legislation was in conflict with either the state constitution or the U.S. Constitution.

As in the *Lewis* case, the court chose to find fault with the African American plaintiff, Carter, for failing to state his claim as specifically or legalistically as possible. In this case, Buskirk claimed that there was not an allegation that the school trustees had refused to provide the means of education for the African American children in the district. Carter had in fact essentially stated this in his claim by saying the authorities had neglected to offer any alternative to the white school to which the children were denied admission, but the court seemed willing to read as little into his petition as possible while offering the greatest benefit of the doubt to the school authorities.

In fact, Buskirk argued that, if there was a cause for complaint, it was *more* likely to be a complaint on behalf of *whites* based on unequal economic rights. Buskirk claimed that people of color received "their full share of the school revenue, although none of it may have been contributed by such class," and that they were entitled to receive their share of revenue "according to number" when districts could not be consolidated to form a school. He concluded by stating that this "privilege" is "not granted to the white class," though in this case the black students had no school in which to exercise the "privilege" of their individual share of revenue, rendering the revenue question somewhat moot.[41]

In making this decision, Justice Buskirk narrated the history of African Americans in Indiana in some detail, including an 1831 law prohibiting African Americans from residing in the state without first securing a bond approved by a township's overseers. Buskirk argued that it was "unreasonable" to suppose that the framers of the constitution, who had denied African

Americans the rights of citizenship, voting, testifying, jury service, and holding office and had also prohibited residency within the state, had intended to provide education for African American children alongside white children in the common schools. Saying that the court would not pass on whether such policies were "wise or unwise" and that they would speak of it "only as a matter of history having a bearing upon the construction of our constitution," Buskirk went on to argue that a cardinal rule of constitutional construction was for courts to give effect to the intent of the framers, as well as to harmonize any portions that conflicted with one another in favor of the intent of the instrument as a whole.[42] In a decision that one historian has likened to the United States Supreme Court's *Dred Scott* case of 1857, Buskirk concluded that blacks were not citizens of Indiana for the purposes of the 1851 state constitution.[43]

> There is but one construction which will preserve the unity, harmony, and consistency of our state constitution, and that is, to hold that it was made and adopted by and for the exclusive use and enjoyment of the white race. Any other construction would convict the members of the constitutional convention and the voters of the State of the grossest inconsistency, absurdity, and injustice. It would be monstrous to hold that the framers of the constitution in adopting, and the voters of the State in ratifying it, intended that the common schools of the State should be open to the children of the African race, when, by the same instrument, that portion of such race as then resided in the State were denied all political rights, privileges and immunities.[44]

Referring to the Supreme Court decisions in *Slaughter-House* and *Bradwell v. Illinois*, Buskirk held that the privileges and immunities clause of Article 4 did not compel the state to allow a citizen from another state to exercise the same rights he had in the state from which he moved.[45] Finally, after a lengthy inquiry into constitutional history and interpretation prior to the Civil War Amendments, Buskirk reached the Fourteenth Amendment. Citing heavily to Justice Samuel Miller's opinion in *Slaughter-House*, Buskirk agreed that the Fourteenth Amendment provided no specific protection for citizens of an individual state or indeed any specific grant of citizenship in a state. Relying on its own opinion in *State v. Gibson*, an interracial marriage case, the court thus reaffirmed its interpretation of the Fourteenth Amendment as granting no authority to the federal government to regulate or control the domestic institutions of a state.[46]

Buskirk interpreted the clause in the 1869 school taxation act providing that schools must be "equally open to all" to mean schools must be equally open to those who were entitled to receive instruction within the schools. Buskirk stated that it was "very obvious" that the phrase "equally open to all" should not be taken literally. Buskirk argued that common schools need only be open to a class of persons designated by the legislature, and not equally open to "everybody, nor to every child." If the phrase were interpreted literally, he argued, it would include all the people of the state, including infants, middle-aged people, the "septuagenarian," and the married.[47]

Separate schools, he insisted, did not amount to a denial of equal privileges to either white or black children.[48] If separate schools could not be provided for children of color because of their small number, he stated, "such other provision is to be made by the trustee for their education as the means in his hands will enable him to do." Buskirk added that since the legislature did not specify the means and the complaint did not aver that the trustee had failed to provide education for the children outside the school for white children, the court could not address the question of what compliance would look like. In response to the *Carter* decision, the Republican Indiana General Assembly in 1877 provided that if a school district did not operate a separate school for black children, they would be allowed to attend white schools, but the ultimate principle of separate schools as "equal" that Buskirk had argued for so adamantly continued to be practiced by local officials and school boards in Indiana and elsewhere.[49]

Taxation Equality and Educational Equality

Decided the same year as the Indiana school taxation act Buskirk dismissed, the *Workman* decision out of Michigan in 1869 was a significant victory for equal education. Joseph Workman's child was described by the court as a "mulatto" who applied for admission into the Duffield Union or Tenth Ward school of Detroit in April 1868 and was refused.[50] There was room for the child at the school, and Joseph Workman asserted that he resided and owned property in the city of Detroit and paid taxes there, including school taxes. In this case, despite the availability of separate schools in other wards of the city, the court granted the father his writ of mandamus in an opinion written by Judge Thomas Cooley. Workman's claim rested on an 1867 Michigan law that provided that "all residents of any district shall have an equal right to attend any school therein."[51] The court in fact was relatively dismissive of the argument that there could be any exclusion with this act in place.

Cooley wrote that it could not "seriously be argued" that with this law in place, any school district could "exclude any resident of the district from any of its schools, because of race or color, or religious belief, or personal peculiarities." Cooley went on to state that "it is too plain for argument that an equal right to all the schools, irrespective of all such distinctions, was meant to be established."[52]

The concurrence by Judge James Campbell argued that the 1867 statute was improperly inserted in the case by the majority and that there were too many variations in the rights of attendance in Detroit schools generally, which this petition simply brought to light. But Campbell argued that otherwise there would not be a case for relief, because the original act of 1841, which required—or at least allowed—separate schools for children of color, would still be in effect. For example, a clause in the 1867 act that gave nonresident taxpayers without schools at home the right to send their children into districts where they were taxed "has tended to make some confusion in the popular mind touching the relative rights of others." Because of the confusion about the "rights of taxpayers in the schools," Campbell decided it was proper for the court to make some explicit declaration, "for no rule of exclusion could be more odious, and none less likely to be sanctioned, than one which should operate against those who, from poverty, were most in need of public aid."[53] Campbell was unwilling to rule against racially segregated schools, but he agreed with the majority that bureaucratic inconsistencies—particularly around taxpayer rights to education—endangered the rights of poor taxpayers and led to confusion.

Workman highlighted for many litigants the power that making a claim as a property owner and taxpayer could potentially have. In a case that reflected the ideals of equal access in the *Workman* decision, Susan B. Clark, twelve years old, of Muscatine, Iowa, brought suit in 1868. Her father, Alexander Clark, who was described as a "resident freeholder and tax payer" in the city for many years, litigated on her behalf.[54] She lived near a neighborhood school in the independent school district organized in the town. Clark brought suit to require the defendant school district to admit her to the white school. The defendants responded that there was a separate school for children of color "in a comfortable building" and that "public sentiment in said independent district is opposed to the intermingling of white and colored children in the same schools, and the best interests of both races require them to be educated in separate schools."[55] Judge Chester Cole wrote the majority opinion, asserting at the start that "in view of the principle of equal rights to all, upon which our government is founded, it would seem necessary, in order to justify a denial of such equality of right to any one, that some express sovereign authority for such denial should be shown."[56] Cole held that the directors had some discretion, but that discretion was limited by "the equality of right of all children" between certain ages. He drew an analogy to Irish or German children, or Catholic or Protestant children, saying that it would not be competent for the board of directors to require these groups to attend separate schools.

He also introduced an analogy to separation based on class, stating that "if it should so happen, that there be one or more poorly clad or ragged children in the district," and public opinion was opposed to their attendance at school with wealthier, well-dressed children, "it would not be competent for the board of directors, in their discretion, to pander to such false public sentiment, and require the poorly clothed children to attend a separate school."[57] Cole continued his analogy to other groups throughout the opinion, arguing that if the words "colored race" were replaced with "English," "Irish," or "German," the same principle would be at issue. Not only would such a limitation of right based on nationality violate "the spirit of our laws," he asserted, but it would also tend to perpetuate national differences and stimulate "a constant strife, if not a war of the races."[58] He concluded that "all the youths are equal before the law."[59] The dissent offered a different interpretation of equality, arguing that the principle of equal rights did not require "that all children of the district should be taught in the same building" but that all had access to "equal school privileges."[60]

While the Iowa and Michigan cases showed promise for equal education claims, cases in New York at this time, like *Dallas*, were consistently pro-segregation. In an 1883 New York case, Theresa B. King, age twelve, had attempted to enroll in a white school in Brooklyn that was closer to her home than the school to which she was assigned.[61] John Gallagher was the principal of the white school. She was refused admission and petitioned for a writ of mandamus to compel admission, which the lower court refused. The court of appeals affirmed the denial of mandamus and held that the local board of education had full authority to maintain separate schools. Chief Justice William Ruger wrote the majority opinion, which extensively praised segregated schools, and claimed that if the argument of the appellant were followed out to its legitimate end, it would also forbid all classification of pupils in public schools founded on distinctions of sex, nationality, or race, which "are essential to the most advantageous administration."[62]

Judge George Danforth dissented, arguing that the case was brought within the spirit and meaning of the Fourteenth Amendment and that King was entitled to be treated the same in the realm of education as she was treated in the realm of taxation.[63] Contrary to the argument of Gallagher and the majority opinion that King would have all the same accommodations and facilities at the school for children of color as she would at the white school, Danforth argued that there was no legal provision that children of color would have "equal or similar accommodations" as white children, "but that she shall not be excluded from any accommodation, advantage, facility, or privilege."[64] Noting that the state was willing to "gather to its treasury" a taxpayer's money "without inquiry as to his color," Danforth argued that it "with like indifference" would accept his vote, subject him to laws, and provide educational opportunity.[65] Danforth put forth the logical but, for its time, radical notion that the equality of taxation as enacted on all residents demanded the equality of other government services as well, regardless of the amount of taxation. In response to the opinion offered by other judges that the discrimination in this case was supposedly in favor of children of color such as King, Danforth responded succinctly "that question may well be left to the child itself."[66]

Racial Construction and the Right to Whiteness in Ohio

Racial construction by school boards and courts was part of the process of establishing the supposedly strict separate schools color line and distributing tax financing accordingly even before the Civil War. The power of judges and white school officials to sort and categorize individuals into simplistic racial groupings often determined a child's educational opportunities. In an 1833 Ohio case, *Williams v. School Directors*, the Ohio Supreme Court chastised a school board for the "shabby meanness" of taxing a "citizen and householder" for the support of common schools, and then excluding his children from the benefits.[67] Racial categorization played an important role in the *Williams* court's defense of taxpayer rights for "white" children. The court in that case noted that "color is very unreliable," and that "it is blood and not color that incapacitates."

The plaintiff in *Williams* was "a citizen, householder and taxpayer of the district for five years," with five children over five years old who were excluded from the school. In part due to his taxpayer and householder status, the court decided to ignore that he was "one-quarter negro" and pointed out that the children's mother, his wife, was "a white woman." Judge Ebenezer Lane, in his opinion, stated that "we think the term white, as used in the law, describes blood and not complexion, and are satisfied with the construction heretofore given. The plaintiff's children, therefore, are white, within the meaning of the law, though the defendants have had the shabby meanness to ask from him his contribution of tax, and exclude his children from the benefit of the schools he helped to support."[68]

In the wake of *Williams*, an Ohio law of 1848 provided for the organization of separate schools for children of color. However, these schools were funded only from a tax levied on people of color and included none of the common school fund, which both white and black taxpayers paid into. In Logan, Ohio, in 1859, Enos van Camp, "a resident householder and taxpayer," petitioned for two "white children" in his house to be admitted to schools, his son and his indentured apprentice.[69] They were refused, and the board of education disputed that the children were white, stating that "the plaintiff is a colored man, being of nearly one-half African blood, and being distinctly colored, and so understood and treated in society, and by the community generally." Additionally, the board made similar statements about the plaintiff's wife, his son "having considerable African blood," and his apprentice. The next chapter will discuss other key cases brought in later decades that questioned the supposed consistency of racial categorization and one-drop rules.

The defendants also stated that the schools organized in the town were for white children alone, that the number of children of color in the district had not ever exceeded ten, and that the money raised on all people of color was reserved by the defendants to be appropriated for the education of the children of color. But no separate school for children of color had yet been instituted in the district.[70] The law of 1853 was, according to the majority opinion in favor of the school board, "conceived in a more liberal and patriotic spirit" by "no longer restrict[ing] them to the miserable pittance collected from the colored tax-payers."[71] Describing the law as therefore "one of classification and not of exclusion," the majority ultimately argued that courts would be of limited value in eliminating "the natural repugnance of the white race" to associating with blacks.[72]

After the *Van Camp* case, in 1871, William Garnes and his three children lived in the township of Norwich, in Franklin County, Ohio, which had just one public school. The children attended this school, but the teacher, under the direction of the school directors, "wholly neglects and refuses to impart instruction to them, or treat them as scholars, and denies them the educational advantages of the school."[73] A separate school for children of color had been set up in a joint district, farther away from the Garnes family than the school for white children.

C. N. Olds argued for the county school directors, claiming that since the *Van Camp* decision of the 1850s, the law had been amended and made "more liberal" and that the school for children of color "is, in fact, equal in every particular, if not superior to the one established for white children." Olds compared himself to the father in the case, asserting that "he has every right and privilege under the school laws of this State that I have." According to his argument, the only difference was that Olds would be required to send his children to one schoolhouse, and Garnes was required to send his to another, leading Olds to ask, "Is that discrimination in his favor or mine? Who shall decide?" He went on to say that "in defining the rights of citizenship ... we do well to remember that social equality is not one of the elements of citizenship."[74] This distinction between social and formal legal equality would later be championed in the *Plessy* case by the impassioned dissent of Justice John Marshall Harlan.

Judge Luther Day refused Garnes's request for a writ of mandamus, deciding the case solely on constitutional grounds since he asserted that both classes of children "enjoy substantially equal advantages in different schools."[75] Day argued that the plaintiff could not dictate where or by whom his children would be instructed without "obtaining privileges not enjoyed by white citizens." Ultimately, Day found that "equality of rights does not involve the necessity of educating white and colored persons in the same school, any more than it does that of educating children of both sexes in the same school, or that different grades of scholars must be kept in the same school."[76] Again, the idea that equality for African American students would necessarily imply a privilege "not enjoyed" by white students would become a mainstay argument for those guarding unequal schools and resources throughout the next century.

Kentucky and the Losses of Winning

State tax policies themselves also came under direct attack in many cases, marking the way a victory in court might lead to no change at all in the actual funding of schools. The State of Kentucky had, in separate enactments in 1871 and 1880, authorized the City of Owensboro to assess an ad valorem tax, not exceeding thirty cents on each one hundred dollars' of property, and a poll tax, not exceeding two dollars on each resident of the city over twenty-one. The tax was specifically for the public schools of the city; the taxes of whites were to be used for sustaining public schools for white children only, and taxes of people of color were only to be used for schools for children of color. The state also authorized Owensboro to issue $30,000 of bonds and apply the proceeds of the sale to building public schoolhouses in the city for the exclusive use of white children, only taxing whites to pay these bonds and their interest. There were five hundred or so children of color and eight hundred or so white children in the city. The taxes assessed in 1882 on whites came to about $9,400, and those assessed on blacks amounted to $770.[77]

The white children of Owensboro had "two excellent school-houses, excellent school facilities, 18 teachers, and a school session of 9 or 10 months in each year." The African American children, on the other hand, had "only one inferior schoolhouse, three teachers, school facilities of every kind very inferior to those of the white children, and a school session of about three months in each year."[78] Judge John Watson Barr, writing for the court, contemplated whether the children of color could sue for their individual share of the school fund, but found that they could not, since there was no undivided share. According to Barr, "all the colored children in Owensboro are entitled to is the equal protection of the laws," which meant that their only remedy was in equity.[79]

But in a follow-up case in equity the next year, trustees of the nonwhite schools filed action against the City of Owensboro to enjoin the city from excluding nonwhite schoolchildren from all the benefits of the taxes raised under the act of 1871.[80] The court held that it had no authority to order the payment of any of the money to the trustees of the nonwhite schools because there was no legislative enactment authorizing such a use, but they enjoined the city from paying out a certain proportion of the money raised. Ultimately, the children of color in Owensboro did not receive a coequal proportion of the school fund, despite receiving, according to Judge Barr, "the equal protection of the laws." The separate taxation laws of Kentucky, which continued to come under judicial scrutiny for decades, are discussed further in the next chapter.

In other taxation cases that came out of the South, the courts sided perfunctorily with the African American plaintiffs, but no remedy was actually granted. When an Arkansas school district built two schools but only hired a teacher for the white school, the court agreed that the directors were required to provide and maintain a school for each race.[81] In that case, however, since there were only three months left in the school year, the court found it "doubtful" that a teacher would be found and the school opened in the remaining time, and dismissed the case. And in Gaston County, North Carolina, in 1886, county commissioners held an election for an additional property tax to increase educational advantages for white children of the district, an election in which black electors were not allowed to vote.[82] The court held that the provisions of the act were indeed unconstitutional because they were not uniform in their operation on taxable property and persons, and they marked a color line among qualified voters discriminating wholly based on race. The court held that this conflicted with article 9, section 2 of the state constitution, which provided that education was to be separate yet equal. The tax, however, had already been levied, so the court dismissed any possibly remedy in the case as moot. Again, winning a case formally might mean nothing substantive would change in the actual funding and resource distribution in the school system.

In an 1892 decision rooted in the rights of taxpayers to equal education, the defendant city barely bothered to put forward an argument, simply stating that "the main controversy involved is too well settled to need argument." In section 5 of "An Act to Amend the Charter of the City of Brookhaven," approved February 17, 1890, the city board of Brookhaven, Mississippi, was authorized to issue bonds of no more than $15,000 for sites, buildings, and furniture for public schools, providing that $3,000 of that could be used for the school for children of color and the rest for white schools. Rather than arguing against segregation, the appellants argued that the separate education of the races "upon equal terms at public expense" was "to be commended." However, the act itself suggested that children of color did not receive equal advantages. The Mississippi Supreme Court affirmed the chancery court's dismissal of taxpayer Chrisman's bill.[83]

When the Mississippi Supreme Court, through Judge Josiah Campbell, attempted to interpret article 1, section 21 of the state constitution of 1869, he stated, "We confess we do not know what its purpose was." Rather than prohibiting distinctions based on race or previous condition of servitude, he argued, "it prohibits *any* distinction, on any ground, for any cause, no matter what, among citizens. It surely does not mean that."[84]

Kentucky's taxation policies were litigated regularly. The Davenport children, through their parents, filed suit against the town of Cloverport, Kentucky, in 1896 for an injunction requiring the town to disburse equally the money collected under Kentucky's 1876 taxation act.[85] The court ruled that there was no constitutional authority for the levy of the tax at all. District Judge Barr found that the act was unconstitutional because "the whole purpose of this act seems to be to raise money by taxes upon the property of white people alone, for the benefit of white children of school age exclusively." That holding, however, meant that the proceeds, which were by then in the hands of the treasurer of the board of trustees, could not be controlled by court order. Ultimately, this meant that once again the court refused to grant anything to the complainants and dismissed their complaint.[86] The victory on technical constitutional grounds may have felt less than helpful to the Davenport family.

Whether North or South, as we have seen, most of the cases protesting segregation directly were lost, despite the repeated assertion of the taxpayer's right to education in any public school. Some scholars have suggested that blacks in the late nineteenth century won all the cases they brought protesting separate taxation, with more mixed results in cases arguing that black schools were unequal.[87] But the taxation cases in this period were often deeply intertwined with issues of unequal funding in racially segregated school systems, and thus were far from overwhelmingly victorious. In fact, though courts may have technically declared separate taxation principles invalid in many cases, the customary practice of racially labeling tax monies and diverting the bulk of tax funds overwhelmingly to all-white schools continued well into the twentieth century, as will be seen in later chapters.[88] The use of the language of equality could formally recognize resource and taxation disparities even as it denied a remedy on the ground and left schools—and communities—in much the same condition as before. Courts maintained and guarded racially uneven expenditures by failing to provide relief even in cases where the African American litigants formally "won" on the merits.

Conclusion

The cases from the latter half of the nineteenth century vary in their outcome. It can certainly be argued that the law was often a space of victory in school cases for people of color in this period. Yet there were also a number of cases in which courts nominally sided with African American plaintiffs but were able to dismiss any remedy as moot, particularly when tax funds had already been (unconstitutionally) collected and (unconstitutionally) distributed. Victory without remedy was hollow, and each victory required a litigant to spend time and money and perhaps risk personal safety in order to pursue the case. Courts were also a place in which the legal foundations for unequal schools were being worked out even as claims to equal education based in taxpayer status were repeatedly asserted. Ultimately, by the end of the nineteenth century, black education had progressed substantially, but the majority of the accomplishments and facilities were either provided by the black communities themselves or wrung from an unwilling state.

In pursuing the "coveted possession" of education, African Americans in the late nineteenth century pursued multiple strategies, from taxpayer funding litigation to direct challenges to segregated schooling.[89] Courts placed the litigants' claims in the context of equal protection and grand narratives of equality before the law, but more often than not they found that the individual demands fell outside the scope of their narrow interpretation of the Fourteenth Amendment. Judicial reasoning also highlighted the weight that would continue to be placed on the "white veto" of black educational access or funding and the power of judges to sort complex individuals into binary racial categories implicitly linked to wealth, property ownership, and taxpaying status. We will continue to see shifting strategies in equal education litigation and taxpayer citizenship, as well as the way in which claims to taxpayer rights to education ultimately facilitated the hardening of lines between race and class categories and the embrace of middle-class-focused litigation strategies for educational access.

CHAPTER TWO

Let Them Plow

Beyond the Black-White Paradigm

One of the only cases to reach the U.S. Supreme Court on school desegregation in the early decades of the twentieth century was *Gong Lum v. Rice* in 1927.[1] Martha Lum was nine years old when her father, Gong Lum, a well-to-do Chinese grocer, attempted to send her to the white school in Rosedale, Mississippi in 1924. She was refused admission by white authorities. The claim made by Lum's attorneys in their lawsuit was that Martha Lum was wrongly listed by white school officials as a "colored" child and sent to the African American school.[2] The lower court agreed that Martha Lum should be allowed to attend the white school, but they were overruled by the circuit court. Lum's attorneys argued that the "petitioner's father is a tax payer" and thus entitled to attend the common school funded from both poll taxes and additional local tax levies.[3]

Gong Lum also asserted repeatedly that "the right to attend said school is a valuable right" and that attending the white school was itself a property right. The Mississippi Supreme Court, however, argued that because intermarriage between "whites" and "Mongolians" had been illegalized in 1892, school segregation would be presumed to follow a parallel track, even if the statutes only classified students as "white" and "colored."[4] The Lums appealed to the Supreme Court without success. Citing *Cumming*, *Plessy*, and *Roberts v. City of Boston*, the unanimous Supreme Court decision held that Martha Lum's exclusion from "schools supported by state taxation" was within the power of state authority and did not violate the Fourteenth Amendment.[5]

While the previous chapter focused on judicial reasoning, this chapter draws from a smaller number of cases in which taxation and school funding were linked to assumptions about class, whiteness, and racial construction. The claims in some cases came from individuals with diverse racial identities that were swallowed up and made invisible by the far-reaching black-white paradigm of Jim Crow–era politics and judicial reasoning. Some of the arguments for taxpayer entitlement to education were made by propertied people of color inside or outside the black-white paradigm, those who would demonstrably benefit from a system recognizing rights distributed based on level of taxable wealth, such as Gong Lum. But other arguments were made by those who were struggling to find a language to fit their hopes for educational equality, and for whom the middle-class language of taxpayer respectability may have seemed the best option to frame that goal.

Yet the claims of people of color to taxpayer rights frequently failed, or won Pyrrhic victories, precisely because "taxpayer" was always already code for whiteness in the political imagination of those in power. And it is perhaps no accident that the ability to bring claims as a taxpayer was sharply curtailed in the same period in which more and more groups (women, African Americans, immigrants) were able to lay claim to that status. Even as courts occasionally expressed sympathy for the taxpaying rights of litigants in various cases, the precariousness of their claims to legitimate citizenship was always rooted in the power of white community members, school officials, and judges to deem them "other" and exclude their children from the benefits they were helping to fund. This "white veto" was virtually always more powerful than the claims of legitimacy emerging out of taxpayer identity.

Class, Race, and the Rights of Taxpayers

In late October 1899, Joseph W. Cumming, James S. Harper, and John Ladeveze, black parents of teenage girls in Augusta, Georgia, came before the U.S. Supreme Court in search of equal justice.[6] Their daughters were of high school age, but Ware High School, the local high school for black students, had been closed in 1897 by the school board. The white high school for girls remained open. The board claimed the closing was due to lack of funds, though it was also likely because the black school offered professional training and a liberal arts curriculum rather than solely trade and industrial education.[7] Indeed, Ware High School was considered a source of pride and potential social mobility by the black community.[8] The black community had made heroic efforts to financially support the school on its own between 1867 and 1872 after the Freedmen's Bureau ended operation and before dual school system laws were passed in Georgia.[9]

In 1880, black community members presented a petition to the school board asking for a high school, a request that had been repeatedly denied. In this petition, the black community offered to self-tax by paying ten dollars per year for each student at the potential black high school. This was the offer that the school board finally accepted.[10] The county school commissioner Lawton B. Evans, elected in 1882, was initially supportive of Ware High School and the instruction it offered. By the late 1890s, however, he began to indicate that he considered the job of public schools to be the education of blacks for "industrial" pursuits, as opposed to the leadership roles that the more academically focused Ware seemed to train for.[11]

The *Cumming v. Georgia* case that emerged from this claim illustrated a demand for equality on economic terms that were understood by the plaintiffs to be intertwined with race. This demand was interpreted by the Supreme Court only in the language of taxation and federalism. A rare segregated education case emerging from the South in this period, *Cumming* reached the U.S. Supreme Court at the very close of the nineteenth century. The three men brought suit as parents of children being deprived access to education, but they also brought suit as property owners and taxpayers. Their class status in this case—propertied African American men with substantial taxable income—formed the basis for their assertion of a right to education for their children regardless of race. By bringing a case based on the respectable and high-status position of "taxpayer" and "property owner," they also demanded a sort of "racial reciprocity" from the court. If the black high school was closed because of lack of tax funds, they argued, the white high school should close too.

Claiming economic citizenship in their community, they argued that a tax benefiting the high school for white girls while the black high school had been closed was an unconstitutional deprivation of their property rights, forcing them to pay in support of a white school they were excluded from utilizing. The plaintiff's motion to advance asked that the school board be compelled to "refrain from carrying on white high schools for the support of which plaintiffs were taxed."[12] Ultimately, they rested their case primarily on this claim of economic rights, with the underlying understanding that the recognition or denial of these rights in Georgia in 1899 was deeply linked to the racially segregated culture in which they lived. The court treated the case as a simple question of local taxation policy and appropriate resource distribution. Treating the parents' and children's race as an irrelevance, the justices found the school board's actions reasonable and appropriate by dismissing the claim of "taxpayer" rights.

Justice John Marshall Harlan penned the unanimous opinion, which agreed with the state court that the school board had neither shown bad faith nor "acted in hostility to the colored race."[13] In the end, the three plaintiff fathers in the case were ordered to pay the school board twenty dollars for the board's legal costs, an amount that also happened to be almost exactly the total amount the three men had already paid the previous year in education taxes for their three school-age daughters who were unable to attend high school.[14] Cumming was a taxpayer with an income of $2,080, Harper an income of $2,550, and Ladeveze "to the amount of $5900," indicating that they were likely among the wealthier members of the black community in Augusta.[15]

Wealthier people of color tended to bring the bulk of cases challenging segregated education, for obvious reasons related to the expense of the legal system, the challenges of drawn-out lawsuits, and the risk of backlash run by anyone litigating these issues. This class homogeneity, however, also had some inadvertent consequences, as in so many instances of legal activism. First, it meant that in a legal world of multiple causes for a claim, wealth, status, and property ownership—and thus taxpaying status—became necessary and convenient bases for the claim being pursued, and any litigant would naturally want to put forth as many bases for the claim as possible. Second, the conflation of taxpayer identity and entitlement to education was solidified and legitimated through the use of this argument in court, even as the outcomes were at best ambivalent for most of the litigants.

Three years prior to *Cumming*, one of the most famous—and ultimately infamous—cases ever to be brought before the court was decided. In *Plessy v. Ferguson*, the majority held that train segregation was legal as long as facilities were "separate but equal," paving the way for the expansion of Jim Crow into all aspects of Southern life in the early decades of the twentieth century.[16] Justice Harlan's dissent in *Plessy* was widely cited in the latter half of the twentieth century as a palliative for the legal wounds inflicted by the *Plessy* majority's endorsement of racial segregation.[17] Yet Harlan's *Plessy* dissent is also notable in repeatedly asserting that there was a difference between legal and social equality, a difference that would perhaps be reflected later in his opinions on school inequalities.[18] Opposing segregation and endorsing a "color-blind" constitution, Harlan's *Plessy* dissent did not influence his decision in *Cumming*. His opinion in *Cumming* refused a challenge to segregation that was brought on the basis of both economic and racial inequality, and unanimously dismissed the plaintiffs' demands.

At one point in the *Cumming* opinion, Harlan indicated that if the plaintiffs had brought a suit that directly demanded a separate but equal school facility and it appeared that the board's refusal to provide one was out of racial hostility, "different questions might have arisen in the state court." Harlan's ability to author a strong dissent against "separate but equal" as a doctrine and then almost immediately dismiss a challenge to completely exclusionary schooling because the claimants did not adequately perform the legal logic of *Plessy* illustrates the tension between the formal legal equality his *Plessy* dissent endorsed and the social equality desegregated education suggested. Harlan's biographer has argued that his opinion in *Cumming* appears to diverge from his dissent in *Plessy* (and in the *Civil Rights Cases* of 1883) in part because he had difficulty treating public schools, with their suggestion of physical and spatial intimacy, the same way he treated public accommodations such as railroads.[19]

Shortly after *Cumming*, the State of Kentucky in 1904 passed a law prohibiting integrated education in any institution and imposing substantial fines on anyone—black or white, student or teacher—found to be participating in such an educational system. This law was directed specifically at Berea College, the state's only integrated educational institution and one founded by a prominent abolitionist prior to the Civil War with the specific goal of educating all who were in need. Indeed, in the late nineteenth century Berea began to recruit poor white students from the region while maintaining its black enrollment, becoming known as a school for poor students of all races.[20] Berea appealed the 1904 law to the Supreme Court, which in 1908 upheld Kentucky's law as within the state's authority to amend corporate charters.[21]

In fact, this case was somewhat of a rarity for its time in limiting rather than expanding corporate rights—when corporate liberty went against state policy on "racial preservation" in *Berea*, the corporation found itself under attack.[22] The state policy on racial segregation was thus aligned with a handful of other Progressive Era reforms that had achieved some victories in courts in limiting the rights of corporations, such as protective labor legislation for women and children. Unlike the *Lochner* decision three years prior, often viewed as the pinnacle of corporate contract protection, in *Berea* the racial fears of whites went up against the free-market rights of a corporation, and the corporation lost.[23] For the next few decades, many cases in which families of color pressed for direct access to or integration of white schools were also lost as courts deployed theories of federalism to allocate school maintenance and funding power to states and local governments.[24] Ultimately, this led to far fewer cases claiming a right to education for students of color in these early decades than had been seen in the hopeful flurry of post–Civil War litigation.

Wealth and the Court of Whiteness

Particularly in such a constrained political time, often the only way families of color could access the courts was if they had access to wealth or property. Herbert Kirby, Eugene Kirby, and Dudley Kirby, fourteen, twelve, and ten years of age, respectively, were the wards of their uncle George W. Tucker, of Dillon County, South Carolina, in January 1913 when they were dismissed from the Dalcho public school. The Kirby children had moved to the county four years prior with their parents and had attended the white public schools in Dillon County for many years. After their parents' death, they had attended the white Dalcho school for "two sessions and a part of a third" when they were dismissed without any statement of cause and were told they would not be received back into the school. Tucker immediately filed a petition on their behalf against the state of South Carolina, alleging that the children were "entitled to attend the said school; that they have all the time been properly dressed, have properly conducted themselves," and that it was very important at their age for them to attend school to prepare them for their duties in life. Tucker also argued that there was no other school to which he could conveniently send the children and that therefore their exclusion would cause them "great and irreparable damage."[25]

A right to education rooted in property ownership and substantial taxable wealth, much like in the *Cumming* case, was again asserted in the *Tucker* case, with the added component of racial identity disputes. Tucker and his attorney based their claim on section 1761 of the Code of Laws of South Carolina of 1912, the same law that the trustees claimed gave them authority to dismiss any child without legal cause. Tucker argued instead that the law distinctly provided for separate schools for white and black children, and that there was not sufficient evidence to show that the children were in fact "of the colored race" but only evidence that they were "children of good behavior and intelligence" who were "white and associated with white people."[26]

Tucker also made a claim on behalf of the children's right to education as owners and taxpayers, in their own right, of substantial property. According to the attorney, the children owned "considerable" property in the district, and paid taxes on it, "including the school taxes levied in the district," and therefore had the right to enjoy the benefit of those school taxes. The board had deemed that there should be separate facilities for the Kirby children "and other children of like situation," but Tucker argued that "there are only a very few, or no other children, of the same class, as the wards of petitioner, in the district," and thus that the board's decision was a deprivation of the children's right to education.[27] We will return at the end of the case to what, exactly, made the Kirby children so special.

Even as the wealth of the children was deployed to assert their right to an education in a white school, their racial identity was the crux of their dismissal from the school. Tucker based the rest of his case on abundant testimony showing that the Kirby children had "always associated with white people" and that their father, in his lifetime, had "owned . . . considerable property in the county and exercised all the privileges of white citizenship." Tucker testified that the children owned a plantation worth $15,000; that their aunt, his wife, was John Kirby's sister; and that both John Kirby and his wife were "said to be white." The testimony also showed that both parents and some of the children were members of the first white Baptist church of Dillon and that the children had attended white schools in the county for many years.

The testimony of John Coleman, the chairman of the board of trustees, revealed more about the children's dismissal, however. A petition had been filed with the trustees objecting to the attendance of the Kirby children. According to Coleman, though Tucker claimed that the children "had never been considered anything but white," it was "generally known that they are not pure Caucasian blood." Coleman's main concern became apparent at the end of his testimony when he stated that "if these children were allowed to attend school others of the class would seek to come in, and our position was that we could not exclude others without these."[28] Coleman alluded to the three hundred acres of property owned by the children in the district, as well as property owned by Tucker and Coleman's own previous business dealings with both Tucker and John Kirby. He acknowledged that because of these economic issues, when the children first entered, "we thought it a business thing to do to let them go to school," but the board changed position when "four others attempted to enter, some of whom were a good deal darker."[29]

According to Coleman, the question of the Kirby children's "mixture of blood" was an issue the board knew without having investigated it, based on "what I have heard people say." Coleman described them as "neither white nor black, but . . . Croatan or mulatto," with the "alleged taint in the blood" coming from their father John's parents. Coleman concluded "from John's appearance we judge that the mixture was not very far back," though "these children have the appearance of white children." The Kirby family was also judged by their associations and half siblings, as Coleman testified that both Mr. and Mrs. Kirby had sisters and half brothers who were "not white" or "colored," while Mr. Kirby "associated with colored people."[30]

According to J. F. Williams, one of the witnesses, Tucker was "a white man," but he had "always heard that [John Kirby] was not clear-blooded," and he claimed that the action of the board, of which he was a trustee, was "decided by the reputation and petition" because "some of the brothers and sisters of John Kirby could not be considered white." Williams also mentioned that the petition to dismiss the children had been carried around by Sam Edwards, whose brother had killed John Kirby. Edwards said first in his testimony that he owned land outside the district and had dictated the petition, but insisted that he "did not have anything to do with the killing of John Kirby, and took no part in the trial." Another trustee, L. E. Dew, predicted dire ramifications for the case and said that if the children were reinstated in the school, "there would be a wholesale resigning of the trustees and a tearing up of the school."[31]

Many of the local residents testified to their objections to the Kirby children attending the school based on their family's reputation as not entirely white, and much of this testimony reflected the powerful role of class and racial identity in the poor white community. Chancler Hatchell stated that he did not "know the ancestry of John Kirby, but by his looks he was not pure white," though "his boy Ed is as white as anyone in the room." Hatchell testified that he was a tenant and not a landowner, and stated that he would take his children out of the school and put them to work if the Kirby children were reinstated. Will Baxley, another tenant who sharecropped on land owned by Coleman, said that he would keep his children at home and "let them plow" if the Kirby children returned to school, since "people say they are not white."[32]

Several other locals testified similarly that they were taxpayers and property owners, and repeatedly echoed the statement that John Kirby "was not considered a clear-blooded white man." John C. Sellers, an elderly resident whose father had written a history of the county, offered the most specific testimony as to the family lineage of the Kirby children, referencing their father's father, "Big John Godbolt," who was "one-eighth mixed blood" and a soldier in the Confederate army. Sellers stressed the white relations of the children and claimed that "the percent of the colored blood in the Kirby children is one-thirty-second" and that John Kirby "didn't associate with negroes," though he knew the Kirby family was "pretty badly mixed."[33]

The court clearly indicated that the question of the children's race superseded any of the claims they might otherwise have made on the basis of wealth or status, particularly if the question of race appeared to threaten the possibility of white children receiving an education. The case also illustrated a more general legal shift in Southern courts toward a "one-drop rule," since the judges cited the South Carolina Constitution, article 3, section 33, which voided the marriage of a white person to anyone having "one-eighth or more negro blood." Still, the court held that they were "unable

to find any good reason why the child of such parents should not be entitled to exercise all the legal rights of a white person."[34] The court then decided, however, that there could still be a distinction made between "those
without negro blood and those with less than one-eighth," when there was
also a provision for equal accommodation.

The court relied on precedents including *Plessy v. Ferguson* to support the
premise that while civil and political rights might be equal, social equality
could not be created or mandated by the constitution, arguing that the law
recognized a "social element, arising from racial instinct, to be taken into
consideration." In support of this "one-drop" classification rule, the court
cited a pre–Civil War case from South Carolina indicating that there was no
precise "admixture of ... blood" that would "make a colored person ... while
another of the same degree may be declared a white man," but that it was
typically established "by reputation, by his reception into society, and his
having commonly exercised the privileges of a white man."[35]

Protecting white children's right to education proved paramount to the
judges, regardless of what they thought of the Kirby children's "reputation
and reception" and despite their substantial taxable wealth. After establishing the vagueness of the rule they intended to adopt, the judges acknowledged that "the testimony shows that the children are entitled to be classed
as white" but held that the board of trustees' decision "was neither capri-
cious nor arbitrary," since equal accommodations would be provided and
the trustees had not acted out of "any feeling of animosity." The court then
reiterated the testimony of many local residents, which they argued showed
that "the decided majority of the patrons would refuse to send their children to
the Dalcho school if the Kirby children were allowed to continue in attendance." Quoting the maxim "The greatest good to the largest number," the
court held that "it would seem to be far better that the children in question
should be segregated than that the large majority of the children attending
that school should be denied educational advantages."[36] The threats of white
parents, particularly poor white tenant farmers, to withhold their children
from school entirely and "let them plow" effectively curtailed the Kirby
children's demand for equal access to education.

Cases pursuing claims of equality of education in Southern courts were
often, as in the case of the Kirby children, only brought on behalf of wealthy
and sometimes light-skinned students for whom claims to privileges associated with whiteness might be treated more favorably. At the same time,
the case of the Kirby children highlights several important trends that would
continue to be important for court determinations of educational inequality

and its connections to racial segregation in the decades to come. First, as has been shown by several legal historians recently, race in this case was a category permanently in danger of losing hold of its own definition.[37] Race might be based on appearance for one witness, on property ownership for another, and on association and acquaintance for yet another, but ultimately the court simultaneously deemed the children white and consigned them to ejection from the white school on the basis of a "one drop" philosophy that was as arbitrary to apply as it was brutally effective in silencing those who might question it.

Second, the court in this case upheld the exclusion of the Kirby children, by its own admission, on behalf of the "best interests" of the other children in the community, whose parents threatened to remove them from school entirely if the Kirby children continued to attend. In the view of the court, then, the Kirbys' class status was shaped in large part by the question of their race. The fluid and overlapping hierarchy of race and class deployed by the judges placed propertied, light-skinned children far enough below the "white" children of sharecroppers that the Kirbys' claim was denied. The effectiveness of the "let them plow" threat in pushing the court to deny public schooling to the Kirby children also indicated how the right to education—and therefore, perhaps, a "right" to move up in class status—was a right courts were especially willing to defend for poor white children. This may have been particularly true in a case in which disparities of wealth and the fluidity of race and racial social networks all came together at once.

But there is one final dimension to the Kirby case that makes it unique in relation to many of the cases discussed thus far. As one of the neighbors, G. F. Bethea, testified specifically, John Kirby was not considered African American, he "was considered a Croatan." The Kirby children were in fact alleged by their neighbors to be "mixed" because of their Croatan Indian ancestry, and their neighbors sought to send them to a segregated Indian school rather than a white school.[38] Dillon County, where the Kirby family lived, shared a border with Robeson County, North Carolina, which was mandated by state law in 1885 to enact three-way school segregation—white, black, and Indian.[39] Indeed, the Dalcho district, where the Kirby children lived, had once operated three separate schools as well, but the Indian school had lost its teachers and closed by the time the Kirby children sought to enter the district as students. They chose the white school, and school officials were content to let them attend for three years before they sought to expel them because of the complaints of their white neighbors.

The black-white paradigm was, in the words of scholars of the *Tucker* case, a lens that lay over the judicial reasoning of any litigation challenging segregation or racial inequality, particularly in a state such as South Carolina. So the Kirbys' Croatan-ness was left virtually unnoticed and unspoken by the time the case reached the state Supreme Court, which described the case in terms of blackness and whiteness, and by decades of journalists, lawyers, and scholars who assumed that the case was solely another example of black and white Jim Crow–era segregation. The Kirbys' multiple sites of identity were conflicting and confusing to the court, which chose to focus on a single binary system that was already well established, a move we will see again in chapter 7 in the *Rodriguez* case decades later. The complexity of and connections between the Kirbys' status as wealthy property owners and position as both outsiders and insiders to the system of black-white racial segregation is also highlighted further in a case a few years later from across the country.

American Indians, Citizenship, and *Piper*

In 1923, Pike and Annie Piper, Paiute residents of Big Pine, California, were facing the end of a protracted legal battle. Their daughter, Alice, was fifteen years old, but she and six other students had sought admission to the Big Pine school district years earlier and were denied due to their Indian heritage. For decades, the U.S. federal government had taken control of Indian children's education by constructing boarding schools, often at an intentional distance from reservations. At these schools, such as the infamous Carlisle Indian Industrial School in Pennsylvania, young people were pushed to assimilate and sacrifice much of their tribal identity, appearance, and language. But after World War I, these boarding schools began to diminish and some closed, including Carlisle, though attendance at boarding schools would surge again in later decades. In the early 1920s, attention turned to the possibility of setting up reservation schools funded by the Bureau of Indian Affairs or, in some cases, integrating Indian children into local public school systems.

The Big Pine Band of Owens Valley Paiute Shoshone, which included the Piper family, had financed their own reservation school at first, making them somewhat of a rarity. The Bureau of Indian Affairs was opposed to this system, and it purchased the Big Pine schoolhouse in 1891 in order to establish a government-run Indian day school. Yet it was quickly apparent that substantial federal support was not actually forthcoming, and the Owens Valley Paiute continued to provide financial support for their school for clothing, lunches, and the like. Superintendent James K. Allen, in his 1899 report to the Commissioner of Indian Affairs, called on the government to furnish the day school and provide necessary equipment.[40] By 1894, only three schools in California had admitted Indian children through the use of tuition contracts with the federal government (in which the government paid the comparable "tuition" to the public school to compensate for the nonresident tax base). In 1903 this number had declined to zero, and the number of schools participating in the federal tuition contract system around the nation was also in decline. The federal government again began to push local public schools to admit Indian children in 1912, and in the 1920s began to appropriate more funding to encourage schools to participate.

For American Indian children, segregation was twofold—between white and Indian schools, and, within schools affiliated with tribes, between taxpaying and nontaxpaying families, often an identity partially determined by the allotment status of the reservation land under the Dawes Act of 1887. The Pipers were valuable as named litigants in part because they could claim status as taxpayers and therefore were able to claim the rights of citizenship that went along with that status. Individual property ownership and taxpaying status provided a basis for a claim to citizenship and education rights in California courts that it had not in South Carolina for the Kirby children, even though school officials still attempted to enforce segregation and exclusion on the front lines.

But another reason the Pipers could make an argument as taxpayers was that, according to the court, many California Indians had been classified by judicial rulings as "Indians who have lost their power of self-government and become subject to state laws," and therefore as U.S. citizens by birth (unlike Indians belonging to tribes with recognized self-governments, who would be granted citizenship in an act of Congress just one year after *Piper*). Because of that recognition of citizenship, the court expressed concern that "Indian children whose parents are taxpayers" were not able to attend the federal Indian school like "children of nontaxpaying Indian parents." Though the justices indicated that the district could constitutionally establish a separate school for Indian children, they acknowledged that such an action would "no doubt . . . add to the cost of the district" but ultimately concluded that those economic questions were not the concern of the court. Alice Piper was a resident, a citizen, and the child of taxpaying parents, and the district could not deny her entry.[41]

American Indians on reservation land had a different dilemma from that of Alice Piper, highlighted by a case that preceded hers by almost two decades. Fremont County, Wyoming, is the historic location of the Wind River Indian Reservation, home of the Northern Arapaho and Eastern Shoshone tribes. Established in 1868, the reservation covers approximately one-third of the county's land base, despite diminishment in a 1906 agreement that ceded some lands to white settlement. In 1902, at the urging of many tribal leaders who had endured the brutal attempts at assimilation in federally funded boarding schools, Fremont County School District Number 21 was created. This was one of the first school districts in the United States that was wholly located on reservation land and that was constructed in part from a special school tax levied on the district's taxpayers.

Because of the special tax status of some Indians at the time, the board of county commissioners then pursued an injunction against the county treasurer to prevent him from paying to the newly created reservation school the taxes that had been collected, claiming that the district was illegally created because there were "no qualified electors" and "no lands upon the reservation subject to state taxation." Indeed, their lawsuit demanded a refund of any taxes that had been paid by those who were subject to the levy. The Wyoming Supreme Court found that the district was legally organized and that it could continue to be funded from taxes, but the complex question of Indian state and federal citizenship and electoral and taxation status continued to limit locally empowered public education, as we will see again toward the end of the book.[42]

Conclusion

By 1923, over two decades after the *Cumming* decision, Georgia had established 275 accredited public high schools for whites and only 2 for blacks.[43] In counties with a student population that was over 75 percent African American, whites received $22.22 per capita, compared with $1.78 for blacks. The NAACP reported that in 1916 the average per capita expenditure for all the Southern states for teaching white children was $10.32, while that for teaching black children was $2.89.[44] During the decades of intense segregation in the early twentieth century, schooling in the South was thus profoundly economically different for poor black children than it was for either poor white children or economically secure white children.

But educational access and funding was also profoundly different for children who fell outside the black-white paradigm of the Jim Crow era, whether Eastern Shoshone children living on reservation land in Wyoming, "nontribal" California Indian children of taxpaying parents, second-generation Chinese American children in Mississippi, or wealthy and multiracial Croatan children in South Carolina. In each of these cases, the assertions of belonging to one side or the other of the black-white paradigm and the judgments rendered by courts helped to further construct racial categories as totalizing spaces in which certain identities were predetermined or simply invisible. At the same time, levels of wealth, property ownership, and taxpayer status were fundamentally important in even allowing many cases to be brought, and the power of claims as taxpayers engendered sympathies within certain courts that highlighted the way the category of taxpayer could serve as yet another code for whiteness and legitimacy in the imaginary of citizenship. But it was always a partial code, revocable whenever there was any suggestion of a white veto from the community, and could never be trusted to guarantee access, justice, or equal treatment.

CHAPTER THREE

We Are Taxpaying Citizens
Separate and Color-Blind

In Covington County, Mississippi, in 1925, separate schools for black and white children were a given. For the African American trustees of Hopewell, the black school district, the profound inequality between their schools and the white schools of the Calhoun consolidated district was a more constant source of frustration. What made it even more frustrating was that many of them owned property inside the territory included in the Calhoun white school district—property they were taxed on for the support of those white schools. In fact, the land included in the black district overlapped with a significant portion of the land in the white district. And all of that overlapping land was owned by African Americans, including many of the trustees. Yet none of the land taxed for the support of the black school was owned by whites, as a result of the careful drawing of district lines.[1]

So they brought a lawsuit, *Bryant v. Barnes* that was unlike many more typical school segregation lawsuits. They sued the tax collector, charging double taxation and arguing that taxing blacks to maintain white schools but not taxing whites to maintain black schools violated the very basis of the Mississippi Constitution's provision for separate (but equal) schooling. Indeed, the trustees charged that the only reason the overlapping areas of African American–owned land were included in the white district's taxable property base was to make black property owners maintain the white school without compensation. They pointed out that it was unnecessary to include that territory in the white district, and that the Calhoun district had sufficient property to maintain its school without doubly taxing the black residents of the Hopewell district.

The trustees lost the case in the chancery court, and they went on to appeal it to the Mississippi Supreme Court. In that court's decision, Judge George Ethridge disputed the trustees' claim that they were being forced to support a school from which they could not benefit. He accused them of "labor[ing] under a delusion as to receiving no benefit from the operation of a white school," and argued that everyone benefited from education. After a discussion of the propriety of property tax levies for schooling generally, Ethridge went on to say that it was of course "not necessary that every child in the county have the same advantages in the way of education that every other child has." Finally, he upheld the lower-court ruling, condemning the trustees to continue paying double taxes to support both white and black schools.[2]

This chapter will examine the litigation brought in the early decades of the twentieth century on separate taxation, as well as lawsuits challenging double taxation in purportedly "color-blind" tax structures. I argue that both separate and color-blind tax systems worked against African American families in different ways, ultimately based on the profound difference in their political power to control the rate of taxation and distribution of funding. There was pushback by many black families to these structures, as seen in the Mississippi case and many others, yet meaningful remedies were frequently unavailable, even when courts proclaimed agreement with the principle of equality.

In these same decades, the NAACP emerged as an organization dedicated to the fight for equality, and separate taxation, funding, and teachers' salary cases constituted some of their earliest battles against segregated schooling. In fact, the most common letters received by the NAACP on education in the first several decades of its existence were from parents or students simply seeking individual financial help for education.[3] And many people wrote the organization requesting assistance in obtaining the schooling for their children that they felt entitled to as "taxpaying citizens," an identity claim that seems quite reasonable in light of the disproportionate tax burden many black families faced from white school taxes.

Separation and Inequality

Different states had many different mechanisms in the early twentieth century for enabling their taxing structures to fund white schools more generously. In some states, such as in Kentucky, North Carolina, and Virginia, whites were taxed only for white schools and blacks were taxed only for black schools, and economic inequality and discrimination did the remainder of the work. Mississippi, Georgia, and Oklahoma, on the other hand, taxed black and white property uniformly for school levies, but they instituted separate—and unequal—levies for the white schools and for the black schools. In effect, this practice often enabled white schools to benefit disproportionately from the inclusion of black taxpayers' payments, due to the strategic drawing of district lines—as in the Mississippi case—as well as significantly different levy amounts for the separate schools. In all of these states, segregated schooling was compulsory by law, as well as enabled by the segregation of tax policy.

Taxation and school equality lawsuits were not especially frequent in general, and they did not occur in all states—indeed, states in the Deep South are almost absent from much of the litigation history, with the exception of a few cases over many decades in Georgia and Mississippi. The lack of litigation itself suggests the difficulty of bringing lawsuits in the first place and the potential backlash risked by those who put themselves forth in opposition to systemic educational inequality. But a few states, Kentucky and Oklahoma in particular, showed disproportionately large clusters of lawsuits, often over virtually the same issues and in many of the same towns and districts over many years.

Despite the limited number of lawsuits, it is possible to draw some tentative conclusions from the pattern of outcomes. In 1935, Gladys Tignor Peterson, Howard Law School graduate and one of the founders of the Epsilon Sigma Iota Sorority at that school, published an article assessing the success and failure of lawsuits brought against segregated schools across the country since the Civil War. She concluded that the overwhelming difference between lawsuits that succeeded and those that failed was whether they directly challenged the practice of separate schooling (a challenge that almost uniformly lost) or whether they challenged the constitutionality of separate taxation or other mechanisms of funding and resource inequality. In the latter cases, she argued, plaintiffs always, or almost always, won, thus suggesting that challenges to taxation were better locations for advocacy groups to expend their strategic resources.[4]

As with earlier cases, however, many of these seeming victories did very little to disrupt the structure of separate school taxation and in many cases failed to even directly remedy the circumstances under dispute. Kentucky is again a compelling example of the most blatant form of separate taxation, and it had more cases challenging separate schooling and separate taxation between Reconstruction and the late 1930s than any other state, as mentioned in chapter 1.[5] Kentucky law provided for mandatory separate black and white schools to be funded by taxes gathered separately by race. Unlike states in which separate taxation was not allowed in the state constitution (such as in Mississippi and Oklahoma), Kentucky's policy appears on the surface to have a greater segregating intent and impact. However, the experience of double and disproportionate taxation in those states with "color-blind" tax systems makes the Kentucky example more complicated to assess.

In particular, the community of Mayfield, Kentucky, came before the courts repeatedly in these decades, like the city of Owensboro, Kentucky discussed in chapter 1. There was a dispute between the boards of trustees for the black and white schools in the city, specifically challenging a Kentucky state statute that designated all corporate property taxes for the benefit of white schools only and demanding that the white board release the proportionate share of funds gathered from corporate taxes to the black board of trustees.[6] In that case, the state court of appeals ruled that the law was unconstitutional, and held that corporate taxes should be distributed between white and black schools based on proportion of students. The court stated that "a corporation cannot be said to have color; it is neither white nor black," and that the attempt by the legislature to treat the race of a corporation's shareholders as determinative of the "race" of the corporation, and therefore of the beneficiary of its tax payments, violated the equal protection clause.

The Kentucky legislature passed a new law in 1920 that provided that certain cities should consolidate their black and white boards of education under a single board, which also meant the consolidation of the school tax fund and the end of separate black and white taxes. White school boards sought ways to escape the implications of this law and avoid consolidation, but the state court of appeals held that they had to implement the legislation.[7] The next workaround by white taxpayers and school boards came the following year, when the City of Pineville consolidated separate schools under one board but refused to make any levies in support of black schools until John Moore, an African American "citizen and taxpayer," filed suit to demand they provide support for black education. After his litigation commenced, the board did finally meet and issue a levy for black schools, but in their later appeal the state court found that the levy was issued "too late" in the year and reversed the lower-court ruling in favor of Moore. While the court did affirm generally that white taxpayers in some cases could be taxed in support of black schools after 1920, in the actual case at hand, the court nonetheless refused to provide a remedy to address the failure of the consolidated board in Pineville to support black schools.

Following this, an unpublished summary judgment opinion in 1926 and a restatement of that opinion in a 1928 case both clarified that, in white independent school districts, white taxpayers could not be made to support black schools within the boundaries of their previously organized districts. In their holding, the court said that a 1926 statute under contention "was never intended to burden that race with the duty to also educate the pupils therein belonging to the race not so organizing."[8] White taxpayers brought another case objecting to the inclusion of black voters in a school tax election in Meade County in 1931, and they won their case at the trial court. On appeal by the board of education, however, the state court of appeals held that black voters should be allowed to participate in the vote, since it was a county common school and all taxpayers would therefore be subject to the consolidation levy.[9] And in a similar case that year, white taxpayers won at the trial court level when they demanded an injunction to prevent the board of education from supporting black schools out of the common fund or paying for transportation to the (geographically distant) black school they had established. Again, the state court of appeals reversed and found that it was appropriate for a common school fund to provide transportation in those circumstances, regardless of race.[10]

What the Kentucky cases highlight is that the policy of separate taxation was contentious for both white and black taxpayers. The two groups brought litigation challenging the practice for different reasons, but in the end the power to control taxation and distribute those resources proved to be the most effective tool for segregationists, and the consolidation of taxing authority under a single school board could in many instances simply mean the empowerment of an all-white school board to limit funding to black schools as much as possible, or at least until a brave litigant could take the case to the state court of appeals. This practice of supposedly color-blind taxation and segregated disbursal was already established in other states in these decades, and in many cases it placed black taxpayers under a double burden.

"Color-Blind" Taxation and Racial Distribution

In Muskogee, Oklahoma, in 1923, Jacob Jones Jr. was a student at Dunbar School, the separate black school within the city. His school, and the other black schools in the district, had a total value of $150,000, while the white school facilities had a total value of $1,393,267.37. Yet though their facility was valued at nearly ten times the value of the black facilities, the number of white students in the district was only a little more than double the number of black students. Per capita, the white schools spent $104.23 per high school student and $65.46 per grade school student, while the black schools spent $43.26 per high school student and $19.53 per grade school student. Classrooms in the black schools were much more crowded, and teachers were paid significantly less. Overcrowding due to the lack of funding for facilities and teachers meant many black children were forced to attend only half time, while the white schools were able to offer an expanded array of courses in electrical wiring, banking and commerce, cartooning, printing, architectural drawing, and many other curricula, none of which could be provided in the black schools.[11]

But for Jacob and his father, Jacob Jones Sr., the final insult came in April 1923 when the black schools were closed for the year, having operated for just over seven months. The white schools continued to run, fully funded, for the complete nine-month session. The Joneses charged, accurately, that this was largely a result of the spartan tax levy provided to fund separate schools that year—1.7 mills. The comparable tax levy to support white schools in the same year was 14.8 mills, almost nine times as much. Both levies were placed on all taxable property, regardless of owner's race, within the county of Muskogee. Undoubtedly, black taxpayers were paying a high price for a tiny fraction of the school fund. Proportionately, for every dollar a black taxpayer paid in school taxes in Muskogee, 90 percent went to fund white schools. White taxpayers, on the other hand, were only contributing about 10 percent of their tax payments to support black schools. This was the system of color-blind taxation at work.

In their suit in the district court, the Joneses demanded a writ of mandamus to compel the school board to reopen the black schools and to restrain the city treasurer from disbursing school funds unequally. The court denied their petitions, and they appealed to the state supreme court. The state court expressed sympathy for their case, calling it "shameful" and saying, "We agree with counsel for plaintiff that equal protection means, not only equal taxation, but equal benefits of the taxes when levied and collected." But they argued that the plaintiffs had not shown that the funding for black schools would still have been inadequate had they been funded at the maximum constitutional rate (under Oklahoma law at the time, 8 mills was the maximum for black schools, with an additional 2 mill option for any common schools as needed). Because of this, the court held, the family could not require the funds collected for the operation of the white school to be used to maintain the black school, and the lower court's denial was affirmed.

Judge Charles Mason, writing for the Oklahoma Supreme Court, went on to state that, from the record, the court believed "that the board of education of the city of Muskogee and the excise board of Muskogee county are deliberately discriminating against the separate schools of the city of Muskogee, and each is trying to shift the responsibility to the shoulders of the other." Throughout the case, the board of education had expressed its sadness about the situation and claimed the excise board had refused to allow the higher mill rate for the higher budget, while the excise board lamented that the board of education could have demanded a higher rate under an Oklahoma Supreme Court case from just the year before.

In that case, the board of education of Guthrie, Oklahoma, had sued the excise board of Logan County in order to compel them to impose an additional levy to support black schools in the city, but they lost the suit in the district court.[12] The board of education had requested the equivalent of a 2-mill levy to support the three black schools, and the excise board had allowed a little over half of that funding. The Oklahoma Supreme Court held that this was a proper remedy under the state constitution and that the excise board had failed to perform its statutory duty—however, since the tax rolls had already been prepared and paid for the year, the court found it "impracticable" to grant the writ at that point and affirmed the lower court's denial, stating simply that they believed that counties would comply with their opinion in the future. Again, as in prior decades, the hollow triumph in this "victorious" challenge to separate taxation systems meant that even if the opinion suggested agreement on principle, as in both the Oklahoma cases, there would be no actual remedy forthcoming. The practice of "color-blind" taxation was often simply the framework on which the experience of double taxation of African Americans was premised.

As education historian James D. Anderson has shown, African Americans in the South from the end of Reconstruction onward were frequently forced into systems of double taxation.[13] Indeed, many predominantly black communities spent the decades prior to the Great Depression paying at least as much in taxes as white neighborhoods, except that black families were paying double and even triple taxes, including privately raised "self-taxes" to support their purportedly "public" schools, which were otherwise languishing due to lack of support from the common school fund into which they paid.[14] While black taxes were incorporated into a common fund that was often distributed by white school boards nearly exclusively to white schools, blacks paid again in privately raised cash donations to build schools, and then often yet again in labor, land, and materials to construct the school buildings. It is unsurprising, then, to find that for many African Americans, their identities as taxpayers were a clear and compelling claim that they sought to utilize in fighting for equal rights and equal resources.

The NAACP and Separate Taxation

A few years after the *Guthrie* and *Jones* cases, Oklahoma continued to implement the funding system the state Supreme Court had called "shameful."

In 1924 NAACP member Amos Daniels wrote to Arthur Spingarn at the NAACP, arguing that many wealthy blacks in the town of Boynton, Oklahoma, had been "fooled by the white Co. Supt. and School Board to vote $80,000 for school purposes, $60,000 to go for whites and 20,000 for colored." Many letters to the organization contained complaints of such a separation of funds in school levies. According to Daniels, "After the election . . . the whites used the whole 80,000 to build them a high school and give the negroes none." After building the new white high school, Daniels said, two more rooms were added on to the building, giving white children a four-year high school with twenty-one units, while black students had no high school at all, "though the school age population is about equal."[15]

Carter Wesley, an attorney in Muskogee, Oklahoma, wrote to Walter White a month after investigating the Boynton case, finding the facts true but not suitable for a test case on the school laws. Wesley then offered as a potential test case the previously discussed situation in Muskogee, where there was "an Independent School District, composed of whites; and a separate School District composed of Colored." The districts coincided geographically, but the law provided that the separate schools were supported by a specific percent of the levy, while the independent district raised funds by a tax on the entire city of Muskogee. Wesley argued that "this means that Negroes are taxed for White schools and the White schools get about ten times as much as the Negroes proportionally." Wesley asserted that "there is no question, but when these facts are properly reflected the law will be declared unconstitutional."[16]

But, again, just a few years later Oklahoma school boards were still implementing disproportionately high rates to support white schools. S. A. McAshan and George McNemee, president and secretary of the Parents and Teachers Club of Vian, Oklahoma, wrote to the NAACP relating the situation of the separate schools in their district in their hope "that the colored children might get all the money that is appropriated for their schools."[17] According to McAshan and McNemee, "Money was appropriated to pay six teachers for eight months, but the directors cut off two teachers in order to save $150 for the white schools." In Vian, they said, "the separate schools are so crowded with large numbers of children that the teachers are not able to instruct all the classes each day." Predating the economic disasters on the horizon, the schools of Vian in 1928 had already lost $150 per month of the money appropriated for the schools, and no state aid had been given to the separate schools. McAshan and McNemee pleaded that "unless legal action is taken at once we shall be given only seven months of schooling this term." While the organization could not follow through on all the complaints of separate taxation and inequality it received, it had begun to develop a range of strategies to test the limits of segregation and separate taxation.

The NAACP was incorporated in 1911 with a mandate "to promote equality of rights and to eradicate caste or race prejudice among the citizens of the United States; to advance the interest of colored citizens; to secure for them impartial suffrage; and to increase their opportunities for securing justice in the courts, education for the children, employment according to their ability and complete equality before law."[18] In response to the nationwide increase in segregation and inequality in education in the early twentieth century, the NAACP also strategically utilized economic arguments simultaneously with demands for racial fairness from the beginning. Many such advocates for school equality eschewed claims of taxpayers' rights in favor of more explicit and expansive linkages between discrimination based on poverty and discrimination based on race.

In a paper on education written in 1921 and noted approvingly in the NAACP files, one author argued that "a nation that pretends to democracy is honor bound to educate all its people, the poorest as well as the richest."[19] He went on to say that it should not be the amount of taxes paid by the different classes that determined the amount of return to them in school appropriations, noting that "poor whites, like the poor blacks, pay little to the government in the way of taxes ... yet schools ... are provided freely for them." This was the dignitarian logic of a right to education inherent in the individual, without reference to wealth, property, or taxes.

The NAACP was all too aware that racially differential tax funding could be used to facilitate and maintain segregated schools regardless of the legal requirements of the particular state. Some of the economic arguments the organization made were rooted in pragmatic, cost-saving approaches designed to appeal to overlapping white and black tax concerns, while others directly challenged the moral nature of separate racial taxation for public schools. When a segregated school bill was introduced in Kansas in 1919, the NAACP sent a letter to the governor that led off with an economic appeal, pointing immediately to the increased taxes and expense a dual school system would require.[20] The same year, in an address in Topeka, Kansas, on the bill, the NAACP speaker stressed that "even where [the] school fund [is] equally divided, separation thereof is [an] economic wrong."[21] In a letter to the Rockville Centre School Board of Long Island, New York, in 1930, responding to a report filed with the board by the Rockville Centre health officer encouraging segregation, the NAACP pointed out that "enlightened communities . . . have long since come to the conclusion that segregated schools increase the cost of education, thus becoming an added burden to the tax payers."[22] Later, in a press note on equal education cases, the organization stated that "these educational cases are significant because they raise the question of the proper use of public tax moneys; a question of as serious importance to the North as to the South, a question which involves not only schools but all publicly supported health, welfare, recreational, and cultural institutions."[23]

The NAACP's attention to unequal funding and taxation was partially a response to calls like the editorial in the *Baltimore Afro-American* in June 1929 titled "Where Are the Leaders?"[24] The newspaper lamented the lack of high schools for black students in Baltimore County despite the ten high schools for the 2,581 white students, "cost[ing] the county taxpayers $243,795 last year." The editors went on to describe the system of "highway robbery" that permitted unequal expenditure of taxpayer funds for segregated schools:

> In plain words, colored taxpayers are being robbed every year of $12,000 worth of high school education. The money is stolen from them by this extra-legal procedure of the school authorities as surely as if the school officials held up the Negro population at the point of a revolver. Highway robbery is a crime when perpetrated by an individual, but a school board gets away with it every year in Baltimore County. As intelligent leadership among Negroes in the county develops, somebody is going to get mad. When that day comes, the county board will be slapped in the face with an injunction by Negro taxpayers, compelling it to show cause why school funds should not be equitably expended. Where are the county leaders? Are they aware that a remedy lies in the courts? How much longer must the common people wait upon them for initiative?[25]

The frustration of the editors with the blatantly unequal funding for white and black students and the belief that courts would provide the remedy for this inequality also illustrated the legacy of the taxpayer suits in the nineteenth-century school cases and the hope that "separate but equal" could be attacked on both fronts.

The other nineteenth-century rationale, that whites supposedly paid more taxes, continued to surface repeatedly in the early years of the NAACP and drew frustrated responses. S. D. Leaward wrote a letter to the editor of the *Commercial Appeal* of Memphis in 1921, describing the disparities in schooling in Mississippi, where there were 525 consolidated rural schools and transportation for whites and none at all for blacks, "though they bear equally the burden of taxation."[26] Though there was an excellent black school in Mound Bayou, he said, the bond for building it was levied on black property only, while the construction of the white school was paid for from a tax levied on all property. Leaward returned continually in his letter to the question of equal taxation, pointing out that the excuse of some whites that they "pay all the taxes" not only was patently untrue with regard to the amount of taxes paid by black Mississippians but also ignored the fact that African Americans did 85 percent of the manual labor of the state. And in a letter to the editor of the *Baltimore Evening Sun* in 1919, William Banister responded to a letter from a white "protective association" that had also claimed that whites paid the bulk of the taxes and thus had the right to live in all-white neighborhoods.[27] Banister called this claim "absurd" because it made "the right of citizens to move in and live in neighborhoods, contingent upon the relative amount of tax they pay." Banister then argued that this principle would mean that a "certain class of whites" would be barred from living in certain blocks because they paid only a small amount in taxes compared to that paid by another class of whites, and he asked, "Are white people willing to accept this principle?"

In majority-black counties and school districts in the Deep South, the problem of unequal taxation and funding was often especially dire, as illustrated in the first two chapters. In the spring of 1919, the NAACP asked J. L. Bond of the Department of Public Instruction in Little Rock, who had worked toward improving school facilities in Arkansas, to look into reports that the school for African American children in Edmondson had been closed and its special district eliminated and annexed.[28] According to NAACP sources, the closure left 515 black children without school facilities. Yet there were only 11 white children in the Edmondson district, and even after combining the two districts, there were only 41 white children. Six of the black teachers, who had been under contract to teach eight months, were cut off with six months of service. The teachers had asked for the remainder of their contract but were denied by a school board claiming lack of funds. However, "the white schools are still in operation, and we are advised that they are to run the full term of nine months." In the Edmondson Special District, the NAACP found, blacks owned and controlled "more than 80% of the land, and pay taxes in proportion," while only five white men in the district owned land. Further, the letter argued, "three of these white men are in favor of the plea . . . to have the school reopened, one is noncommittal, and one of them opposes the opening of the school." The black residents of the district believed that it was due to the opposition of this one man that their schools had been closed.[29] The same "white veto" exercised against the Kirby children in South Carolina just a few years earlier effectively shut out these 515 black children from access to school facilities.

Frustration with the need for philanthropy to attempt to compensate for the meager tax funding provided for black schools in many states also led to calls for African Americans to migrate to other parts of the country. In 1923 the Rosenwald Fund spent $40,000 in four high-need counties in Southern states to build 125 black schools. In a *Chicago Defender* editorial from that year entitled "Paying Their Bills," the paper expressed appreciation for the Rosenwald Fund but questioned why "Northern capital" had to be sent into the South to pay for schools that "should receive their sole support from the taxpayers of that section."[30] Stating that the South should be ashamed of that state of affairs, the editorial concluded that if "black taxpayer[s]" were not receiving the same educational facilities for their children as white taxpayers, they should prepare to migrate to locations with better conditions. For many reasons, including Jim Crow inequality in Southern states, tens of thousands of African Americans had been migrating to cities in the North and West in these years. And, by the 1930s, the Great Depression exacerbated these educational inequalities even more deeply.

"We Are Taxpaying Citizens"

In 1936 the only schoolhouse for African American children in Bladenboro, North Carolina, mysteriously burned down, not for the first time. A. E. Monroe, a local resident, wrote to the NAACP national office to ask for help in rebuilding the school yet again after "they burnt it." Monroe closed his brief letter with a simple plea: "We are taxpaying citizens."[31] A few years before, Alice Timms similarly wrote a letter to Arthur Spingarn of the NAACP asking him to look into school segregation in her small Oregon community. This policy of segregation was being enacted in the small lumber town of Vernonia by "a Southern lumber company" that had built a mill there. The Southern school principal refused to admit black or Filipino students to the high school, and Timms was outraged. She closed her appeal by arguing that "we own our home in Klamath and I realize that part of our taxes are helping Vernonia as much as any other place in Oregon and I do not see why our people have to go to the expense of sending their children to some other town or keeping them out of school when they are entitled to just as much as any white people."[32] Asserting both her economic citizenship as a taxpaying and home-owning individual and her membership in an African American racial community that was entitled to equal treatment with whites, she also pointed out the added economic costs that families were forced to incur because of race-based segregation policies.

Many people were writing to the NAACP requesting help in obtaining the schooling for their children that they felt entitled to as "taxpaying citizens" in these years. The letters sent to the NAACP and the first handful of school cases brought through the organization illustrate in the realm of education litigation what Risa Goluboff has termed the "lost promise" of the NAACP's labor litigation to assert both economic equality and civil rights.[33] Since litigation combating segregation had waned in the wake of the *Plessy* decision, the newly founded NAACP focused its limited resources on battling educational inequality under the rule of "separate but equal." The organization's legal strategy eventually changed to center on integrating schools, but its early cases—both those brought by it and those from individual parents and families—indicate the ongoing struggle to obtain equality from courts and schools. These demands for educational equality were frequently tied to both racial and economic discrimination of those requesting aid, but by the time a handful of cases reached the courts in the 1930s, the legal strategy typically centered on race and taxpayer (middle-class) status, including in the spate of NAACP cases seeking equal teachers' pay in that decade. One of the key points that these sources highlight is the continuing claim by many African Americans to identities as taxpayers, identities that were particularly linked to the right to education for many individuals.

A common refrain in the unsolicited letters received by the NAACP in these early decades was simply that the writers were taxpayers, and had a right as taxpayers, and therefore citizens, to equal education. In a letter from Nottoway County, Virginia, in 1922, which was left unsigned because of the authors' fear of retribution, a group identifying themselves as "legal tax payers" complained that they had been deprived of a school for nearly five years.[34] The parents had been asked to raise money to build a school, and when they did, it was only in operation four days before it was burned down. And in a letter in 1936, Alphonzo Lee of Montgomery County, Maryland, argued that the school board's unequal payment of teachers was unfair both to the teachers and to "all other taxpayers of this County."[35] Lee restated his identity as a taxpayer two more times in the letter, emphasizing that since blacks were being taxed for education on the same basis as all other citizens, "the standard of education for our children should be as high as that for all other children."

In addition, the issue of access to schools through funding for transportation was of crucial importance for many people writing in to the organization in these decades, particularly since segregated schools were often placed long distances from their population. When Philadelphia school officials were considering moving Central High School to a distant neighborhood, a local citizen pointed out that even if the school were still legally accessible to the young black men who made up 40 percent of the school's population, the new location would render it economically unfeasible to attend.[36] The majority of the students "belong to the poor working class families whose parents are wage earners, days' workers and domestic servants." Despite the technical availability of the school to the children, "they will never get there . . . they cannot afford that amount of carfare even where it is only 75 cents for one boy." Central High School had actually been built in 1836 specifically in order to provide an accessible education to "boys from all classes of society." The plea ended by acknowledging that of course "the easiest solution of the problem" was to build a new school on the outskirts of the city, "if the problem involved were only to educate . . . the middle and upper class of the citizenry without regard to the problems confronting the families of the under privileged." And Raymond Pace Alexander, a prominent civil rights attorney who participated in many key NAACP school cases, used the argument of "unneeded and improper expenditure of taxpayers' money" in Berwyn, Pennsylvania, schools to fight segregation. In that case, the school board was requiring that every African American child be enrolled in the Mount Pleasant School, while "the board is permitting every white child to be sent by bus to Strafford at the expense of the taxpayers."[37]

School boards in the North, just like those in the South, were overwhelmingly white and thus were able to make decisions that had a profound impact on funding, transportation, and basic access to education. Mary Scruggs of Gary, Indiana, wrote to the NAACP in 1927 saying that she was opposed to the present proposed site for a high school "for the children of the colored citizenry of Gary" because "it is unfair to the colored taxpayers of the city of Gary."[38] Ultimately, she said, "the unchristian, unjust principle of the whole scheme would prompt no civilized body of thinking people to make such a move even to suggest [sic] a place like that a high school for any children unless it was with malice and aforethought for a people for whose children they wish to see perish from the face of the earth."

School Funding and the Depression

During the Great Depression, many African Americans found themselves completely shut out from any of the school funds raised through state and local taxes. A majority-black county in Virginia, which reportedly had more African American tenant farmers than any other county in the state, was denied money for school transportation for black children in 1930.[39] Local citizens raised money and purchased school buses, which they operated for four years through what a reporter described as "self-imposed taxes." When a school official asked one poor farmer without children of his own why he was so interested in buses, the farmer responded that he was an American citizen who paid taxes to run schools so "all the children, black and white, are mine." He went on to say that "when the war broke out the other day, you didn't ask me why I was fighting. We black men fought to defend black as well as white." The farmer concluded by saying that he didn't want to see either white children or black children have to walk to school; rather, he wanted to "see 'em all ride."[40] These "self-taxes" had been utilized in many black communities from Reconstruction onward to build school facilities and maintain teaching staff when funding was refused by the state.[41] The practice of self-taxation overlaps closely with the experience of double taxation that ironically led to its necessity.

The Great Depression led to numerous tax resistance movements. By one historian's account, there were even more such organizations created in the 1930s than in the 1970s modern tax revolt.[42] In many cases, such as the ongoing organized tax strike in Chicago from 1930 to 1933, real estate and property taxes were the central focus of rebellion. And because many homeowners and companies went into default on their property taxes during the Depression, school funds were extremely difficult to collect in many communities by the mid-1930s.[43] In the fall of 1938, the state of Ohio was forced to close its schools for six weeks due to lack of funds, which meant several school systems simply did not pay their teachers, leading to a wave of strikes.[44] In letters sent to the NAACP in 1934, residents complained that many teachers had not received their pay for the 1933–34 school year in Georgia, even as other letter writers continued to seek financial aid from the NAACP to attend teacher training school.[45] At a time when black teachers could not be sure of receiving even the unequal salaries they were battling over, the teaching profession was still seen by many as the best ticket into the African American middle class, a class divide that was continuing to grow within the African American community during the height of Jim Crow.[46]

Calls for the reform of the now-precarious property-tax finance system grew in the 1930s, leading one education scholar to argue that the Depression had highlighted how incapable property taxation schemes were of financing education, claiming that "we are still in the ox-cart and stagecoach days" in terms of school funding.[47] The lack of funding was particularly brutal for African American schools, which already struggled with limited resources and deteriorating facilities. In Chicago during the Depression, school authorities explicitly funneled limited school funds to white schools, leading to severe overcrowding and often dangerous conditions in black schools.[48] A. L. Foster, executive secretary of the Chicago Urban League, a sister organization to the NAACP, stated at one point that his seventh-grade son "has never gone to school a full day."[49]

School segregation and funding inequalities in the North in this time period illustrated the eventual implications of a system of simultaneous race and class discrimination. As Davison M. Douglas has shown, while Northern school segregation had often reflected residential segregation, at the turn of the twentieth century it was "far more deliberate," despite being in frequent violation of state law.[50] Though most Northern states prohibited school segregation and many Northern courts enforced these statutes when asked, white insistence on segregated school systems led to a political and cultural system of segregation that effectively found ways to skirt the relatively vague laws.[51] After the Great Migration, growing racial antagonism manifested in a dramatic increase in white demands for segregated schools in the North, and school segregation increased in much of the North during the first two decades of the century and then increased even more sharply after that.[52] These black schools in the North were usually older, more overcrowded, and in worse condition than the white schools.[53]

Legally permitted racial segregation in the North and West—segregation that was formally forbidden or absent from statutory law but was nonetheless practically enacted by institutions and actors with legal authority—has been more difficult to track historically precisely because of its seemingly more informal nature.[54] Yet its effects on students subject to separate and underfunded schools were likely quite similar. In Philadelphia, for example, school officials simply ignored the 1881 law forbidding segregation and designated separate schools for black and white students.[55] Chicago school officials did not formally acknowledge racial segregation at any point, instead introducing complex (and more "forward-looking") segregation devices such as the transfer system and the gerrymandering of school districts.[56] By 1930 approximately 27,700 of the 36,962 black children enrolled in Chicago schools attended "practically segregated schools."[57]

Schools in the South continued to struggle during the Depression under a distribution of tax funds that was simultaneously racial and economic— white local leaders ensured that fewer funds would flow to segregated black schools, maintaining their poor conditions and justifying them with the rhetoric of color blindness and equality. In the words of the South Carolina State Teachers Association, this desire to avoid improvement of black schools was rooted in an old belief that "to educate a rural Negro was to spoil a good field hand."[58] Annie Mae Hall, a teacher in Newton, Georgia, wrote to the Urban League in 1935 to request help in getting a school building.[59] Despite white leaders' statements that the black community "could get their old building after some bonds were paid off," the old white school building had then burned from "an unknown origin" right after a new $26,000 white schoolhouse was built, and no one had responded to the black community's requests for school tax funds since then.[60]

Late in 1934, Louis Campbell of Coeburn, Virginia, wrote to Walter White for help in pressuring the county school board to build a black high school that it had been promising for years. He closed his plea by commenting that there was no legal help nearby to obtain a hearing for the case of the local children who were unable to attend high school, since "generally, lawyers around mining districts are employed by corporations, and do not care to handle welfare cases."[61] Campbell continued to write to the NAACP over the next several months, repeatedly requesting assistance and investigation of the situation. Though initially not receiving a response (and writing follow-up letters subtly chiding the leadership for its inattention to what he described as a "well-disciplined army"), Campbell ultimately received letters and a visit from NAACP leaders to examine the situation.

Eventually, under pressure, the school board did pass an order allowing funding for the construction of black schools. Following this, however, they quickly met again and rescinded their previous order so as to use the funds for transportation instead of building.[62] Despite another series of letters from Campbell, White, and others, a bus system was ultimately created— for white children only. Finally, after further pressure, the school board agreed to fund private transportation for black students who qualified to attend the closest black high school. The first class of students that could have taken advantage of this transportation, however, were deemed "insufficiently prepared" to attend high school by the board, which required them to repeat grades of elementary school instead.[63] In a follow-up letter to

White in 1938, Campbell lamented the continuing lack of school transportation in his area, saying that "what federal aid that they could get" was "throttled by the county officials."[64] Finally, he noted the differential treatment based on wealth, arguing that the division superintendent of schools was the ultimate source of the problem because "he has nothing to fear but the tax payers, the big tax payers."[65]

Teachers' salary differentials were among the earliest locations of litigation for the NAACP in the area of educational equalization, particularly when funds were cut by local school boards during the Depression. Part of the zeal for teacher salary cases also likely stemmed from the middle-class membership focus of the association and its desire to win more teachers to its cause.[66] A Maryland resident wrote to the organization to offer to serve as a plaintiff in a teachers' salary case as both "a citizen" of the county and "a tax payer" of the county.[67] In Durham, North Carolina, African American teachers regularly earned less than half the salary of their white counterparts in 1905.[68] The difference between per capita salary expenditures on white and black teachers in segregated school systems increased from 52.8 percent in 1900 to 113 percent in 1930, according to one report.[69] And in 1935, Sidney R. Redmond, a prominent African American lawyer from Saint Louis, offered Charles Hamilton Houston a series of legal theories on which to base salary equalization litigation, concluding with the straightforward argument that since blacks "pay taxes as well as the whites . . . it is discrimination to use their money to pay white teachers more."[70]

W. B. Gibbs Jr., a Maryland elementary school principal, wrote to the organization in 1936 to describe the "starvation wages" of black teachers in comparison to the wages of white teachers—in Maryland, a first-year white elementary school teacher made $1,000, while a black teacher earned $522. To those whom he imagined saying, "You have chosen the profession, why complain?" Gibbs responded that "the complaint is being advanced solely from an economic standpoint."[71] One pastor in Atlanta, urging teachers to fight cuts in black teachers' salaries by up to 30 percent in 1934, predicted that "one of these days we shall bring the whole question to the courts and thrash out this matter for unequal pay for equal work in our educational system, as well as an unjust and unequal distribution of school funds gained from taxpayers' money."[72]

A frequent claim made by newspaper editorials was that the black community and black children were treated unequally because of the way taxes were appropriated for teachers' salaries. In a *Baltimore Afro-American* editorial from January 1920, the newspaper argued that the recommendation by the state board of education to pay white teachers $300 to $450 a year more than black teachers was "robbery, pure and simple."[73] The editors went on to say that there was not a tax that fell on white Marylanders that did not fall with equal weight on blacks, and that when black citizens did not pay taxes directly as owners of property, "they [paid] it as purchasers of goods and as renters of property." And when the Democratic successor to Huey Long, Senator Allen J. Ellender of Louisiana, disapproved of the Harrison-Black-Fletcher education bill to increase federal aid to education in 1937, he told a reporter from the paper that "there isn't any need for a lot of your witnesses to come to these hearings asking for equal distribution. Races take care of their own first, and if there's anything left, you can have some of that." The *Baltimore Afro-American* editors responded by saying that Ellender's comments were a rare public admission of the "highway robbery" of many white Southerners in relation to the double taxation of black people, describing it as "a swell idea of public trust—to use taxpayers' funds, to which all persons contribute, to take care of the schools of a certain color first!"[74]

Conclusion

In the small town of Oyster Bay, Long Island, in the fall of 1938, it was reported in the local newspaper that a "tax-payer" at a taxpayers' meeting said he was "sick and tired of paying taxes for a school filled with 'foreigners'" and suggested that the village schools were too good for Italian, Polish, and African American students.[75] Two Italian American, two Polish American, and two African American students in the school were immediately elected to a student strike committee, and they presented demands for an apology to the head of the local school board, Myron Jackson. The children told him that if he wouldn't disclose the name of the insulting "taxpayer," they would demand the apology directly from Jackson, and went on to lead a strike of over three hundred students in protest of the statements.[76] Like those children, many African Americans subjected to limitations on voting, unequal school funding, segregated education, and double taxation fought back against those systems in the early decades of the century. And while they did not necessarily win most of these cases, their battle built the foundation for a broad and ambitious litigation strategy that the NAACP would move forward with in the ensuing years.

It is evident from the cases in these decades that the power to set tax rates and distribute the tax fund, to paraphrase John Marshall in *McCulloch v. Maryland*, was the power to create and to destroy, and white school boards and excise boards claimed that power and wielded it to maintain vastly unequal white school facilities and salaries.[77] Yet what also shines through in the cases from this period is the consistency with which the general principle of separate taxation was refused by courts—and, despite this, the consistency with which these same cases had to be brought back to court, again and again, over many years. Despite the judicial rulings describing separate taxation as unconstitutional in many states, the number of repeat cases itself suggests that these rulings were not being implemented on the ground by either tax collectors or school boards. Separate taxation created its own structures of inequality, as evidenced in Kentucky's example, yet the "color-blind" inequality of double taxation in many ways proved even more insidious and became more widespread as time went on precisely because its racially inequitable character was hidden behind seeming neutrality.

Tellingly, in the *Bryant* case in Mississippi discussed at the beginning of this chapter, double taxation of black families was held to be constitutional when used to support white schools. But in Muskogee, Oklahoma, just two years previously, claimants' request for equal funding for the black school from tax funds designated for white schools was refused. It is difficult to avoid the conclusion that in many places, black taxpayers were being intentionally subjected to double taxation in order to buoy the budgets of the white schools, even as white taxpayers were freed from responsibility for the support or equalization of black schools. Far from the myth of white taxpayers subsidizing black education, which would help fuel the white backlash after *Brown* discussed in later chapters, black taxpayers spent decades consistently overpaying just for the opportunity for their children to attend poorly funded schools. Ironically, in several Southern states, the common pool of white and black taxes only began to flow in a more meaningful way toward school construction or funding for black children when white politicians scrambled in the years preceding the *Brown* decision to stave off potential desegregation orders, as will be seen in the following chapter.

CHAPTER FOUR

A Drain on Taxpayers

Graduate School Segregation and the Road to Brown

R. I. Brigham, self-described as a "white educator," argued in 1946 in an article in the *Baltimore Afro-American* that segregated schools were "a drain on taxpayers" and were "costly and wasteful" to Missouri.[1] The straightforwardly economic argument that separate schools were ultimately a waste of taxpayer resources was deployed in various ways by the NAACP and many other advocates in the graduate school segregation cases as a conscious strategy to force the fiscal hand of segregationist states. For example, in 1936, the *Richmond Times-Dispatch* argued that black Virginians deserved "justice" in pursuit of graduate or professional training. The problem was evidenced by the unequal treatment of a "colored citizen and taxpayer [who] must stand the entire expense of securing graduate and professional instruction in some other State.... The white citizen and taxpayer, on the other hand, may attend any one of several State-supported institutions."[2] While the *Times-Dispatch*'s remedy was to have the state set aside $10,000 to enable African American students to pursue graduate education outside the state, the *Baltimore Afro-American* quickly pointed out the absurdity of this remedy: "If it is really a matter of economics, isn't it strange that it never occurred to the authors of such a proposal that it would be even cheaper than that to open the doors of the University of Virginia and other lily-white State institutions, where facilities already exist?"[3]

This chapter examines the shift in the NAACP's litigation strategy at the height of the Great Depression and the organization's focus on black students' access to white schools as a remedy for unequal facilities, as well as the ways in which taxpayer citizenship continued to be asserted as a fundamental basis for rights in these cases. The NAACP's new litigation strategy centered on the integration of education at the most elite levels of professional training, rather than the frequently poor and either rural or urban school districts and teacher equalization litigation of previous cases. This emphasis on the achievements of African Americans in professional training was perhaps understandable from a team of professionally educated lawyers, but it also served to further solidify a middle-class taxpayer strategy and the racial liberalism that would reach its pinnacle in *Brown*'s focus on the isolated harm of racial prejudice, disconnected from other structural inequalities such as unequal taxation and funding.

Though the NAACP was sensitive to both economic inequality between white and black schools and the formal and informal structures of racial segregation that created the separate schools to begin with, there was ongoing dissension at the highest levels of leadership about whether a focus on legal victories over school segregation should take precedence over an approach that focused on economic disparities and community organizing. This debate came to a head in 1934 when W. E. B. DuBois resigned from the NAACP after writing a series of editorials insisting that the organization could not maintain complete opposition to segregation while also supporting racial pride and community self-organization.[4] Lloyd Imes of New York wrote to the NAACP shortly after DuBois's resignation, saying that "for one who hates segregation as much as I do, I had rather have Dr. DuBois' 'segregation' than all the so-called 'anti-segregation' of his opponents."[5] Arthur Spingarn wrote to Walter White around the same time, saying that the resolution on segregation passed by the NAACP board was both "revolutionary and weak, because it expresses disapproval only of enforced segregation, whereas our historic attitude has been to regard all segregation as an evil, even though in some cases we are forced to submit to it."[6] This chapter will frame the new educational litigation strategy of the NAACP, which focused on categories of formal race, middle-class racial liberalism, and graduate school segregation as a primary point of attack, as well as the pressure the organization's litigation placed on tax funding in many states by making segregation as costly as possible in the buildup to *Brown*.

Gaines and the Road to *Brown*

In 1936, an aspiring young black law student named Donald Murray won the right to attend the University of Maryland Law School after an NAACP legal battle that made it all the way to the Maryland Court of Appeals.[7] In the *Murray* case, the NAACP followed the new strategy, proposed by the internal Margold Report, of pursuing graduate school admissions, knowing that the "equalization" of graduate school opportunities would be so cost prohibitive for most states that they would have no choice but to admit qualified black students or turn them away completely. Thurgood Marshall, who had been forced to commute long hours from his home near the University of Maryland to Washington, D.C., for law school, saw the case as a particularly personal triumph.[8] The Maryland Court of Appeals was careful to distinguish the Supreme Court's precedent in *Cumming* and, though they found in favor of Murray, was also cautious in asserting that "equality of treatment does not require that privileges be provided members of the two races in the same place." Ultimately, the court held, "the state may choose the method by which equality is maintained." *Murray* was the first case in which the NAACP achieved its goal of court-ordered integration, and it would prove an important foundation for the decision in the *Gaines* case a few years later.

Lloyd Gaines, described as a "handsome" and "rail-thin" young man, graduated as his high school's valedictorian in just three years, and he sold magazines door to door to help pay for his college education at segregated Lincoln University.[9] When he applied to the University of Missouri Law School and was denied in 1936, the same year as the *Murray v. Maryland* decision ordering "equalization" of graduate opportunities, the NAACP believed it had found the next perfect test case for graduate-level segregation across the South. Missouri was one of the only states that provided an in-state black state university, but funding for the black state university and the white university was extremely disparate. Missouri had, in the fiscal year ending June 30, 1934, distributed $3,125 of federal funds to Lincoln University and $405,642 to the University of Missouri.[10]

Taxpayer status was an important component of the NAACP's arguments in the early stages of the case. In Gaines's initial petition to the Boone County Circuit Court, he asserted that he was "a citizen of the United States and of the state of Missouri, resident of the city of St. Louis, and a taxpayer."[11] The next point in his petition argued that the curators of the University of Missouri performed their function "with funds derived in large part ... from taxes collected from the citizens at large in the State of Missouri, including petitioner."[12] In further arguments, Gaines and the NAACP extended their implied claim that his basis for the suit was in part rooted in his taxpayer status by asserting that the agents of the university had deprived him of his property without due process, referring to the taxes he had paid to the state, from whose general fund the university drew its operating costs.[13]

The university did not treat the claim of Gaines's taxpayer status as irrelevant, though the Supreme Court ultimately would. Gaines's position as a taxpayer was repeatedly contested by the attorneys of the university as the case went on. The curators of the university quickly denied that they had "any knowledge or information thereof sufficient to form a belief as to the truth of the allegation that relator Gaines ... is a taxpayer; and respondents therefore deny that relator Gaines is a taxpayer."[14] They then went on to deny that they had sufficient information to believe that the operating funds were derived in part from "taxes (if any) collected from relator" and therefore denied that any funds used were in fact partially from Gaines's own taxes.[15]

In the hearing before Judge W. M. Dinwiddie of Boone County Circuit Court in September 1936, NAACP attorney Sidney Redmond asked Gaines specifically about his identity as a taxpayer during direct examination. Redmond asked Gaines first if he was a taxpayer, to which Gaines responded, "incidental tax." When Redmond further asked Gaines what taxes he paid, Gaines replied that he paid "sales tax, internal tax on luxuries, and amusement tax."[16] Since Gaines was a student, taxpayer status was more difficult to prove if the definition of a rights-bearing "taxpayer" was someone with a well-paying, full-time job. While it would be impossible to show that Gaines's incidental taxes were not included in the university's general tax-based fund, the fact that he was not a property owner appeared to encourage the university to dismiss his taxpayer identity.

The circuit court eventually found in favor of the university, and, as in similar previous cases, awarded the university their costs from Gaines.[17] Gaines petitioned for a rehearing by the Missouri Supreme Court while pursuing Supreme Court certiorari. The NAACP attorneys now took the testimony that the university admitted "foreign" students, except people of African descent, as a basis for a new kind of taxpayer citizenship claim, arguing that Gaines, as a "Negro citizen taxpayer," was helping to provide this publicly funded education "for said whites and foreigners."[18] Since the tuition and fees paid by other students did not even cover the operating costs of the law school, attorneys argued, they had to be "supplemented by public tax money, which appellant is compelled to pay in part without an opportunity to participate in the benefits therefrom."[19]

Gaines's assertion of taxpayer citizenship was thus closely tied to an understanding of a right to education as a property right belonging uniquely to taxpayers or citizens, reminiscent of *Gong Lum*, discussed in chapter 2. When Gaines appealed to the Missouri Supreme Court, they flatly rejected the idea that as a "citizen and taxpayer of Missouri," he had a "proprietary interest in the University of Missouri" and was thus being deprived of his property rights without due process of law. The court found that black taxpayers were entitled to school advantages "substantially equal" to those provided for white citizens of the state. But, the court continued, "equality and not identity of school advantages is what the law guarantees to every citizen."[20] NAACP attorneys filed a petition for certiorari to the Supreme Court in which they again repeatedly asserted that Gaines was both "a citizen and taxpayer of Missouri."[21]

The case reached the Supreme Court late in 1938 and was decided relatively quickly. By a six-to-two margin, the court struck down the Missouri Supreme Court ruling against Gaines on Fourteenth Amendment equal-protection grounds. The opinion held that if a state provided a law school or other type of education to white students, it must supply the same thing to black students, either through a separate institution within the state or at the same institution with white students. Since Missouri had no separate black law school in the state, the curators were ordered to admit Gaines for the following year. Though far less famous than its descendant, *Brown*, the *Gaines* case emphasized the importance of the equality rule of *Plessy* in a way that was very different from the *Brown* approach. Rather than asserting that legal separation was itself the basis of inequality because of the stigma that attached to the segregated individuals, as the *Brown* court did, the *Gaines* opinion exemplified the same reasoning that would be used several decades later to overturn sex-segregated higher education.[22] By focusing on "intangible" aspects of education that could not be replicated, such as in-state location, faculty connections, reputation, prestige, and the like, this kind of legal rationale in many ways indicated that "identity" of privileges *was* in fact required in order to achieve educational "equality"—at least in a graduate school setting. In the *Gaines* opinion, the court was particular in noting that the many debates consuming the lower courts—which included whether Gaines qualified as a "taxpayer" in various ways—were "beside the point."[23] Instead, what was crucial was that a privilege was provided by the state for one set of students at a level of quality that another set of students were not able to obtain because of their race.

Though the NAACP had no choice but to agree to dismiss the case once it returned to the lower court due to Gaines's mysterious disappearance, the legal victory reinvigorated the legal campaign against school segregation, especially for the new general counsel for the NAACP in 1938, Thurgood Marshall.[24] The victory was also meaningful to a broadening community understanding of what school desegregation represented. In a letter to the court in 1938, responding to the *Gaines* decision, the Reverend A. R. Vanlandingham of Danville, Virginia, argued that African Americans were "segregated, jim crowed, denied our political rights, disfranchised, and taxed without representation [*sic*]." According to Vandlandingham, all Southern blacks wanted was "social equality," including "equal chance, equal pay, equal political privilege, equal education facilities, equal homes, equal streets and economical freedom."[25] NAACP letter writers responding to the case similarly complained about the tax burden of segregated universities. A Saint Louis attorney wrote to his senator in 1939 asking him to vote down a separate university funding bill then under consideration in response to the *Gaines* decision, stating in all capital letters that "this bill would create a staggering tax burden" and that, "from the standpoint of a taxpayer, I denounce this bill to the high Heavens."[26] But despite the attempt by various states to forestall desegregation remedies, the wind was changing. Within less than a decade, several more cases came before the Supreme Court involving graduate school segregation.

The High Cost of Graduate School Segregation

Though efforts to pursue litigation and locate willing plaintiffs were delayed by World War II, the NAACP found its next test case in Ada Lois Sipuel, who applied to the University of Oklahoma Law School in 1946 and was denied based on her race. Unlike in Missouri, school integration was a criminal offense in Oklahoma. The Oklahoma Constitution of 1941 made it illegal for anyone to operate a school in the state that received both white and black pupils, and anyone who did so could be convicted of a misdemeanor and fined between $100 and $500.[27] In addition, the constitution ensured that every day such a school was open would be counted as a separate offense, and provided for misdemeanor convictions and daily compounding fines for any instructor teaching in a school that had both white and black students.[28] While providing no criminal punishment for African American pupils, a third constitutional provision banned white students from attending a school that included black students, again creating misdemeanor penalties and compounding fines for any white student who did so.[29]

The NAACP's attorneys continued to make an argument that taxation was an important basis for a claim to educational rights in their petition to the Oklahoma Supreme Court, in which they asserted that "the University is a part of the educational system of the State and is maintained by appropriations from public funds raised by taxation from the citizens and taxpayers of the State of Oklahoma."[30] The Oklahoma Supreme Court held, based on the state's policy of segregated education, that the university authorities had acted appropriately in denying Sipuel admission. Judge Earl Welch argued that the university was correct, since the schools had been instituted separately and "maintained by voters and taxpayers and educators and patrons of both races as if for the greater good of both races in Oklahoma." Recalling the "reciprocity" rationale of many late nineteenth-century judges, he concluded that this was equal treatment under the law, since "a negro child or pupil may not enter a white school nor a white child or pupil enter a negro school."[31]

Local authority was repeatedly connected in his opinion to the local and state tax base for public education. In discussing the question of whether "equal facilities" were actually being provided to Sipuel and other black students, Welch admitted that "the benefits and burdens of public taxation must be shared by citizens without discrimination against any class on account of their race." However, he said, relying on *Cumming*, when it came to education in schools maintained by state taxation, that was an issue for the states, and federal authority could not be justified in interfering unless there was a "clear and unmistakable disregard of rights."

But Welch also repeatedly couched his decision in language about "fairness" to taxpayers. By arguing that the state had authority to protect taxpayers' fiscal interest in efficiency and financial security, the court assumed that the decision not to build a black law school was presumptively economic and therefore benign. Though the state had authority to create a separate black law school, the court found that if it had "in fairness to all taxpayers" deferred building one until the need "was made manifest," it was not fair for a black student to then claim relief that went against the state's express policy of educational segregation. According to Welch, the outside-fund scholarship plan to send black students to other state universities did not "necessarily demonstrate" discrimination against African Americans, despite the *Gaines* decision. Welch argued that "financial consideration, the saving to taxpayers, is not controlling, but is important to both races."[32] He continued to assert that it was likely the wish of taxpayers and pupils of both races to create an outside fund for scholarships in order to efficiently utilize taxpayer funds.[33] In fact, he concluded that it could be the case that a black student "who receives education outside the state at state expense is favored over his neighbor white pupil rather than discriminated against in that particular."[34] Ironically, given his defense of taxpayer rights, Welch himself was convicted of income tax evasion years later and forced to resign from the judiciary after one of his fellow judges admitted that he, Welch and another judge had taken more than $150,000 to decide cases a certain way.[35]

But for all Welch's efforts, courts do not generally like to be overruled, let alone have their prior rulings ignored by those lower on the judicial hierarchy, and the Supreme Court perhaps least of all. When the case reached the Supreme Court in early 1947, the *Gaines* precedent decided a decade prior was clear, and the outcome was not especially in doubt. After Thurgood Marshall argued the case on the same equal-protection grounds—and virtually the same facts—as the *Gaines* case, the court took only four days to reach its decision, overturning the lower court in a few succinct paragraphs and citing only *Gaines* for support. The *Sipuel* decision was the first in what would become a long line of unanimous school desegregation decisions reaching through *Brown* into the early 1970s.

Within two years, two more cases were before the Supreme Court, both involving graduate school segregation. Like Ada Lois Sipuel, George McLaurin, who already had a master's degree in education, also sought professional training at the University of Oklahoma, this time a doctorate in education. He was admitted—after litigating his initial denial on the *Sipuel* precedent—but the Oklahoma legislature had acted quickly to ensure that when African American students were admitted to previously white university programs, education would still be administered "separately."[36] So, McLaurin was required to sit at a separate desk in the hallway just outside the classroom with a Reserved for Colored label; he had to sit at a separate desk on the library mezzanine; and he had to sit at a different cafeteria table and eat at a different time than other students. When he sued the university demanding equal treatment, the Oklahoma Supreme Court denied his claim and he appealed. Before the hearing at the Supreme Court, where the state was aware it was likely to lose, the university altered these original "accommodations" to allow him to sit in a designated row *inside* the classroom, to study at his separate desk in the library on the *main* floor of the reading room, and to eat at his special designated table *while* other students ate. The court found these alterations irrelevant and held that he "must receive the same treatment at the hands of the state as students of other races."[37] In particular, the court argued that such restrictions impaired his ability "to study, to engage in discussions and exchange views with other students, and, in general, to learn his profession." Again, in an extension of the discussion of qualitative differences in conditions begun in *Gaines*, the court seemed close to holding that all aspects of (graduate) education had to be truly substantively equal for equal protection in education to be achieved.

The final major school segregation opinion prior to *Brown* was announced the same day as its corollary, *McLaurin v. Oklahoma*. Herman Sweatt had applied to the University of Texas Law School in 1946 and was denied admission because he was black. He brought suit to compel his admission under the *Gaines* precedent, and the trial court agreed that he had been denied equal protection but gave the state six months to supply substantially equal facilities rather than mandating his admission. While his case was pending, Texas announced the construction of a new law school for African American students, which was opened within a few months, but Sweatt refused to enroll. On the question of whether the facilities at the two schools were "equal," the trial court and court of civil appeals affirmed that they were. The Supreme Court granted certiorari after the Texas Supreme Court refused to consider the case, and, building on *Gaines*, *Sipuel*, and *McLaurin*, it issued another unanimous opinion that chipped away at the "equality" definition of the "separate but equal" standard and stated there was much more to equal protection in education than numbers of library books— "reputation of the faculty . . . position and influence of the alumni, standing in the community, traditions and prestige" were all crucial.[38]

By the late 1940s, Charles Hamilton Houston was confident in describing in a newspaper essay the legal strategy discussions taking place in the NAACP in the wake of its victories in these cases. He described a black war veteran "and Baltimore taxpayer," Leon A. Norris, who had applied to the Maryland Institute for a degree in teacher art training and was refused based on race. Though the district court decided that the private school couldn't be compelled to accept qualified black students, "the court suggested that Norris might litigate in the Maryland State courts the question whether the city and State can appropriate public money to a private corporation which draws the color line." According to Houston, the NAACP was still deciding "whether to appeal the Federal case, or to start a new taxpayer's suit in the State courts to enjoin the appropriations."[39] But the rationale of local control of tax funds was not so quickly abandoned. The *Gaines* opinion had emphasized that the right denied to Gaines, and the constitutional protection he was entitled to, was only as an individual. Asserting that "petitioner's right was a personal one," the court repeatedly reiterated that it was "the individual who is entitled to the equal protection of the laws."[40] The dissent by Justice James McReynolds, joined by Justice Pierce Butler, had quoted Justice John Marshall Harlan's statement in the *Cumming* case that "the education of the people in schools maintained by state taxation is a matter belonging to the respective states, and any interference on the part of Federal authority with the management of such schools cannot be justified except in the case of a clear and unmistakable disregard of rights secured by the supreme law of the land." In a comment that hinted at the dissenters' suspicion of the cases' motivations, Justice McReynolds recounted with approval the out-of-state tuition option Gaines was offered to enable him to study law, and then tartly followed this with the statement, "if perchance that is the thing really desired."[41]

Graduate school conditions were thus key to many of the NAACP's education victories in this period, and particularly variations in quality and equality, from enormous differences in facilities and faculty down to the specific location of a desk or cafeteria table. In some respects, it was probably easier for a Supreme Court made up of elite-trained lawyers to identify the qualitative importance of nuanced differences between different law school facilities and experiences. And it was probably easier for an NAACP team made up of elite-trained lawyers to argue for the necessity of each intangible benefit that encompassed the law school experience and ensured success in a legal or professional career. Taxpayer-funded higher education was an important strategic focal point for establishing the logic that separation invariably led to inequality. But public schools at the elementary and secondary levels were in another category of resource disparity entirely, and the inequalities between and within schools were growing during the 1940s as school construction ground to a halt during the Depression and World War II. The NAACP, meanwhile, was drifting further from discussions of economic civil rights in general as racial divides within the labor movement and the middle-class focus of the NAACP's leadership combined to leave behind its earlier forays into labor and employment litigation in the 1940s.[42]

Spending for Segregation

After *Sweatt* and *McLaurin*, Southern states began to ready themselves for the possibility that elementary and secondary public school segregation itself might be overturned by the court next. In 1950, the NAACP sought an injunction against officials in Clarendon County, South Carolina, to prohibit them from maintaining segregated schools. The complaint was filed on behalf of the "parents and taxpayers" of Clarendon County against the trustees of the school district containing the segregated schools.[43] R. M. Elliott, Clarendon County superintendent and named defendant in the *Briggs v. Elliott* case, claimed that black students were not entitled to school transportation because blacks did not "pay enough in taxes" to warrant a school bus.[44] Under the imminent threat of desegregation litigation, however, tax funds abruptly materialized to build new schools for African American children and improve transportation and facilities. South Carolina underwent an intense program of school consolidation in the early 1950s, going from 1,200 school districts in the state in 1951 to 102 in 1955 by eliminating one-teacher schools in rural areas and providing "substantial equality" of transportation for African American students for the first time.[45] James F. Byrnes, governor from 1951 to 1955, spearheaded the campaign. The state went from spending $36 million a year on education in 1951 to spending $65 million by 1954, largely on new construction projects. Property taxes were not adequate, the governor soon realized, to actually provide any semblance of substantive equality in school conditions in short order, so the state chose to levy a sales tax to raise most of the funds. But the *Briggs* case from South Carolina, which would eventually be consolidated into *Brown v. Board of Education*, was an example of enormous funding and resource inequalities that could not be remedied with a few years of higher taxes.

At almost the same time that the NAACP was litigating for equal graduate school conditions and Southern states were scrambling to improve public school facilities, one of the first cases addressing Mexican American segregation and what would later be described as "de facto" segregation was decided. Jim Crow laws had been silent with regard to the segregation of Mexican American schoolchildren, but early on states such as California had developed a method for dealing with this silence. Similar to the way in which many states in the North segregated schools by race through custom, location, and funding despite such segregation being technically illegal, local authorities in California relied on custom and fictional language tests to designate some schools as strictly Anglo and others as Mexican American. In California, the district court decision in *Mendez v. Westminster School District of Orange County* ruled this widespread school segregation of Mexican American students unconstitutional, setting a precedent that would be cited eight years later in *Brown*.[46] In *Mendez*, the California court did not, however, have to address *Plessy v. Ferguson*'s precedent, precisely because California did not legally *allow* segregation of Mexican American students. The state education code did allow school boards to segregate "Indian," "Chinese," "Japanese," and "Mongolian" students. While these provisions of California law were quickly jettisoned the year after the *Mendez* decision, the fluid nature of "de jure" and "de facto" segregation in California foreshadowed the adaptive methods of school segregation that would become widespread in the decades after *Brown* and that will be discussed further in chapter 6.

Another of the cases that would be consolidated into the *Brown* litigation was *Gebhart v. Belton*, a suit from Delaware. *Gebhart*'s complaint attacked segregated schools on the basis that the parents of black students were citizens and taxpayers of the school districts and were being required to "bear certain burdens and forego certain advantages, neither of which is suffered by parents of white children."[47] *Bolling v. Sharpe*, the Washington, D.C., case that was decided separately but issued the same day as *Brown*, was filed on behalf of "taxpayers whose children have been refused admission to Sousa Junior High School in Washington."[48] This case was particularly galling for many in the community, who saw 6,508 surplus seats in the white schools and 122 extra teachers "costing the taxpayers $541,924 in salaries," while black schools in the DC school system had more students than white schools and were overcrowded and underfunded.[49]

Brown itself, when the ruling was announced to a still, silent courtroom, was not a decision connected to facilities inequality or funding inequity. Rather, the case defined inequality in terms of psychological harms—intangible, though certainly no less real for those experiencing them—and held that it was because of these inevitable effects of state segregation on children's "hearts and minds" that separate would always be unequal. However, psychological effects were in many ways some of the most amorphous and difficult-to-measure ramifications of segregation. Unequal facilities, inadequate funding, and disparate access and resources were also, arguably, inevitable—and measurable—results of state-sponsored segregation in the vast majority of communities, results that the Supreme Court had identified clearly in the case of segregated graduate and professional schools. But the legal demand for strictly defined identity categories was ingrained in both the way in which the case was brought and the way in which it was decided.[50] Part of this was certainly a strategic decision to forestall the undoubted response of many Southern states—as South Carolina's example shows—that they would spend any amount of money in order to maintain segregation. However, the *Brown* court also created a new paradigm of "inequality" for school segregation decisions, one focused on the personal harm inflicted on the student's "heart and mind" by the state-sponsored rule. It would prove to be both morally and historically compelling, as well as extremely slippery to rely on as legal precedent for litigating equality in many later cases.

Racial Liberalism and Unequal Resources

The *Brown* decision has been controversial since before it was even handed down, though the reasons for criticism have varied. Derrick A. Bell Jr. has famously claimed that *Brown* was the result of a confluence of factors pushing white liberals to momentarily identify their interests in containing communism, domestic resistance, and economic security with the desegregation movement, a moment that quickly ended.[51] And, as Mary Dudziak has persuasively argued, the *Brown* decision was powerfully connected to the foreign policy impetus to deflect Soviet propaganda regarding racial segregation, whereas substantive economic differentiation was part of the very system the United States was fighting the Soviet Union in order to maintain.[52] Indeed, several prominent legal theorists recently "rewrote" the decision, most often by including an affirmative declaration of the constitutional right to education as the basis for their revised ruling, a rationale largely missing from *Brown* that would have a profound impact on later litigants, as discussed in chapter 6.[53]

Lani Guinier in particular has argued for an understanding of the legal strategy of racial liberalism in *Brown* as one that centered only on psychological stigma and thus focused on the unacceptability of individual prejudice rather than systemic inequality. This focus on race and formal segregation left behind the legacy of the pursuit of equal educational resources discussed in the first half of this book. In the "court-centered universe" Guinier describes, desegregation, which should have been a strategic tactic in order to obtain more equity, became itself the end goal.[54] By facilitating what would become a "doctrinal distinction between race and class that lifted unequal resource distribution out of the constitutional canon," the court's reasoning also forestalled political coalitions around economic inequality across racial lines.[55] And Neil Gotanda has argued persuasively that the "color-blind constitutionalism" at play in the law since Justice Harlan's famous deployment of the phrase in his *Plessy* dissent "matured" in *Brown* as a doctrine of formal race.[56] Marking what Gotanda describes as the maturation of formal race ideology, the *Brown* decision has had a significant impact on law and legal reasoning, perhaps even greater than its ultimate impact on segregated school systems themselves.[57] These arguments suggest that the *Brown* decision, having served its historical purpose of highlighting the psychological damage of racial prejudice, has in fact done relatively little to remedy glaringly racialized economic inequalities in education.

Justice Robert Jackson, formerly the U.S. chief prosecutor at the Nuremberg trials, was also known for his stinging dissent in the *Korematsu* decision, in which the court upheld the military's decision to intern Japanese American citizens. Jackson had argued in his *Korematsu* dissent that once the court validates an exercise of racial discrimination by rationalizing it under the Constitution, "the principle then lies about like a loaded weapon," waiting for the hands of future authorities to "expand it to new purposes."[58] Jackson would also prove to be one of the most difficult votes for Earl Warren to sway in the *Brown* decision. In a memo sent by Jackson as the cases consolidated under *Brown* were under consideration, he argued that the court "cannot overlook the fact that for three quarters of a century it has been the law of the Constitution as declared by this Court that the negro is entitled to equal facilities if they are separate."[59] At the same time, Jackson acknowledged, the court's ruling to that effect "has remained in a large part of the country a dead letter." In explaining this, Jackson argued that the way in which the equality aspect of *Plessy* had been roundly ignored indicated that a legislative remedy was superior to a judicial pronouncement.[60] His argument was rooted in the blatant lack of equality in schools despite the judicial ruling in *Plessy* mandating equal accommodations:

> One needs only to be a casual traveler in many parts of our country to see for himself that the facilities provided for negroes are not equal to those provided for white pupils and while in any particular case, we should be guided by the evidence in the record, we need not, on a matter of nationwide common knowledge, be so dumb as to pretend absence of knowledge. Why has the separate but equal doctrine remained a dead letter as to its equality aspect? It has remained an empty pronouncement of policy because it was declared and supported heartily only by the judicial department which has no power to enforce its own decrees. The pronouncement had no concrete application to any particular school district until some negro of that district brought an action to enforce his equal rights under it. This was costly, it was time consuming and it was impossible for a disadvantaged people to accomplish on any broad scale.[61]

Jackson expressed concern that the court could not contribute constructively to the process of building integrated school systems, a process that would have to be largely performed by local or state action, which would then involve decisions of "taxation, the sale of bonds, taxpayers' votes or other affirmative actions."[62] In order to avoid throwing the issue completely to the states and localities, according to Jackson, congressional action was necessary to "make provisions for federal funds where changes required are beyond the means of the community, for mixing . . . will impose the largest burden on some of the nation's lowest income regions."[63] Jackson returned several times in his memo to a concern about where the money would come from to make integration feasible, given that "the white schools are good, the Negro schools poor." In what would prove to be a prescient assessment of the complex interrelationship between economic desegregation and racial desegregation, he argued that shifting white pupils to poorly funded or dilapidated black schools would be a measure "not likely to be accepted without strong local opposition."[64] Jackson did not, however, have to be convinced that education was a fundamental right of citizens. He argued instead that the "place of public education has markedly changed" since the time of the Fourteenth Amendment.[65] Indeed, Jackson argued, education was now both a right and a duty of citizenship, not a privilege for a handful of elites.[66]

The overall impetus of the unanimous court, however, which would eventually include Jackson, was toward a declarative ruling that enabled at least a small degree of public desegregation for legal, moral, and, certainly, political purposes.[67] In fact, as the letters received by the justices in the wake of the *Brown* decision reveal, even the court's minimal, surface efforts at desegregation were unacceptable to many whites, North and South, who translated their disapproval into a discourse of taxpayer rights. And the deeply intertwined structures of racial taxation and school segregation across the country would prove highly resistant to the *Brown* doctrine of limited formal racial equality under law.

Conclusion

In the wake of the *Brown* ruling, the Oklahoma Association of Negro Teachers Committee on Integration proposed the adoption of a state constitutional amendment that would increase tax levies and allow the money to follow African American students on a per capita basis.[68] The Urban League instead focused most of its efforts on eliminating or reducing housing segregation, in the hopes that educational integration would follow residential integration.[69] Doing so, they also noted the difference between the "desegregation" imperative of *Brown* and real integration. In assisting local chapters and Northern school districts toward this goal of complete integration, the national Urban League office explained that "this difference in emphasis presupposes a difference between desegregation and integration. The one is eliminating legal barriers that prevent free use of school facilities by Negro children. The other is a more positive process, one that seeks to make the public school system an effective vehicle of democratic education."[70]

Desegregation was certainly not the same as integration, but it was a powerful symbol. In an eighteen-year period between 1936 and 1954, the NAACP's attack on graduate school segregation had culminated in what had seemed, at least to many, the impossible. *Brown* altered the political—if not the educational—landscape almost immediately. But the decision and its legal ramifications were also rooted in an identification of "formal race" and Southern-style "legal" school segregation that had little impact on the complexities of residential school segregation and property-tax-based funding inequalities. While attention to specific aspects of the educational opportunities provided to students was critical for the NAACP in securing the Supreme Court opinions in the graduate school cases, attention to the equality of primary and secondary education was strategically minimized in the struggle to achieve a strong ruling against formal racial segregation laws in *Brown*. The next chapter will take up the response to the *Brown* decision and the way in which that response channeled the anger of segregationists into a fierce claim of white taxpayer entitlement.

CHAPTER FIVE

The White Man's Tax Dollar

Segregationists and Backlash

As the Supreme Court was debating *Brown v. Board of Education* in early 1954, Harry A. Johnston wrote a letter from his home in Alabama to Justice Robert Jackson. Johnston wrote to lament the possible desegregation ruling anticipated from the court, saying he spoke on behalf of "the tax-paying citizens as individuals, as well as parents," who, he said, did not want to have to accept blacks "on an equality basis."[1] Ultimately, one of the most common refrains in the grassroots debates around judicial desegregation from 1954 to 1970 was precisely Johnston's claim—that those speaking in opposition to desegregation were *the* taxpayers and had a legal right as "tax-paying citizens" to an all-white educational experience. The same argument that African American citizens had attempted to deploy before the *Brown* case was now put forth vehemently by segregationists as the reason *Brown*'s ruling should not be implemented. The ramifications of this racialized entitlement could also be seen on the ground in the Prince Edward County case in Virginia, where public schools were cut off from taxpayer funding for years.

This chapter argues that the discourse of "taxpayer citizenship" legal consciousness was consistently deployed by segregationists defending racial inequality in the wake of the *Brown* decision in 1954. While previous chapters discussed how African American individuals and families before *Brown* had used "taxpaying citizen" language to argue for the right to education, segregationists on the defensive after the ruling claimed the right to unequal and separate schooling based on an assumed difference in taxes paid by white and black taxpayers. Despite the lack of evidence that whites were actually paying more or disproportionate levels of taxes, the argument proved rhetorically powerful precisely because it appealed to white beliefs in racial superiority, including their presumed status as the "real" taxpayers. This legal consciousness of taxpayer citizenship and taxpayer rights to education built on the unequal structure of property-tax school financing to entrench fiscal inequality in public schools even as the formal legal protections for racial segregation were eroding. Ultimately, by linking the right to education to taxation, these white "taxpaying citizens" facilitated an idea that public school resources should legitimately be linked to the tax payments and taxable wealth of a person or a racialized community. They also laid claim to an identity as *the* taxpaying population, rendering invisible many African Americans' actual experience of double taxation and disproportionate support of white schools, as discussed in chapter 3.

This consistent use of "taxpayer" legal consciousness by segregationists contributed to the racialization of taxpayer status and solidified fiscal inequalities in education by implicitly tying educational benefits to the amount of taxes paid. Even though courts did not formally recognize taxpayer status as a sufficient basis for a legal claim in these decades, taxpayer identity was specifically connected to the perceived right to education in letters and court documents during the desegregation era. For people of color, this right was usually framed as access to education equal to that provided to white students. For whites, it was often the right to access superior education in comparison to the educational resources provided to black and other minority students.

In the first section, I examine how the initial responses to *Brown* in defense of segregation were consistently framed in terms of taxpayer citizenship and the rights of whites to unequal and better-funded schooling. Next, I look at the response to the *Brown* decision in the courts, particularly in the lengthy litigation from Prince Edward County, Virginia, which was rife with tax policy implications. Finally, I return to the reaction of segregationists to these education cases by tracing the deeply racialized "taxpayer" rebellion in the 1960s.

While other work examining the threat of a taxpayer revolt in the 1960s and 1970s has focused mainly on the compelling links between party political leaders and the suburban taxpayer anxiety of homeowners, this chapter argues that taxpayer identity was also linked before this to a legal consciousness that obscured class divisions while simultaneously elevating those with more taxable income to a position of more rights, particularly education rights, in a "marketplace of citizenship."[2] This chapter looks at the specific way public school taxation, as an obligation and a perceived source of rights and citizenship, was transformed into a deeply felt form of white racial consciousness in response to the school desegregation cases of the civil rights era. Ultimately, it was precisely the way in which taxpayer citizenship was utilized as an argument for separate education rights in this period that made it a category of exclusion.

Segregationists and Taxpayer Rights

In recent years many historians of the civil rights era have turned their attention to the development of conservative politics and Southern white resistance to school desegregation, often focusing on community organizations such as the White Citizens' Councils that sprang up all over the South in the wake of *Brown*.[3] These authors have richly explored the way in which white moderates attempted to protect public schools as an institution while simultaneously moving farther and farther into white-enclave suburbs, and the shock and anger that was felt by many die-hard segregationists at the series of decisions that removed legal barriers to racial interaction in classroom space. In these works, the importance of parental rights, the right to association, the language of "freedom," and arguments for federalism and "states' rights" is identified, and these elements are discussed as some of the formative components of the anti-integration movement. But, as I argue in this chapter, one of the other constant refrains emerging from letters sent by segregationists to the Supreme Court after *Brown* was also specifically the defense of taxpayers' rights to education that had previously been put forward by many African Americans for very different reasons. Kevin Kruse has noted that whites leaving Atlanta for suburbia in the 1950s in the wake of court-ordered desegregation "fought to take their finances with them," articulating many of their demands in the language of tax resistance and taxpayer rights.[4] Taxpayer identity would prove to be a powerful movement-building tool for growing and refining the rhetoric of the segregation movement in the 1950s and 1960s, with repercussions into later decades. Eventually, as Joseph Crespino has argued, taxpayer-rights controversies such as the one over the IRS's investigation of private religious schools in the 1970s helped create a sense of persecution that motivated and consolidated the emerging conservative Christian movement at the time.[5]

The letters sent to the Supreme Court justices in response to the desegregation cases from *Brown* onward compose some of the thickest Supreme Court archives of popular legal ideas, with the possible exception of the archive of letters around reproductive rights cases. The use of taxation and taxpayers' rights as a principle to uphold segregation in these letters was often implicitly premised on the idea that African Americans proportionally paid less in taxes, and therefore were not entitled to the same benefits as whites. Whites repeatedly asserted that they paid more taxes than blacks and therefore had the right to be heard by courts and legislatures. This sense of "buying" services from the government through tax payments was tied in their rhetoric to an idea that African Americans were lesser taxpayers and therefore lesser citizens.

In the immediate wake of *Brown* and for many years afterward, very little integration actually occurred. A group of Supreme Court law clerks wrote a joint memo on the *Brown* case in 1954 in which they examined the different possible outcomes of the decision and argued that a twelve-year-long gradual desegregation plan would be permissible—not far from the time it actually took before most schools began integrating in earnest. However, they acknowledged that it might give too much weight to the gradualists to explicitly state that position in the opinion.[6] They concluded that, "practically speaking, it seems more important at the present time to get a few Negroes into white schools than to require overall, immediate desegregation, unacceptable to white Southerners."[7] In fact, as the letters received by the justices in the wake of the *Brown* decision reveal, even the court's minimal, surface efforts at desegregation were unacceptable to many whites, North and South, who translated their disapproval into the rhetoric of taxpayer rights.

Often "white rights" and "taxpayer rights" were conflated explicitly. Aura Lee, who wrote to Justice Hugo Black in 1956, asked him "why you feel it is your right . . . to ignore the civil rights of those whites who cannot afford to send their children to private schools."[8] Lee felt she had been "pushed" out of Harlem, her home, by African Americans and repeatedly asserted that it was "poor whites" who were particularly suffering, and in many cases were "forced" to integrate because of poverty. She also claimed that "many whites have gone uneducated in the South for lack of proper schools" and told Black it was "high time to fight for the civil rights of the poor white man in this country." She concluded by identifying poor whites specifically as taxpayers, demanding that Black say "that poor white taxpayers are entitled to enjoy some all-white places, if they so desire."

The idea that desegregation would "harm" black students due to financial constraints was embraced by many in support of segregation. A public school teacher from Missouri wrote to Justice Earl Warren as he was deliberating in *Brown* and argued against integration despite his "deep affection" for African Americans.[9] Asserting that student bodies should be "homogenous" for the purposes of education, he also claimed that "the white race pays for more taxes which go to educate and help the Negroes than do Negroes themselves, so it can hardly be said the whites are niggardly toward the Negroes." In another letter, a South Carolina man argued that "no tax-supported elementary schools at all" would be the inevitable result of the decision, a prediction that had some basis in South Carolina's recent legislation. He also went on to argue that both black and white citizens of the South "cannot be forced to pay taxes in support of a low level communism in public schools," a doctrine that would, according to him, "deprive each of the equal and best learning opportunity guaranteed him by the Fourteenth Amendment."[10]

A sense of paternalism toward African Americans was often connected to the belief among whites that the public tax funds really "belonged" to whites to distribute. According to one South Carolina man, "Statistics prove that the Negro pays only about six percent of their educational costs." He claimed that the feeling of white people was that they loved and respected black people and wished to "protect and care for them"; he believed that by "buil[ding] churches for them, help[ing] with their church expenses, [white people] have practically educated them."[11]

Segregationists repeatedly identified whites as supposedly the only—or only meaningful—taxpaying group. A grocer in Memphis claimed that African Americans would not have made the progress they had "had it not been for the whites" and argued that in his area the black population was "37%" but they "support much less than 20% of the taxes and responsibility of the city or Federal government."[12] A factory manager from Georgia claimed in 1957 that blacks in the South were "living off 'the fat of the land'" and "doing wonderfully well, being educated at the expense of the white people."[13] He claimed that African Americans should be thanking whites, since "their children are being taken care of at the expense of the white people." One woman argued that virtually all aspects of African American life in the South, from education to welfare to recreation, "are *most largely* supported by white taxation and contributions, as you must know," and that integration would end up harming blacks and hurting their educational opportunities. Another note from a white Southerner asserted that "all was being done" for African Americans, and that "even more money than for whites is being spent."[14]

Segregationists sent numerous letters to the court protesting *Brown* by arguing that their rights as white people were being violated and often asserting that the injured parties from the decision would be not just whites but almost as often the poor. This was a category that, when implied to be "deserving," also seemed to overlap only with white racial status, as in Aura Lee's invocation of the "poor white taxpayer." Many whites asserted their right "not to be forced together" as a primary entitlement of citizenship.[15] In some cases, letter writers openly resented that the "right of association" defended by many segregationists as the basis for maintaining segregation was something much more available to the rich "of both races" than to the poor.[16] An Alabama woman wrote to Justice Black in 1956, upset that "the financially independent can always *be independent* but there is all the poor and those who are not so poor but not able to get around the group schools."[17] Others repeatedly listed "poor" parenthetically when discussing the hardships desegregation would cause for "white people."[18]

Segregationists defended their rights as taxpayers from Northern cities as well. A Michigan writer was upset that when an African American received "his benefits" in education, it "force[d] the rest of the people to give up whatever they might happen to receive, as their share in equality."[19] These "deprived" whites of the North, according to the author, were dependent on Southern courts to find a way to evade the Supreme Court decision. One anti-integration diatribe expressed frustration about the transformation of Chicago neighborhoods from white to black in "northern style integration."[20] In one exception to the tendency of whites to leave the city as blacks moved in, the author identified Trumbull Park, Chicago, as a place where "the white man's tax dollar ... is being used amply to keep 'integration' alive." The writer of this letter also argued that the measures some states had taken to remove public funds from integrated schools would "impose an extreme hardship" on African Americans, since, the author claimed, "their schooling is primarily a result of white tax dollars."[21]

Anxieties about the impact of *Brown* on poor whites were widespread, particularly among those who in some cases were struggling to maintain a hold on the valuable commodity of whiteness.[22] Tulio Vasquez, self-identified "Racial Expert," wrote to Justice Black from Puerto Rico shortly after the *Brown* decision to assert his opposition to desegregation on a combination of racial and economic grounds.[23] First, Vasquez identified himself "as a part of the white population of our United States of America," and then he returned repeatedly to his concern with taxation, arguing that "95% of taxpayers within the United States" were white people, and that segregation could not be abolished without their direct consent because "money of white taxpayers shall not be used against the general wellfare of white taxpayers [*sic*]."[24] Segregationists also defended their rights as taxpayers from many places outside the South. An angry parent from Washington, D.C., claimed that the only choices he had were to teach his son to "sharpen his boy scout hunting knife to have to use it in the classrooms and hallways" or to send him to a private school that would cost more than a thousand dollars a year while, he complained, he would still be "paying taxes in the district for school support which I cannot even use."[25]

If many white letter writers constructed themselves as the only taxpaying class, they also understood themselves to be the group with control of the distribution of tax funds. In an address to a Virginia club, one white Southerner stated that he was "sure" the Supreme Court realized that they did not have the power to compel a state or local government "to levy taxes to support a system of schools which is offensive to a majority of the people in the area affected, and which they will not support."[26] He continued to argue that if desegregation was pushed, "the minimum reaction will be that appropriations will be drastically reduced and the level of education materially lowered." Ultimately, he said, this would mean that the quality of education provided to both black and white students would be lowered, but "people will not elect representatives to levy taxes and make appropriations for projects to which they are opposed."[27] Indeed, almost immediately in the wake of the *Brown* decision, many school districts began to remove funding entirely from public schools rather than accept any future possibility of integration.

Backlash to *Brown*: Taxes in Prince Edward County

Despite the legal framework's surface revolution in *Brown*, the fundamental rules of racially and economically segregated schools and funding systems remained largely intact and, if anything, gained a veneer of new legitimacy and neutrality after school segregation was perceived to be a thing of the past.[28] In providing what Charles Payne has called "a milestone in search of something to signify," *Brown* provided cover for the continuation of many of the same unequal property-tax funding systems instituted decades earlier—but it was crucially different in the kind of response it provoked, as legal historian Michael Klarman has argued.[29] As discussed in the last chapter, the *Brown* case was a consolidation of five cases, one of which had emerged from Moton High School, a profoundly underfunded all-black high school in Prince Edward County, Virginia. In terms of taxable funding disparities, there is a clear and consistent parallel between the Moton case and many of the other cases in this book. The conditions at Moton High School were so terrible that a student strike was famously led by Barbara Rose Johns in 1951 to protest the lack of funding for black schools from the all-white school board.[30] The difference in valuation of school property in

1950–51 in Prince Edward County dramatically illustrated the extreme levels of inequality in facilities and resources obtained through local property taxes. The valuation per pupil for Moton was $306.54; for the nearby white town of Farmville, it was $1,679.31.[31] The rest of Virginia was also deeply unequal in funding and resources—in one Virginia county, there were twenty-four schools with only one teacher in 1951.[32] All were segregated black schools.

The Moton school case out of Prince Edward County would prove to be one of the most difficult for desegregation advocates to pursue. As was true of most districts after *Brown*, the county had interpreted "all deliberate speed" to mean that it did not have to take any affirmative action toward desegregation. The sense that superior white schools were an entitlement of white families was partially rooted in a taxpayer citizenship notion of reciprocal or proportional rights based in the assumption that whites paid disproportionate amounts of taxes. In what was an early precursor of an organized tax revolt, the board of supervisors for the county had passed a resolution on May 3, 1956, declaring it to be "the policy and intention of said board in accordance with the will of the people of said county that no tax levy shall be made upon the said people nor public revenue derived from local taxes shall be appropriated for the operation of public schools in said county wherein white and colored children are taught together under any plan or arrangement whatsoever."[33] Local control of schools, for many white residents of this county, meant white control of schools, as seen through the lens of taxpayer citizenship and the assumption that whites paid more in taxes. Indeed, one Virginia editorial during the Prince Edward County litigation opined that occasional efforts to improve the state's education system sometimes "bore fruit," but that "often the plea for more school money was denied on the ground that it would be used to educate the Negro."[34]

Virginia spent much of 1955 and 1956 debating the Gray Plan of State Senator Garland Gray, the head of the Commission of Public Education, which was approved with large margins by voters in a referendum on January 9, 1956. Gray proposed a constitutional convention to change the Virginia Constitution to allow public funding for tuition grants for private schools. In opposition, *Baltimore Afro-American* journalist Louis Lautier argued that "the education of children in private schools is not the responsibility of taxpayers."[35] He also argued that such laws authorizing tuition grants would "cost Virginia taxpayers thousands of dollars which could be better spent in improving the public schools of the state."[36] In 1956, as Virginia's gover-

nor Thomas Stanley was pursuing his own plan (the Stanley Plan) to withhold state funds from any schools that integrated and to provide tuition
grants for private education wherever public schools were closed, the
Baltimore Afro-American reported that a "taxpayer's rebellion is afoot in
answer." Though stating that the revolt wasn't organized yet, the paper
indicated that many taxpayers in Arlington, Norfolk, and Charlottesville
were "spearheading the revolt" to not pay state taxes.[37] Black taxpayer revolts, however, did not gain the momentum or the attention white taxpayer
revolts did in later years.

Throughout Virginia in 1958, over thirteen thousand children were unable to attend school still in late October as a result of Governor James Lind-
sey Almond's orders to close all public schools under court orders to
integrate. State delegate Robert Whitehead argued to teachers at a meeting of District C of the Virginia Education Association that massive resistance had to be scrapped not because he supported integration but because
"the white children are by law being denied public school, but it is being
provided by law for the colored children at taxpayer expense. This is discrimination against the white people on account of race."[38]

The controversial "race tag" on taxes—applied in local jurisdictions haphazardly throughout the Jim Crow era, as discussed in chapter 3—was still
being discussed statewide by Virginians as a potential solution to the *Brown*
decision in the late 1950s. In testimony before the Perrow Commission in
1959, J. B. Mason, a building contractor from Lynchburg, argued that
Virginia couldn't operate segregated schools as long as it had an integrated
treasury. His proposal was to preserve segregation by keeping the school
funds segregated by race and under control of that race, "with each system
to operate from funds paid by its race's taxpayers."[39] Segregationists were
able to argue both sides of the race-tagged tax question, however. The removal of the race tag on school funds in South Carolina in January 1962
was seen by black papers as "a major shift in strategy by the Administration in
its effort to maintain school segregation," similar to the rush of construction
discussed in chapter 4 as a precursor to *Brown*.[40]

Thus, in another carryover from the segregated property tax systems implemented after the Civil War, the race tag was still in use in Prince Edward County—local tax records were still being categorized based on race
in many communities with segregated schools. During the lengthy series
of appeals taken in the *Prince Edward* case in the years after *Brown*, Ver-
non C. Womack, commissioner of revenue for Prince Edward County, suggested the possibility of a white tax revolt in his testimony. He stated that

he was "familiar with all the taxpayers, I believe, in the county, and we have about fifty-fifty; fifty percent of our number are white and colored."[41] Womack then testified that "chaos would result" if desegregation were ordered in 1958:

A: I believe the white people just would not be able to take the change, because in my work I have complete knowledge of the tax situation in our county and the percentage of the taxes borne by the Negro people is such a small percentage of the total, and the population being about equal, I just feel like the white people just would not be able to put up with it.

Q: Do you mean that they would refuse to provide the funds for the schools?

A: Yes, sir.[42]

When he was cross-examined by NAACP attorney Oliver Hill, Womack admitted that he "strongly opposed desegregation personally." Hill then challenged Womack on his implication that whites paid "a great deal of taxes" and blacks "do not pay." When Hill pressed him on the question of business taxes and asked where the major department stores, wholesale plants, and other large businesses were listed, Womack stated that they were "listed as white taxes . . . unless it is a Negro business." Hill then questioned him about the Hub department store in Farmville, which had both white and black customers and a large sales volume. The business tax for the Hub, Hill argued, was carried as "white taxes," despite Womack's admission that blacks "contribute[d] to the payment of those taxes" by shopping and purchasing items there.[43] The indirect taxes paid by blacks had been subsumed into white resources and used to bolster the claim of white taxpaying privilege.

The litigation continued as school officials repeatedly sought ways around the judicial rulings. In November 1961 the district court granted an injunction preventing the payment of "tuition grants" and "tax credits" for private school "contributions" as long as the public schools remained closed.[44] There were no schools available for black students from June 1959 until 1963, when a voluntary association conducted classes as the Prince Edward Free Schools in some of the old public school buildings. Of the 1,700 children who attended these schools, "fewer than nine" were white, while 1,300 white children attended the racially exclusive Prince Edward School Foundation schools during the 1963–64 school year. The state board of education adopted a resolution on July 1, 1964, that authorized retroactive tuition grants for parents who had paid for "private non-sectarian schools" in the previous school year. The next day, they were enjoined by the court from processing or paying these grants. A little over a month later, the Board of Supervisors of Prince Edward County decided to pay "scholarship grants" to parents of white children in the county for the next year's tuition. Immediately, the board notified the white parents, had them "make applications" for the grants, got the applications processed, and had the checks written and delivered before nine o'clock the next morning.[45]

As a result of the school board's actions, the checks for most of the $180,000 of "scholarship grants" were cashed before any of the black citizens of the county even knew the prior day's meeting of the board of supervisors had occurred.[46] The plaintiffs argued that this constituted state action "beyond peradventure." The board appropriated $375,000 for tuition grants for children to attend the foundation schools, though the 1959–60 operating expenses for the schools was a little more than $300,000. According to the plaintiffs, it was clear that tuition grants were being used by the board of supervisors to send tax funds to the foundation, enabling the operation of segregated schools.[47]

The issue of equality of facilities was crucially important in the Prince Edward County litigation, since without well-funded facilities, even white parents who did not especially care about segregation would most likely choose to send their child to the better-funded private white school if it were free to them. After a five-year closure, the board was forced by court order to appropriate $189,000 for public schools again. The NAACP attorneys compared this amount for the education of 1,600 black children (and a minuscule number of white children) with the $375,000 appropriated for 1,300 white children at the foundation schools. As the attorneys argued, "It was then apparent that the Board of Supervisors was insuring the operation of maintaining segregated schools by giving the parents of every white child the Hobson's choice of accepting a grant for payment of tuition at the Foundation's exclusively "white" school or accepting the lot of Negro children by attending the public schools which the Federal courts required to be operated with approximately one-half the money which previous experience indicates to be reasonably necessary."[48] As the NAACP recognized, the rush to pay the tuition grants (which were increased substantially) was to avoid the increase in poor white parents who would send their children to the integrated public schools if they could not afford foundation school tuition.

In this case, the district court held that the county's public schools could not be closed to avoid the effect of *Brown* "while the Commonwealth of Virginia permits other public schools to remain open at the expense of the taxpayers."[49] The district court postponed making an order that would compel schools to open if they were not reopened by September 1962. When the case finally reached the Supreme Court in 1964, a unanimous court spoke through Justice Hugo Black in saying, "That day has long passed, and the schools are still closed."[50] Black then described the schoolchildren's access to equal education in clear rights-based language, stating that the district court should make an immediate order "to assure these petitioners that their constitutional rights will no longer be denied them" and arguing that the phrase "deliberate speed" could no longer be used to justify "denying these Prince Edward County school children their constitutional rights to an education equal to that afforded by the public schools in the other parts of Virginia."[51]

The ruling in *Griffin*, the final Prince Edward County decision, was the most firm the court had issued yet, however, and Black's words forced many reluctant school systems to finally take action—albeit ten years after the *Brown* ruling. In his statement concluding the case, Black seemed to suggest that the right to education could and even should mean equality of all school resources, at least in cases in which racial motivations were the cause of the inequality. Black, a native of Alabama, would continue to receive constant letters from "betrayed" segregationists for the rest of the time he was on the bench.

"Taxpaying Citizens" and White Entitlement

Implicit in the majority of correspondence to the court from segregationists during the 1960s cases was again the assumption that whites paid more in taxes, and that this meant whites were entitled to a different level of rights and representation. In particular, desegregation remedies were seen by many letter writers as a direct violation of their "taxpaying citizen" rights to well-resourced local schools. One woman wrote to the court pushing for an amendment outlawing communism, complaining that communists were "threatening schools, that if they don't integrate now you will cut off their federal aid."[52] She was angered even at the idea that the aid was "federal," claiming that "those monies do not belong to the federal government; they have no legal right to withhold any monies from government agencies; monies which were paid into the government by the very people being threatened." And in a 1967 letter, a Louisiana woman was upset that private schools were not to be allowed to receive grant-in-aid, asking if Black did not think "white people" had rights, since, she argued, "we're tax paying citizens too more so than Negros."[53]

The connection between taxpayer citizenship and (increased) rights to education and schooling was made repeatedly, often by imputing lack of effort or another stigma to the perception of African Americans as paying less in taxes. One notecard expressed bitterness at the *Alexander v. Holmes County* decision ordering immediate desegregation of Southern schools in 1969, claiming that "white people pay most of the taxes always have and always will."[54] A Mississippi woman identified the families in her area who were losing their "rights to their public school system" as "hard working citizens who have been paying taxes for many years."[55] She was, however, convinced that the public schools were her right as a citizen, asserting that "private schools are not the answer to this problem in any area." A North Carolina woman offered Justice Black a "history lesson" in a 1969 letter, arguing that Southern blacks worked on farms "because they loved the land and did not want the full responsibility of owning and running their own farms."[56] She went on to claim that every black man after the Civil War ended "was given forty acres of land and a mule.... It was up to them after that." She concluded that since African Americans "did not have to pay taxes like the white man," the actions of the court were "Communistic." She was especially angry that "our government is going to spend hard earned tax money to use in training Black people" to do jobs that "thousands of white people" had not been trained to do.

Many letters were specifically frustrated at the poor quality of the schools at issue in the cases. A Maryland woman was angry about the federal government threatening Prince George's County with the withholding of "$12,000,000 (our tax money)" if they did not show sufficient effort toward integration. She was also upset that the University of Maryland was attempting to arrange more scholarships for African American students in order to comply with integration requirements, "again our tax money I think."[57] She concluded that "millions of students and parents white and colored are being taxed to death to support schools which are unsafe and poor." An Alabama woman wrote to Black that she thought the government was "giving everything to the poor (as they call themselves)" and that "we can't get help from the Government or from the poor but yet we work ourselves down to pay taxes like the rich."[58] She accused the court of not "even check[ing] to see how the schools are here and because someone was telling the truth and you didn't like it your [*sic*] making our children pay."

Sometimes letters expressed subtle threats that tax funding would be withheld from schools that were accessible to nonwhite students. In a letter exemplifying the identification with middle-class respectability and taxpayer entitlements, Black was asked by a Mississippi state representative, "How [do] you expect middle-class people to react to your decision affecting our local school district(s)?"[59] The letter writer planned to put his children in private school and said he was "increasingly reluctant to spend more tax money" because "the middle-class people who break their backs paying the bulk of income, sales and property taxes to support schools" were "fed up" with federal involvement in school desegregation. He also said that the court decision would lead to decreased willingness to vote for bond issues, tax increases, or bigger appropriations for schools. After accusing "limousine liberals" in Washington, D.C. of sending their children to private schools, he argued that "the real tragedy will be that those people who need the help the worst, educationwise, the colored people and the poor whites, probably will be hurt the worst by the backlash which will inevitably occur."

The perceptions regarding class and racial intersections expressed many of the whites who wrote to the court suggested that the intersection of class with blackness in the eyes of whites meant welfare, lack of taxpayer status, and undeserved rights, whereas the intersection of class with whiteness was viewed by whites as signifying the "deserving" poor, or "deserving" middle-class or working-class taxpayers. Even when white parents sought to distance themselves from overt racism, the inequalities between schools were a clear baseline of discontent for them and a framework for articulating their sense of proprietary ownership of both public schools and the tax fund. One father giving a speech at the Concerned Parents Association of Charlotte claimed that he was not opposed to integration, but he was wealthy enough "to buy a home near the school where I wanted my children to go. And I pay taxes to pay for it. They can bring in anybody they like to that school, but I don't want my children taken away from there."[60] Angry at the court's insistence on affirmative steps to integrate, one "northerner" likened the court's action to "the days of Robin Hood—*taking* from one and *giving* to another."[61] One letter writer expressed the common sentiment that the decision had "wrested control of the schools from the local people who pay the taxes" and transferred the power to the federal government.[62] He was especially upset that many parents would "doubtless . . . spend their life savings and even borrow money" in order to send their children to private schools, all because African Americans claimed "the white schools are better than the Negro schools."

Busing decisions provoked a great deal of "taxpayer" and "homeowner" response from individuals who felt the rights they had "paid for" were being violated. A Florida man was frustrated by busing decisions that, he claimed, injured "the Tax Payers who elected the one who appointed you to your high office" and "the working mothers and fathers who now must hire one to care for their children during their return from the shortest school session in my history."[63] He argued that his "Constitutional Rights" were being "impaired" when a court or the government could tell him "where I as a Tax Payer shall send his children to school. . . . I have lived and worked hard for what I have and intend to retain them." A Denver man described himself as "a homeowner and a taxpayer who has worked hard all of his life to be able to pay the taxes and other costs of living in one of Denver's better residential areas with correspondingly high taxed neighborhood schools."[64] His "deep fear" was that his son would be bused to "a school of much lower standards and run down facilities than the ones that I have helped pay for." An Oklahoma City woman felt that it had always been "the sacred privilege of each American family to either buy or rent a home in the school district that the parents wanted their children to attend school in." She asserted that she was "not anti-black" and suggested that the courts "bring them to her son's school. . . . That's all right with me as long as my son can still attend the school he rightfully belongs in."[65] One North Carolina woman argued for a parent's right to "send a child to the nearest school," saying that she and her husband "worked hard to buy our home which we did in order to be near a school."[66] Home ownership served as a helpful code for wealth, whiteness, and property-tax-paying status in these neighborhood school arguments.

The idea of spending money on any education for black students was a common source of frustration. This was particularly true for poor whites, such as a Florida man who wrote to say that since "education is going to be impossible at Campbell Park School," he was "desperately trying" to enroll his children in private schools.[67] If he could find one, he said it would cost him $215 per month, "a staggering figure" when compared to his $875 take-home pay. Another Florida man sent a letter saying that he did not think it right that "the Supreme Court should order our educational funds be spent on new busses rather than new schools."[68] An angry letter from a Rhode Island man was passed on to Justice William Brennan from Justice Byron White with a sardonic prefatory note asking, "You want this printed as an appendix to the school cases—right?"[69] In his lengthy diatribe, the author of this letter condemned the courts for the "failure" of integrated schools "year after year, while we continue to pour the taxpayers' millions down an educational rathole."[70] An Atlanta man was angry about the "untold millions of dollars in school buildings and home and business investments" that were being lost "by parents and other taxpayers as a result of the present 'police state' over public education."[71] A North Carolina woman wrote to the court to ask them to make the guidelines for school integration "the law of all the land (North as well as South)" and to ask why they were spending "this extra tax money for such an unnecessary purpose when so much is needed for necessary things."[72]

Again and again, taxpayer identity was asserted as a way to demand rights and consideration by the courts in the busing cases, as well as a way for whites to assert a racialized class identity that marked them as middle class and hardworking. One woman asked for "some kind of consideration as parents and tax payers."[73] Another man described his opposition to busing as a "long-silent suffering tax payer."[74] An "angry taxpayer and mother" wrote from Queens in 1970 to share her negative opinion of busing African Americans "from very bad and middle income areas.... These youngsters are very bad."[75] She was furious at plans to "down zone" her county with low-income housing but said she wouldn't mind having "a few" blacks on her street "if they're decent and I'm not outnumbered."

In addition, however, the letters indicated the ongoing interconnection between racial segregation and fundamentally unequal educational conditions, a connection that indicated that the roots to the opposition to busing and desegregation were sometimes located both in racial animosity *and* in concern over poorly funded school facilities. Integrating white students from well-funded schools into schools with deteriorating facilities provoked backlash, as Justice Jackson had predicted, and solidified racial resentment, often expressed through the language of taxpayers' rights. A North Carolina woman argued that the "huge expenditures of money and effort would provide no educational gains," and she feared that white leaders would bolt to suburbs and private schools rather than bus.[76] A Florida woman was upset that "we have listened for a long time to sad tales" that teachers were underpaid because of lack of tax funds, but tax funds were being found to bus children to faraway schools.[77]

Ultimately, the loud clamor of "taxpayer citizenship" claims from defenders of segregation overshadowed those few who wrote in to suggest openness to integration or that taxation could perhaps imply equality, of rights and of resources. Carolyn Gaither, who identified herself as black, wrote of how African Americans "loves their school just as good as whites do," and argued that blacks "pay taxes and have sons in Vietnam and all part of the world to service for country, but . . . this thing call[ed] hatred won't ever die."[78] And Anne F. Rutledge, expressing a white moderate's wish for gradual integration and concerns about the run-down facilities her children were bused to, wrote to say that "husbands and fathers work, pay the tax increases" in order to live in the communities with the best schools for their children.[79] She said she had sincerely "kept an open mind regarding busing," but when she finally went and saw the condition of the school facilities assigned to her children, "I felt true rebellion toward each of you."

Taxpayers and Taxeaters

Some African American commentators at the time were also still troubled by the combined economic and racial problems that had contributed to *Brown*, which they argued *Brown* did not ultimately address, a criticism that would arise again in later decades. According to an editorial by Davis Lee, a black editor from Newark, New Jersey, modeling integration on the system of Northern cities would still be detrimental to the African American community. While Newark's population was 20 percent African American, only 70 of its 2,200 teachers were black and not a single principal was. He compared this to Georgia, which employed 7,313 black teachers and paid them nearly $15 million in salaries in one year.[80] Arguing for Southern blacks to have "their own schools, but equal facilities," Lee warned that integration could lead to millions of dollars in lost income for the African American community as black teachers lost their jobs, and asked whether such an "economic licking" was worth sending black children to integrated schools.

Prior to the *Brown* decision, Representative Adam Clayton Powell Jr. of New York had opposed appropriations of federal funding to separate school districts as "federal subsidization of segregation" and particularly as a "tremendous waste of taxpayers' money" to support segregated schools. Powell argued that government funding sent to Jim Crow schools meant that "we are called upon to take at least a quarter of a million dollars out of the pockets of taxpayers who live in those parts of the country where there is no segregation in schools to pay for racial segregation in Maryland and Virginia."[81] A few years later, in defense of the Powell Amendment, Powell appeared on a Sunday-night ABC radio show, *America's Town Meeting of the Air*, to say that the amendment would not force integration on defiant states. Instead, he said, "it merely forces the Federal treasury not to aid and comfort the defiant school districts with your money—the taxpayers' money."[82]

Ultimately, the NAACP and Representative Powell would disagree over whether to include an anti-segregation amendment to bills extending authorization of federal funding for building and operating public schools in 1958, with Powell ultimately deciding to refrain from adding the amendment "because he wanted to see the bills passed." The NAACP expressed disappointment in this decision, stating that "a whole lot of taxpayers want to see no part of their tax dollar go to the support of jim-crow schools."[83] The frustration with the continued use of federal government funds to help finance segregated Southern schools that engaged in "massive resistance" campaigns was also expressed on behalf of Northern taxpayers, with Louis Lautier of the *Baltimore Afro-American* arguing that the money the government was "pouring" into segregated schools "comes from taxpayers of the North" and that "Southern states take out of the Federal till more than they put in."[84]

Yet many African Americans were also still arguing that taxpayer status claims could work to their advantage in ending segregation. When state governments threatened, as in Arkansas in 1959, to give "taxpayer's money to a private, segregated school," the NAACP was "ready to object."[85] In several suits, taxpayer status was invoked to fight against policies of segregation. In the case of San Francisco in 1962, a "taxpayers' suit" was filed to block the decision by the board of education to fight a lawsuit by the NAACP that argued that local schools were operating with de facto segregation. The San Francisco taxpayers specifically sought to enjoin the board from using the "neighborhood school pattern" argument in court in defending itself against the NAACP.[86] In Frankfort, Kentucky, in fall 1962 a group of local residents met with the school board after twenty-four black students were denied admittance to a purportedly desegregated school. In the meeting, they threatened litigation, saying, "We hate to waste the taxpayers' money and so we're making this appeal."[87]

In September 1961, Roy Wilkins of the NAACP, along with Arnold Aronson of the National Community Relations Advisory Council, submitted a report to President John F. Kennedy detailing the role of the federal government as what they called "a silent, but none-the-less full partner in the perpetuation of discriminatory practices" with relation to federal grant-in-aid to segregated schools and other programs. The report highlighted that in 1960 over $1 billion in federal grant-in-aid had been used in a discriminatory manner by eleven Southern states, aid that the authors argued had been "paid for by all taxpayers alike."[88]

But spending to maintain segregation was not limited to the South. In Chicago in 1962, School Superintendent Benjamin Willis was well known for refusing to acknowledge that segregation existed in the city at all. The *Chicago Daily Defender* described the six mobile classrooms he had erected in one neighborhood to avoid having to take measures to integrate schools as "Willis Wagons." Describing the situation as "horrible," the paper stated that "the taxpayer's money is being used to re-enforce the containing wall of segregation which Mr. Willis has erected." Yet, they argued, "our taxes go toward the support of the public schools," and therefore they had "a right to be heard."[89]

President Lyndon B. Johnson delivered a special message to Congress entitled "The American Promise" on March 15, 1965, in which he introduced the Voting Rights Act. In response to the march for voting rights in Selma, Alabama, a mere week before, Johnson said he spoke for "the dignity of man and the destiny of democracy." Johnson closed his address with a discussion of "the purpose of This government." He began by referring to his first job after college, teaching in a small, poor, Mexican American school where the children knew "the pain of prejudice." Johnson used the end of his speech to highlight the importance of education and to make a call for uplift from poverty, saying, "I want to be the President who educated young children to the wonders of their world. I want to be the President who helped to feed the hungry and to prepare them to be taxpayers instead of taxeaters."[90] Even in the introduction to one of the most important pieces of civil rights legislation in U.S. history, the image of a ravening maw of poor and implicitly black people "eating" the contributions of "taxpayers" was indelible and haunting.[91]

The "Worthy Poor" and State Action in Private Schooling

The court would continue to be the last hope for those rebuffed by educational administrators and local school boards, and the question was now frequently about where to draw the line on at what point state action had created or facilitated segregation. A case from Philadelphia that was the first Supreme Court school segregation case brought after *Brown v. Board of Education II*, *Pennsylvania v. Board of Trusts* represented the complicated intersection of race and poverty that arose in identifying this line and surfaced the narrative that separated the "deserving" poor from the "undeserving."[92] Stephen Girard, one of the richest men in America at the time of his death, had left the city of Philadelphia money and land to build a private school for "poor white orphan boys" from the area in his will in 1830. One of the stated purposes of Girard's will and the construction of Girard College was "to diminish the burden of taxation upon the inhabitants of the City."[93] The first bequest in Girard's will was for a quarterly sum of money to be paid from his estate and trust (which came partly from a slave plantation he owned in New Orleans) to his "black woman Hannah," whom he also freed.[94] At the time of Girard's death, Philadelphia had fewer than 9,900 black inhabitants, out of a population of around 80,500, who under the law of the time were not considered citizens. By the time of the 1965 lawsuit, the city had 582,400 African American residents, out of a total population of 2,060,400. The forty-five-acre location of Girard College specified by Girard's will would eventually become "the center of the most densely concentrated area" of black population in Philadelphia.[95]

In the complaint against Girard College in 1965, the attorneys for Ruby Bond's son Alan, Marie Hicks's sons Charles and Theodore, Ardella Scruggs's sons James and Henry, and Charlotte White's sons Tyrone and Terry asserted that each of the boys, a "poor male orphan between the ages of 6 and 10," was denied admission because the trustees "deemed him not to be 'white.'"[96] The college had first opened in 1848, and by 1943, the board of city trusts determined that the capacity of the college was two thousand students, but enrollment by 1965 was only seven hundred. The NAACP organized a daily picket line manned by young working-class black men from the neighborhood around the college in front of its ten-foot-high walls.[97] After many months of picketing and police presence, Pennsylvania governor William Scranton appointed two attorneys, William Biddle and William T. Coleman, to file suit on behalf of the State of Pennsylvania to force the college's trustees to break Girard's will and admit black boys.[98]

Biddle and Coleman repeatedly linked the principle of combating both poverty and racial discrimination to the best interests of the city and the desire to keep the state from participating in unconstitutional behavior. The attorneys claimed that "the need of the City of Philadelphia for the eradication of poverty and ignorance among its Negro population today is identical with its need for the eradication of poverty and ignorance among its white population in 1830."[99] The way in which the trust was being administered by the current private trustees was itself antithetical to Girard's objectives, they argued. They claimed that Girard had described his bequest in terms of "white" boys as a result of the actions of the State of Pennsylvania and the United States as of 1830.[100] In effect, they argued, his private will entrenching racial segregation was the result of state action encouraging and facilitating discrimination based on race—such as slavery and segregation—at the time he wrote it. Biddle and Coleman argued that although both the state and national governments had subsequently repudiated those policies, they were still being perpetuated in the performance of Girard's will.

In addition to the intriguing argument that state policies of racial discrimination and segregation should be understood to have a legal impact lasting past their expiration once they became enshrined through private individual choices, the attorneys argued that the city had been directly involved in the operation of Girard College from 1848 to 1959, directly supervising its operation, managing the property, hiring staff, planning curriculum, and admitting students or denying them admission based on race. In their discussion of state action, the attorneys argued that common law and the statutes of the commonwealth were themselves what allowed Girard to create a charitable trust that continued to exist 134 years after his death. The actions of the state in waiving the rule against perpetuities for public charitable trusts and in exempting Girard College from all taxation gave state sanction, according to the attorneys, to the discriminatory policies of Girard College. The total amount in taxes that Girard College saved over this period was estimated at over $12 million.[101]

The will had been altered frequently over the years, eventually creating a more inclusive definition for the category of "orphan" to encompass children with only one living parent. In addition, students had been admitted who "were not 'poor' within any reasonable construction of that word." Several other provisions of the will were unenforced by the time of the lawsuit, including the provision that students were to be "indentured out" until they were twenty-one years old and the rule that students were to have no further contact with family members after entering the school. The orphans' court permitted these deviations by agreeing that the strict application of the terms of the will "would be impractical in contemporary society," which led the attorneys for the state to argue that the policy of racial exclusion was similarly "impractical in contemporary society."[102]

The Girard College battle was hard fought, and in many ways it was a battle over who would be defined as the "worthy poor"—white orphan boys or black orphan boys. The City of Philadelphia was removed as a trustee by the Supreme Court in 1957 because, under the Fourteenth Amendment (after *Brown*), the city would not have been constitutionally able to exclude applicants based on race.[103] Though the goals of the college were originally to combat poverty through education and to "diminish the burden of taxation, now most oppressive especially on those who are the least able to bear it," the poorest residents of the city were perversely excluded.[104] The number of applications from poor "orphan" white male students from Philadelphia had declined so significantly over the years that the trustees had actually had to search outside the state for students and had relaxed the definition of "poverty" for admission in order to fill the student body even partially.

Biddle, in his oral argument before the court, first asserted that "this insistence on a White restriction . . . is destroying the usefulness of the college."[105] Acknowledging that "it has caused no end of turmoil and racial feeling in Philadelphia," he reminded the court that "Mr. Girard set up this plan in his will because he wanted to help Philadelphia." Finally, he argued, the city had obligations to aid dependent and neglected children, many of whom might fall under the definition of "orphan" provided for by Girard College but would be turned away because of their race. When asked at a pretrial examination how to determine whether an applicant was poor, trustee Karl R. Friedmann called it a "fairly relative word" and said the trustees tried to judge each case "on its own merits," which may involve "the number of children, obviously the age of the children, the condition of the mother's health, her employability, the state of the economy at the time, many, many factors."[106]

When the case reached the Third Circuit Court of Appeals in 1968, the court of appeals described the "amazing effort to maintain Girard's discriminatory status" even after the Supreme Court ruling of 1957 that the city could not administer a trust on a racially biased basis.[107] According to the court of appeals, the "ironic result" of the prompt removal of the city trustees by the commonwealth orphans' court and that institution's subsequent assumed power over the reappointment of trustees to administer Girard's will was that "Pennsylvania's involvement with Girard College is far more powerful than was provided for by Mr. Girard." The court concluded that "given everything we know of Mr. Girard, it is inconceivable that in this changed world he would not be quietly happy that his cherished project had raised its sights with the times and joyfully recognized that all human beings are created equal."[108] Girard College, at last, began to integrate in 1968. Female students were admitted in 1984, and black female students are now the majority of the student body at the school.

Conclusion

Several years after President Johnson's invocation of "taxeaters" and "taxpayers," in the summer of 1970, Mrs. John Fawcett Jr. of Oxford, Mississippi, wrote a letter to Bishop Paul Moore, chairman of the Committee of

100, which supported the NAACP Legal Defense Fund. She said she was responding to a fund-raising letter stating that there had been progress now that almost 40 percent of Southern black students were attending formerly all-white schools. Rather than progress, Fawcett claimed that Bishop Moore was "unaware of the actual situation. You are not helping the good black. You are destroying him." Following these ominous words, she invoked repercussions of biblical proportions, saying, "Hell, your Excellency, is paved with good intentions. Those 'poor,' to whom you are directing all your attention, are no longer the 'poor.' We, the taxpayers, are the 'poor' today. Our schools have been taken away from us."[109]

This letter illustrates the legal consciousness of many white segregationists in the 1950s and 1960s that taxpayer status was a symbol of whiteness, and that taxpayers were engaged in a market relationship of purchasing public services from the state, which led them to conclude that black families (who, many assumed, did not "pay taxes") should be excluded from full citizenship rights. Indeed, this pervasive implication even permeated presidential rhetoric in the invocation of the specter of "taxeaters." The concept that black schooling was "a result of white tax dollars" was a common refrain among those upset by desegregation decisions, as illustrated in this chapter. In part, this is evidence of the way in which an ideal of "taxpayer citizenship" inherently categorizes levels of citizenship and rights based on the individual's (or identifiable group's) level of wealth and assets, at least in a system of bracketed taxation. But it is also tied to the unique nature of school taxation systems. Unlike other public services, school taxes are one of the only areas in which people are generally allowed to directly vote and choose how much they are taxed for a specific benefit. This unique sense of "public decision making" and local control contributed to a connection for those who benefited from better schools—most often whites—between the quality of their schools and the proportion of their taxes. Having access to better-funded schools itself became evidence of having contributed more in taxes, an argument impossible to counter for groups whose community schools had long been poorly resourced. And in the case of many white schools in the Deep South, black taxpayers had likely disproportionately paid into the resources provided for white education over the years, rather than the reverse. But the assertion of white taxpayer entitlement as a rhetorical move also enabled the more public tax revolt of the 1970s to claim that it was simply a color-blind suburban homeowner argument for local control, rather than a movement rooted in the politics of racism, segregation, and white flight.[110]

The story of racial segregation in public schools and the legal battle to overcome it from *Brown* onward has been told many times before as a battle over race and rights. This chapter argues, however, that this legal battle was also strongly connected to a racial consciousness of taxpayer rights that would have an important effect on later possibilities for demanding educational equality in the courtroom. Ultimately, white segregationists shared an emphasis on the perceived centrality of taxpayer status for claiming the right to education and for defining African American families out of the category of citizenship. The identity of "taxpayer citizen" did not have a legally important meaning—few cases in the twentieth century were won solely on the basis of taxpayer status claims—yet it was powerfully important in the legal consciousness of citizenship for those arguing about school segregation. This framework of claiming citizenship and rights through a rubric that could, by its nature, be defined in terms of wealth, in terms of who pays more and who pays less, would return to haunt the attempts in the next decade to secure truly equal education for poor children and children of color.

CHAPTER SIX

Taxpayers and Taxeaters

Poverty and the Constitution

As the schools in Prince Edward County were closing down and diverting the public school tax fund to private options rather than submit to desegregation orders, not far away a similar case was brewing in Newport News, Virginia. During that litigation, the Newport News school board's attorney, Archibald Robertson, pointedly asked a city official how much of the public relief fund "goes to Negroes and how much to whites." After pressing for the answer that "ninety percent" of the "aid to dependent children, general relief and foster care" went to African Americans, Robertson tried to then ask about illegitimacy (not yet a protected constitutional category), which the court refused to allow.[1] This case illustrates the explicit connections made by many whites between the receipt of welfare benefits and lesser citizenship status, as the local school board's case for funding private schools for whites from taxpayer dollars consciously drew links between race and poverty in an attempt to frame African Americans as less deserving of school funds. The "taxeater" of President Lyndon B. Johnson's speech was quickly transformed into a black woman reliant on government benefits, an image that would return again and again in political imagery in the ensuing decades.

The connections drawn by many whites since the Reconstruction Era between higher levels of poverty in a community and assumed lower tax-paying levels in that community—connections that supported the assertion that those identified with that community were less entitled to the rights of citizenship—were further entrenched in the wake of the long-delayed expansion of governmental benefits to poor African Americans in the 1960s. Yet if chapter 2 highlighted how frequently cases brought by people of color against unequal and discriminatory tax structures in the early twentieth century were by necessity brought by property owners and those with means, this chapter will illustrate the way in which, for a brief moment in the popular "rediscovery" of poverty in the 1960s, there was a brief window into a vision of overlapping and *simultaneous* claims of racial discrimination and economic injustice. At the same moment, there was also a continued push to frame poverty as synonymous with race and therefore with a lack of "taxpaying citizen" rights.

This chapter will examine the emergence of requests for the treatment of poverty as a protected constitutional class in the 1960s, as well as the poverty cases' frequent racial components, which the court would refuse to acknowledge, even as "taxpayers" writing to the bench expressed their frustration with "welfare rights" cases in combined racial and economic terms. It will end with a discussion of the court's last unanimous school desegregation case, in which the cracks in the court's emphasis on eliminating racial segregation were beginning to show, cracks that will become more apparent in the next chapter. In these cases, the court was frequently confronted with intersecting segregation and inequality, but it consistently focused on remedying only the formal system of racial segregation, leaving the inequality of school resources and property tax funding to the side.

Scholars have recently begun to examine more fully the growth of conservative, suburban politics in the 1960s and have identified several key trends in the formation of this movement. Identification as a "middle-class" person and a homeowner was particularly important for suburban parents, North and South, who wished to maintain public schooling but did not want to see their children bused into city schools.[2] In some cases, the gradual loss of systems of state-sponsored racial hierarchy and white supremacy was felt by many whites as traumatic, a sense reflected as well in many of the letters written to the court in this time.[3] Additionally, scholars of the "new suburban history" have studied the development and growth of socioeconomic and racial divisions between the largely (though not completely) white and middle-class suburbs and predominantly low-income black or Latino urban areas.[4] Historian David Freund has argued that residential segregation by Northern liberal whites who moved to suburbs while simultaneously supporting civil rights resolved this conflict by developing a new language of free-market choice and home-owning property rights tied to citizenship.[5] I identify an additional component of taxpayer identity that was strongly linked to both opposition to busing and opposition to welfare rights cases or any case seen as helping the racialized poor.

Finally, welfare historians in recent years have focused attention on the importance of the welfare rights movement and the grassroots organization of welfare recipients around ideas of rights and citizenship.[6] Welfare was a particularly fertile ground for the conservatism of a taxpayer rights paradigm within a "marketplace of citizenship" rhetorical attack. If citizenship and the rights thereof were understood to be tied to status as taxpayer and amount of taxes contributed, welfare recipients composed a category that would be automatically labeled as undeserving. Felicia Kornbluh specifically analyzes the link between the pursuit of welfare rights and the contested right to consumption, a link that can be seen as in many ways contributing to and reflecting the link between taxpayer status and rights.[7] Indeed, given the developing postwar system of "consumer citizenship" Lizabeth Cohen has described, citizenship divisions rooted in purchasing ability themselves naturalize citizenship distinctions based on wealth.[8] Without the ability to link race and poverty as categories deserving overlapping protection, particularly in the realm of educational equality, poverty became simply a natural outcome of private choice and the marketplace of meritocracy.

Poverty, Suspect Classifications, and Fundamental Rights

Once race was established as a suspect class in the *Brown* decision, a two-tiered framework of constitutional scrutiny was born. If the legislation in question did not involve race (or, later, national origin), it was presumptively valid under the rational-basis test's extreme degree of *Lochner*-haunted deference. The rational-basis tier of scrutiny was essentially a judicial rubber stamp for a variety of laws, while the heightened-scrutiny tier would only be activated if race or national origin was visible as a category in the legislation. In 1968 the Warren Court began formally expanding the categories to which it extended strict scrutiny in equal-protection cases to include alien status and national origin.[9] At the time, many advocates believed that poverty was a likely area for equal-protection expansion, reflecting the inadequacy that many of the justices perceived in the rational-basis scrutiny process. Various Supreme Court rulings in the 1950s and 1960s suggested that the court had in fact already declared poverty a suspect class by drawing clear parallels between poverty and race, the paradigmatic suspect class.[10] Indeed, the court's opinions in several cases listed poverty as a standard suspect class that triggered strict constitutional scrutiny, just like race, and one prominent legal scholar at the time described this series of decisions as an "egalitarian revolution" in the protection of the rights of the poor.[11]

In 1956, in the first major case suggesting constitutional protection against wealth discrimination, the court held that indigent criminal defendants had a constitutional right to a free transcript of their trial for use on appeal.[12] One of the cases relied on by the justices in the *Griffin v. Illinois* decision was an Oklahoma Criminal Court of Appeals case from 1913, in which the Oklahoma court had held that an indigent defendant had the right to appeal. In that case, the Oklahoma court had stated that, "it is true that appellant is only a friendless Negro without money[,] . . . but the law is no respecter of persons." The court went on to say that courts "cannot look to the color a man's face, the size of his pocketbook, or the number of his friends."[13] Justice Hugo Black, writing for the court in *Griffin*, emphasized the historical rationale for its opinion and quoted extensively from this decision, as well as from the Magna Carta and the book of Leviticus, in arguing that "providing equal justice for poor and rich, weak and powerful alike is an age-old problem."[14]

In a set of facts that would parallel later debates on the right to education (or the right to vote), the court held that though a state was not required by the Constitution to provide appellate courts or appellate review at all, if it did grant appellate review, it could not do so in a way that "discriminates against some convicted defendants on account of their poverty."[15] Another parallel with future debates on educational "equality" versus educational "adequacy" is illustrated by the early drafts of Black's opinion in *Griffin*, which repeatedly argued that states must provide "full appellate review for the poor"—not simply the bare minimum. After revisions offered by Justices Tom Clark and John Marshall Harlan II, however, the words "full appellate review for the poor" were struck out to replace "full" with "adequate."[16] Justice Harlan's dissent argued that in a parallel scenario in which "indigents" were specifically listed as excluded from a free state university, that example would "deny them equal protection," while the more subtle and ordinary requirement of tuition fees "surely would not, despite the resulting exclusion of those who could not afford to pay the fees."[17] The outcome was the same, but the wording made the difference to Harlan. The strand of jurisprudence evident in Harlan's dissent in *Griffin* remained strong throughout the 1960s decisions, suggesting—without explicitly stating—that in a capitalist country, punishing a state for treating rich and poor differently based on their ability to pay was inappropriate. This theory would reemerge more pointedly on the court in the early 1970s.

In two 1963 cases, the court held that indigent defendants had the right to court-appointed counsel both at trial and on direct appeal.[18] Justice Harlan's dissent in the second case chastised the court majority for its "new fetish for indigency."[19] Harlan again argued that while, under the equal protection clause, the states were not allowed to explicitly name different applications of law for rich and poor, it was a very different thing to claim that they could not adopt a law "that may affect the poor more harshly than it does the rich." Harlan argued that to imply such a thing would suggest that perhaps the state could not "levy a uniform sales tax[,] . . . charge tuition at a state university[, or] . . . fix rates for the purchase of water," since each of those actions would create a financial burden that would be more difficult for the poor or indigent to manage.[20] Whatever was meant by "equality," for Harlan, it did not and could not require the state to facilitate an equal playing field for rich and poor alike.

Annie Harper was a single African American woman in 1965 who had supported herself for most of her life by doing household or domestic work. As she grew older, her only regular income came from Social Security benefits. She could not afford the $1.50 poll tax—most of which was used for public schools—demanded by Virginia law. She, along with others, would eventually pursue her case to the Supreme Court to appeal the denial of her right to vote, claiming that the tax had a disproportionate impact on African Americans due to the large percentage of the poor who were black.[21]

The plaintiffs in *Harper* were unquestionably poor. Another plaintiff protesting the Virginia poll tax was a black grandmother who provided day care for seven small children, five of whom were her grandchildren. Curtis Burr; his wife, Myrtle; and their nine children were entirely dependent on his income from the construction trade, which was irregular and insufficient for the family of eleven. Though the Twenty-Fourth Amendment had eliminated the use of the poll tax in federal elections, Virginia, Alabama, Mississippi, Texas, and Vermont all still had versions of the poll tax for state elections in 1965.

The appellants argued from the court's other voting jurisprudence that the protection of the First Amendment extended beyond its particular words "to protect from abridgment concomitant personal rights necessary to make the express guarantees of the provision fully meaningful."[22] The appellants relied on 1960 census figures that showed that 27.9 percent of all families in Virginia had incomes below the poverty line—22.4 percent of white families and 54.1 percent of nonwhite families, illustrating what they described as the "commonly known fact that there is a higher proportionate incidence of poverty among Negroes than among white persons."[23] The United States argued in its amicus brief that any tax levied on voting limited "a fundamental right impermissibly," but they were careful to note that it was for this reason that the "basic vice of the poll tax system cannot be cured—as could, perhaps, a law that merely discriminated against poor persons—by exempting indigents from the burdens of the law."[24] But the premise that the ability to pay taxes was closely connected to the rights of citizenship was clearly present in the state's case. According to a tax assessor from Virginia, the poll tax provided "a simple and objective test of certain minimal capacity for ordering one's own affairs and thus of qualification to participate in the ordering of the affairs of state."[25]

In its decision in *Harper v. Virginia State Board of Elections* in 1966, striking down the Virginia state poll tax on equal-protection grounds, the court stated that "lines drawn on the basis of wealth or property, like those of race, are traditionally disfavored."[26] Justice William O. Douglas wrote the court's opinion in *Harper*, arguing that the "Equal Protection Clause is not shackled to the political theory of a particular era" and stating that in the consideration of what constituted discrimination, "we have never been confined to historic notions of equality."[27]

Justice Black dissented vigorously, defending his participation in the court's 1937 decision to uphold the poll tax and arguing that if the case was only about class, not race, the plaintiffs should lose. He pointed out that "the Court's decision is to no extent based on a finding that the Virginia law as written or as applied is being used as a device or mechanism to deny Negro citizens of Virginia the right to vote on account of their color."[28] Black assumed that this meant the majority agreed with the district court that "this record would not support any finding" that the Virginia poll tax law had a discriminatory racial effect, because if it did, he argued, that "would of course be unconstitutional." Though the appellants had strongly argued that racial discrimination was an integral component of the economic discrimination of the poll tax, Black was accurate in describing the majority opinion as solely rooted in discrimination based on wealth, not on the combination of wealth and race discrimination alleged by the plaintiffs.

The decision in *Harper* declaring the poll tax unconstitutional did "not mean a great deal" in a practical sense, according to one media outlet.[29] It involved only a handful of states, and as the country gained in affluence, more blacks could pay the tax and afford to vote. But, according to an ABC radio broadcast at the time, the decision meant more than that because it ruled that there was such a thing as "economic discrimination."[30] Further cases in the 1960s seemed to confirm this sense that the *Griffin*, *Douglas*, and *Harper* cases had confirmed poverty as a constitutionally protected legal category. The quiet implication that poor people, people who did not own property or pay large sums into different tax systems, were still full citizens and fully guaranteed equal rights was immediately controversial.

In *McDonald v. Board of Elections* in 1969, the court decided not to apply strict scrutiny to a question of absentee ballots for medically incapacitated prisoners because the distinctions in the absentee law "are not drawn on the basis of wealth or race." But the most lingering moment of the decision was when Chief Justice Earl Warren, writing for the court, stated as an aside that "a careful examination on our part is especially warranted where lines are drawn on the basis of wealth or race, two factors which would independently render a classification highly suspect and thereby demand a more exacting judicial scrutiny."[31] Following this, he cited *Douglas v. California* and *McLaughlin v. Florida*. *Douglas* was the case stating that indigent defendants had the right to counsel on appeal, and *McLaughlin* had announced a presumption against all racial classifications. By citing these two cases to support an argument that either wealth or race would "independently render a classification highly suspect," the court seemed to clearly be naming the poor a suspect class. They did this, in large part, by emphasizing the parallels between race and poverty as status categories in need of protection. They did not, however, examine the intersections within these categories themselves, as in the case of *Harper*, nor did the structure of the formal discourse around race or poverty lend itself to such an analysis.

The new, two-tiered approach of constitutional scrutiny that emerged with the confirmation of race as a suspect class offered solutions to two long-running problems.[32] In one area, it empowered the court to potentially strike down racial classifications without the need to deploy the convoluted rationale of *Brown*, with its focus on psychological harm and its inability to fully commit to either racial discrimination or educational equality as its premise. And in all other areas of law, the deferential rational-basis standard left the court free from any implication that it was just rampantly striking down legislation that was personally or ideologically unpopular with members of the court. Otherwise, the court risked comparison with the conservative *Lochner* era and the "nine old men" who had received so much criticism in the 1930s for constantly invalidating protective regulatory legislation.[33] But poverty as a suspect class with the power to strike down state laws that discriminated against the poor threatened to be so revolutionary in application that this momentary window of possibility did not last more than a few years.

Welfare and Working-Class Backlash in the 1970s

After the turning point of 1968, including the election of Richard Nixon and the corresponding rightward turn in the administration's attitude toward the War on Poverty, the court quickly began to step back from the high points of its jurisprudence on both protection for the poor and desegregation, exemplified by *Harper* and *Alexander*, respectively.[34] Though a few decisions were rendered in the early 1970s in favor of welfare recipients, poverty was no longer discussed openly in opinions as a clear suspect class that automatically triggered constitutional attention.

Goldberg v. Kelly was an important Supreme Court case in 1970 that held that a welfare recipient was entitled to an evidentiary hearing prior to termination of welfare benefits.[35] In the words of one scholar, the case reflected "a brief shining moment when it appeared thinkable that some version of a welfare state was not just a constitutional possibility, but a constitutional duty."[36] Justice William Brennan wrote the court's opinion, arguing that welfare recipients were entitled to procedural due process and that "we have come to recognize that forces not within the control of the poor contribute to their poverty."[37] Ultimately, the majority held, the interest in protecting "public tax funds" did not outweigh the needs of the individual welfare recipient to maintain food, shelter, and basic necessities.

A Spokane man wrote to Brennan to express his gratitude on behalf of what he called "the 'Silent Majority'" for his opinion in *Goldberg*, stating that, though he was not himself a welfare recipient, he did "understand the plight of these people."[38] He felt that welfare recipients were "ridiculed, kicked around," and "degraded" because they provided good "kicking posts for politicians who scream 'public assistance' when the taxpayers demand an accounting of their tax money." Indeed, one such politician, Arkansas representative Wilbur D. Mills, chairman of the House Ways and Means Committee for many years, would often abandon his occasional reticence on nonbudgetary issues to argue, like President Johnson, for the need to transform people on welfare from "taxeaters" into "taxpayers."[39]

A number of letters were sent to the court in response to their indigency jurisprudence, asserting taxpayer rights and making racialized comparisons and assumptions. After *Goldberg v. Kelly*, one writer complained that "our hard-earned tax dollars pay the salaries of the U.S. Supreme Court . . . but all I see and hear are giveaway anti-poverty programs, welfare for anyone who wants it."[40] Another letter complained that it was "us decent and loyal citizens that are being taxed to the hilt, so these crumbums, can live off the fat of the land."[41] Claiming that "many Negroes and Puerto Rican families are put up in luxurious hotels" and also given government food stamps, the author claimed that if "anybody should be entitled to get [such benefits] it should be us tax payers who are keeping those chislers [*sic*] on relief, and living off the fat of the land." A Brooklyn woman was incensed at the *Goldberg* decision, claiming that "it is unfair and unjust to tax heavily those who do work."[42] She was furious that "honest, upright citizen[s] be continually raised taxes" to provide for "ignorant masses," who, she insinuated, "could stop our former privileged free school system."

Shortly after *Goldberg*, a group of female welfare recipients who wished to apply for divorces but could not afford the court filing fees pursued their appeal to the Supreme Court in *Boddie v. Connecticut*.[43] Justice Harlan wrote the majority opinion narrowly upholding their right to have the filing fees waived. He particularly stressed the nature of marriage as uniquely tied to the state in finding that the Connecticut requirements discriminated against indigents regarding a fundamental right. Justice Douglas concurred but believed the majority focused too specifically on marriage; instead, he argued, "rather definite guidelines" had already been set out for equal-protection analysis. He proceeded to list the categories and cases requiring additional constitutional scrutiny: race, alienage, religion, poverty, and caste. While the court considered the *Boddie* decision, many younger lawyers interested in poverty "saw the court as their best hope of social change" for protecting the poor.[44]

Those who wrote to the court on the *Boddie* decision were often working-class whites who continued to represent an antiwelfare taxpayer identity. A New York man thanked Black for his dissenting vote in *Boddie*, stating that he was tired of the burden of welfare recipients being placed on "the tax paying working class."[45] A California woman was concerned after *Boddie* that the court had created "a new privileged welfare class at the expense of those who work."[46] Suggesting her own class position, she especially wanted to clarify what the meaning of "indigency" was—particularly whether someone who received the same amount of money in a paycheck as others received in a welfare check would be considered indigent. One woman who opposed the *Boddie* decision signed her letter to Black as "a member of the working class" and said she was happy to see that "one leader of our Supreme Court is speaking up for the working people."[47] She also asked him in particular, "Where does the status line for being poor end and that of being rich begin?" She felt that "the harder we work," the more "we" have to pay taxes to support welfare, which she argued meant "the working class is becoming tax poor." She wanted to know when working-class people would "qualify to have our divorces and court costs paid for by the State!" Another woman took the *Boddie* decision to mean that "the so called *poor* can now do anything they want."[48]

As seen in these letters, *Boddie* seemed to especially infuriate those working people who were clearly struggling themselves to make ends meet. Helen M. Mattice of New Jersey felt that the decision meant that the expense of divorce for the poor would now be paid by "hordes of overburdened taxpayers like me."[49] She believed that "scores of these poor" were living better than she was, and she proceeded to list all the things she couldn't afford, such as dental care, cleaning supplies, healthy food, auto insurance, or a color television set. She was also upset that the "taxes withheld for their support are inequitable" because, as a single person, she was taxed at a higher rate. She was angry that she and other "really poor people" who were receiving "insufficient remuneration" were being "ravaged by the inroads of the taxation for the poor." She demanded justice for the "blue collar, low paid white collar worker," who she said "is also a citizen," even as she acknowledged that "no one should starve or be in want in this great country today."

Despite Black's dissent in *Boddie*, once the decision was reached, he argued that it should not be limited. Though he disagreed that the right to seek a divorce was "fundamental" enough to warrant the decision, he argued in a memo that "the need to be on the welfare rolls or to file for a discharge in bankruptcy" was no less a "fundamental" right and, as such, should have the attorneys' costs paid by the government.[50] In addition, he said that he could "not believe that [his] Brethren would find the rights of a man with both legs cut off by a negligent railroad less 'fundamental' than a person's right to seek a divorce," arguing that court costs in civil lawsuits should also be covered for the indigent under the *Boddie* precedent.[51] He construed *Boddie* to mean that indigent people were entitled to court-appointed counsel in divorce cases, and he believed there was "no fairness or justice in a legal system" that limited governmental assumption of civil court costs to divorce cases and prevented it "in other civil cases which are frequently of far greater importance to society."[52]

Choosing between Categories: Race or Class

By the 1970s there was a strong sense that the pendulum of rights creation had begun to swing the other way on the Supreme Court. There was also further evidence of the law's inability—in both its liberal and its conservative wings—to deal with multiple sites of identity. The two shifts may in fact have had a great deal to do with one another—once systems found to violate a particular or categorical rights claim learned to adapt themselves, and in fact began using the language of rights in their own interest, then all rights claims became simply competing voices on an equal terrain.[53] *James v. Valtierra* was a 1971 Supreme Court case alleging racial and wealth discrimination in a California law, article 34, requiring local referendums prior to the construction of low-income housing.[54] A three-judge district court panel had found in a 1970 decision that the law violated the equal protection clause, but the Supreme Court overturned that ruling, while refusing to connect the race and class discrimination claims despite the evidence offered.[55]

Justice Harry Blackmun indicated in March 1971 that his "inclination is definitely to affirm" the lower court in *Valtierra* because "the plan is a thinly veiled attempt to avoid the availability of low-income housing."[56] He mentioned that the court below and the appellees "try to work in a racial overtone as well," which, he stated, "may or may not be present in the case," but if so, "it makes affirmance all the more in order." He did not subscribe to the idea that there was a heavy tax burden on the local community, since the federal government was the source of the funds, but he was careful to state that he was not saying that "low-income housing is the answer to everything."

Blackmun's law clerk, Daniel Edelman, disagreed with Justice Black's opinion that referendums were a democratic tradition by pointing out that the "malapportioned legislature and the poll tax may have been fine old democratic traditions, but they violated equal protection."[57] The measure discriminated against low-income persons, he argued, and it meant "little" that a previous case involved a racial classification "and this case does not." He did not understand how discrimination against low-income persons seeking housing "can be differentiated from discrimination against indigents," a distinction that, according to Edelman, Justice Harlan had drawn at oral argument by suggesting that "individual appellees in this case have considerable incomes through welfare assistance and hence, are not indigent." Edelman argued that indigency was determined by the magnitude of the cost involved, and since the appellees were, by definition, people unable to afford decent housing—and were receiving welfare—he did not see how discrimination against them could "stand on constitutionally firmer ground than racial discrimination."

The claims of intersecting race and poverty discrimination were mentioned or discussed at nearly every level of the proceedings. The NAACP Legal Defense Fund filed an amicus brief in the case arguing that article 34 established an impermissible racial classification, a "badge of slavery," under the Thirteenth Amendment, and denied rights to hold property.[58] In his bench memo on the case, Edelman noted that the plaintiffs in a corollary case, *Hays et al. v. Housing Authority of San Mateo*, were also poor persons, "predominantly Negro," on the waiting list for public housing in San Mateo County.[59]

One of the main justifications the appellants offered against low-income housing was that it would lead to the "loss of property tax revenues without compensating new revenues."[60]

The appellees argued that article 34 violated the equal protection clause by denying poor persons "the use of ordinary law-making procedures" and, most importantly, by "authorizing and encouraging a racial veto over distribution of federal funds for public housing."[61] Though they admitted that the article did not explicitly mention race, they argued that it was "simply a means of creating a white middle-class veto over black and brown, lower-class immigration into the traditional havens of residential segregation." They went on to claim that "the Constitution forbids sophisticated as well as simple-minded modes of discrimination."[62] Both the U.S. and the New York attorneys general supported the appellees in this case, with the New York attorney general arguing explicitly that article 34 "imposes a special burden on poor persons and Negroes and other disadvantaged minorities."[63]

Despite the two simultaneous claims of discrimination in the case on the basis of race and poverty, the court's majority opinion dealt solely with the claim of racial discrimination, which it rejected. The extremely brief opinion, written by Justice Black, opened by stating that "these cases raise but a single issue."[64] The opinion compared the California provision to a 1969 case in which the City of Akron had amended the city charter to require that any ordinance attempting to regulate racial discrimination in real estate could not take effect until it had been passed by a city voter referendum.[65] The court held that the Akron provision was an unacceptable classification based on race, but in *Valtierra* the majority argued that "the record here would not support any claim that a law seemingly neutral on its face is in fact, aimed at a racial minority."[66] Indeed, according to Black, "provisions for referendums demonstrate devotion to democracy, not to bias, discrimination, or prejudice."[67] The majority thus disposed of the claim, and the case, by only addressing the question of race discrimination, and finding there was no explicit intent to formally discriminate, without reaching the lingering question of poverty as a suspect class that still remained open for the court.

In opposition, the equally brief dissent in *Valtierra*, written by Justice Thurgood Marshall and joined by Justices Brennan and Blackmun, dealt *only* with the question of wealth discrimination, without mentioning the claim of racial inequality, perhaps strategically. Contending that singling out the poor to bear the burden in the law constituted invidious discrimination in violation of the equal protection clause, the dissent said that "of course" states are prohibited from "discriminating between 'rich' and 'poor' as such in the formulation and application of their laws." Marshall chastised the majority for subjecting the article to "no scrutiny whatsoever" and treating it as if it were "a totally benign, technical economic classification." Marshall then pointed to the court's own precedents in wealth discrimination in cases such as *Douglas*, *Harper*, and *McDonald* and argued that "it is far too late in the day to contend that the Fourteenth Amendment prohibits only racial discrimination; and to me, singling out the poor to bear a burden not placed on any other class of citizens tramples the values that the Fourteenth Amendment was designed to protect."[68] *Valtierra* shows the beginnings of the court's incapacity to deal with race and poverty as anything but mutually exclusive categories, even in instances of residential zoning segregation that had been judged invalid in earlier cases and legislation.[69] This treatment of race and class discrimination claims as separate culminated in the *Rodriguez* decision discussed in the next chapter.

Though neither the majority nor the dissent discussed together the dual nature of the discrimination at issue in *Valtierra*, the public response had no trouble tying the threads of race and poverty together and identifying the intersecting motivations behind the referendum law. One letter's author complained about low-income housing and how the black middle class "also" wouldn't want "able bodied lazy bums" living next door.[70] The author demanded a stop to "the lies of racism" when the problem was "living standards." Finally, the writer suggested that "poor whites" be moved into a wealthy black neighborhood in Washington, D.C., and claimed that "these people cheer poor blacks into middle class white areas but reject poor whites in their neighborhood." Another letter writer acknowledged that the "provision for referendums may be an expression of racial prejudice" but claimed that that was "a human failing that we, unfortunately have to live with."[71] And, since it was the taxpayers in the area who "without doubt" provided the funds "used to erect such subsidized housing," they should "have a say regarding how public funds are spent in that area." Finally, he claimed it was a positive thing that the Supreme Court was "aware" that others besides "the poor, and the black" have rights as well, since there was "no inherent virtue in a black skin, or poverty either," just as there was no inherent virtue in wealth.

An Arizona woman wrote to compliment Black and the court on their "stand" to keep people from being "forced to have slums in well-kept neighborhoods."[72] She was upset that "people spend life-savings to have nice homes, only to be crowded out by trashy shantys [sic]," and then noted, perhaps defensively, that the "slum-class" was "not only minorities." She then cited a "fine" African American family nearby who feared having low-income housing move in near their "nice home and pleasant surroundings." She concluded that unless "planned housing" was protected, "never will any minority reach the goal" of dignity and homeownership this family had achieved.

Not all who responded to the case were opposed to low-income housing or supportive of the court's decision. One letter writer was frustrated at the majority opinion, calling it an "American 'apartheid,'" and referred to the warning of the Kerner Commission, "now apparently moving forward with the blessings of the U.S. Supreme Court."[73] Calling the decision a serious "backward step" for the country, he imagined the potential ramifications of the decision. He asked the court whether now communities could vote to exclude "all apartments with rents under $250; housing for the handicapped . . . all housing for the elderly or the mentally or emotionally disturbed."[74] He viewed this as a way in which certain groups could "attempt to transform themselves into rich ghettoes without any of 'those groups' which might incur social costs."

A New Jersey letter writer was upset at Black's lack of empathy for the poor who were in need of housing, asking Black somewhat sardonically why he thought public housing had been blocked up until then "by all the Taxpayers' Associations in the country."[75] Though the author asserted that he or she would not be eligible for low-income housing, rent was an increasingly heavy burden with "a landlord on my back." Finally, the letter writer suggested that if there "was any justice in the courts . . . you would all have a whack at being poor for a while. . . . It is delightful, and so slimming."

The media also illustrated that the case could not be isolated to either race or class discrimination alone. An editorial in the *Pittsburgh Press* argued that the cause of the failure of so much public housing in previous decades was the practice of "cramming thousands of poor families (many of them black) into multi-stories apartments in the bleakest parts of our cities."[76] The authors concluded that unless housing barriers were lowered soon, "the 'devotion to democracy' Justice Black so heartily commends will be simply another exercise in exclusion against the black and the poor."

Desegregation and Unanimity, North and South

As illustrated by the Prince Edward County case in the previous chapter, from *Brown II* throughout the 1960s, the court grew progressively more impatient with the delaying tactics of school districts in implementing deseg-regation. In 1958, the court had refused to grant "additional time" to Little Rock, Arkansas, to work toward desegregation after white segregationists forced President Dwight D. Eisenhower to call in the National Guard.[77] This decision signaled that the court was willing to push further toward true desegregation than the "with all deliberate speed" fuzziness of *Brown II* would suggest. A decade later, in *Green v. County School Board of New Kent County*, the court declared "freedom-of-choice" plans inadequate to com-ply with the mandate of *Brown* and asserted that state-compelled dual school systems had an affirmative duty to eliminate racial discrimination "root and branch."[78] Then, the U.S. Department of Health, Education, and Welfare and the State of Mississippi in 1969 asked for additional time to implement the department's recommendations for desegregation in the state, and the Fifth Circuit granted a stay. In *Alexander v. Board of Education of Holmes County*, the court issued a short per curiam opinion stating that the ques-tion of the case was of "paramount importance, involving as it does the denial of fundamental rights to many thousands of school children," and holding that segregation must be ended at once.[79]

The Nixon administration came into office the same year as the *Alexan-der* decision on a series of promises to the "silent majority" of suburban white Americans that taxes would be lowered and "states' rights" would be recognized.[80] An editorial in 1969 chastised the administration for "play-ing with matches" by encouraging the "die-hard white South" to believe that there would be a "way out" of desegregation.[81] In addition, the editors pressed the administration to give financial assistance to incentivize deseg-regation rather than "reinforc[ing] the pieties of Southern resistance," ar-guing that doing otherwise had thrown the responsibility on courts.

Cities in the North could be battlegrounds for segregation struggles as intense as many of those seen in the South. Southern newspapers frequently noted the "double standard" they perceived from Northern liberals, espe-cially those living in major cities who sent their children to private schools.[82] The *Jackson Daily News* especially targeted the example of Washington, D.C., where the Department of Health, Education, and Welfare reported that 99.1 percent of black students attended majority-black schools in 1970. The paper singled out Ted Kennedy, George McGovern, Clifford Case, Eugene McCarthy, Thurgood Marshall, and James Farmer, all of whom, it claimed, sent their children to "expensive (as high as $1900 tuition) private day schools rather than having them attend the predominantly black public school system of Washington, D.C." The editorial also highlighted Indiana, where there were fifty-seven schools with a black enrollment over 80 percent and forty schools with black enrollments of 99 to 100 percent, even though African Americans were only 9.8 percent of the state school population.[83]

Southern senators pushed to require the Department of Health, Education, and Welfare to terminate racial segregation in "at least ten Northern states," as well as Washington, D.C.[84] The department's own figures showed that Ohio's racial segregation was very similar to Indiana's, with 105 schools that were 98 to 100 percent black. On the question of de jure segregation, the Southern states were more ready to point out that the majority of Northern states had laws "at one time or another" that sanctioned or required segregation. Mississippi senator John Stennis demanded that the department "apply the same rules for desegregation" in the North and the South but argued that "the federal government has been persistent in its policy of avoidance of the issue in the North." Stennis, whose arguments' effectiveness was perhaps hampered by his own history of stridently defending segregation, claimed that "if segregation is unlawful because of the 1954 decision of Brown v. Board of Education, it is illegal whether or not it results from de jure or de facto reasons and it is illegal whether it occurs in the North or in the South. Make no mistake about it. Let there be no misunderstanding. There is no real difference between segregation in the North and the South."[85]

Certainly those who wrote to the court in favor of school segregation were also prepared to point out that the North had many of the same aspects of segregation that courts were condemning in the South. A Georgia man wrote to Justice Black and Justice Warren E. Burger in 1969 "requesting as a tax payer to know where your children and/or grandchildren go to school."[86] Many letter writers also expressed possessiveness about tax funds and taxpayer-funded facilities. One retiree who "played golf about three times a week" complained to Justice Black that he felt "discriminated against" because he would be bumped into a higher tax bracket if he accepted a teaching post at Mississippi State University.[87] Mrs. James W. Marley of Montgomery, Alabama, interpreted the *Brown* decision as saying that "all facilities operated by tax funds must be available to all citizens."[88] She lived between two air force bases, both operated "by tax payers money," and even though three-quarters of the people in her town were veterans, they were not allowed to use the facilities. She was also offended that enlisted men and officers were "segregated" from each other in the armed forces, even if they were related to each other, and wanted everyone to be allowed to use the same facilities, especially since "our tax money is paying for all the facilities used by the officers."

Two women from Oklahoma City wrote to Justice Brennan in 1969 in response to the increase in district court orders for busing, claiming they had contributed to the struggle for access to public facilities by African Americans, which "is their right and we shall defend it now as we did then."[89] They then asked "how we can possibly be discriminating against them now in our schools when any predominately white school in Oklahoma City is open to them by transfer, with transportation paid by our school board." They were particularly upset that despite the constant "shortage of funds for public education," desegregation would require a "vast amount of money" to provide the necessary facilities, and they believed voters would vote against the extra school levies if they were for desegregated facilities.

And even as the court was deciding how far it would extend its jurisprudence on the rights of the poor, school equality and desegregation cases continued to come forward. The "school cases" of the 1970–71 term were consolidated under a case from Charlotte, North Carolina, in which the district court had ordered the county school board to bus students in order to affirmatively desegregate the schools, which were overwhelmingly segregated.[90] Some newspapers in the South hinted that, despite the court never having "heard a Northern school case," the ruling in *Swann v. Charlotte-Mecklenburg* "could be phrased" so as to apply throughout the country.[91] As will be seen in the concluding chapter, the remedy of busing children to affirmatively desegregate was a necessity in many Northern cities as well. Many school districts in the South had a long tradition of busing children far away to maintain segregation.[92] Children from Sturges, Mississippi, where there was a white school, were routinely bused 46.5 miles each way to the closest black school in Maben, Mississippi. In one Atlanta suburb throughout the 1960s, black children were bused 75 miles round trip daily to attend segregated schools. The Department of Health, Education, and Welfare had compiled a table of busing data in various districts during the 1968–69 school year and found that only a small number of counties would have to increase their busing to desegregate, while the rest would have the same amount of busing or less.[93] The color of the children on the buses was the primary difference; the number of buses stayed essentially the same.

In a transcript of one of the court's conference meetings on the school cases in October 1970 with the instruction "To Be Destroyed," several of the justices revealed their general leanings on the segregation cases as they began to consider *Swann*.[94] Though the case seemed to be about the use of busing as a remedy in a dual system, the debate was about the tension between discrimination and equality, the right to a quality education versus the right to send a child to a neighborhood school. The discussion also revealed the tendency to define "desegregation" for the South in terms of what Northern schools already looked like.

Douglas agreed that the issue was narrow and the "nub of the case" was busing, but the question for him was, "What is the power of the Court when there is no act of Congress and the situation is one which the Court has said violates the Constitution?"[95] He did not feel the remedy of busing was too extreme when, "if this were in the anti-trust area, we would give broad scope and support to attempts to remedy." Justice Harlan argued that "these decisions are as important as the original *Brown* litigation." He concluded with his fervent hope that "the federal courts eventually can get out of this school business."[96]

Justice Byron White agreed with Justice Potter Stewart that racially identifiably schools were acceptable, stating that a school board "can do as it wishes by way of educational policy," whether it chose to racially balance or not.[97] Ultimately, he argued, equal protection was "no guarantee of the right to go to school with the opposite race throughout one's educational career." According to White, the court "need go no further than the point at which things would be had there been no *de jure* factor." Justice Marshall argued vehemently to the contrary that there was "no such thing as freedom of choice. . . . Nowhere has a white child asked to go to a Negro school." He disagreed with Justice Stewart that the court had "gone far enough" and said that he could not "call any northern system today unitary." He went on to argue that "the only time a black child knows he is getting an equal education is when he is in a white school." Blackmun tried to emphasize that equality was the key to these cases, and that "racial controversy" would recede when equality was achieved.[98]

Black sent around a draft opinion partially dissenting and partially concurring with the court's initial decision to uphold the busing remedy, arguing that the Constitution did not "require a racial balance or necessitate the abolition of every all-black or nearly all-black school."[99] Justice Black expressed many concerns about the power of the court to enforce busing, stating in one letter to Burger that in particular he "gravely doubt[ed]" the court's constitutional authority to "compel a State and its taxpayers to buy millions of dollars worth of busses to haul students miles away from their neighborhood schools and their homes."[100] One of Burger's law clerks, however, argued that state officials were frequently ordered by courts to expend funds, such as when a court orders a retrial of a convicted defendant or when damages are awarded against an official for violating civil rights.

And if a court ordered a school board not to build a particular school because it would increase segregation, "this order may cost the school board money" and "some of these orders may eventually require the state to raise taxes," but there had been no order to levy taxes in the Charlotte case.[101] Justice Lewis F. Powell, who would take over Black's seat by the time of the *Swann* ruling, was sympathetic to Black's feeling against busing. Prior to his appointment to the court, Powell had in fact served as special counsel and principal author on an amicus brief filed on behalf of Richmond and Norfolk, Virginia, against busing in the *Swann* case.[102] Arguing that the Virginia cities had "done all that they could do," he expressed similar concerns about taxpayers' willingness to vote for school bonds if busing were enforced.[103] Since his role in the case had been analyzed very publicly in his confirmation hearings, he was especially loath to write on the case or later busing cases, knowing that "an antibusing tirade" from a former education official in a segregated Southern school system would not be welcomed.[104]

Justice Blackmun's deliberations in *Swann* are revealing in understanding the way in which Northern contexts of segregation (and "ethnicity") would come to be defined as benign and therefore beyond the reach of the methods used to desegregate the South. His arguments also illustrate a focus on equality of conditions that the court would prove unable to integrate into its decisions for remedying the segregation in schools. Blackmun, who grew up in a small town in Minnesota, stated that it seemed to him that "ethnic concentrations are basically *de facto*," listing as examples "the large Italian community and the German community in St. Louis, the Bohemian community in New Prague, Minnesota, the German one in New Ulm, Minnesota, and the heavily concentrated Scandinavian areas in northeast St. Paul."[105] Blackmun did not feel that "racial balancing per se" was a constitutional prerequisite, stating that the "real key to this is equality . . . in staff and facilities, in curriculum, in opportunities." He believed that once equality was achieved, racial balancing would recede and become "completely meaningless." Indeed, he argued, the court should be able to imagine "that happy day when a school district is unitized and yet might have an all white or an all black school."[106]

The idea that the cases presented the question of a remedy and not a "right" to racially balanced education was popular among many of the justices. One of Blackmun's law clerks speculated about the question that might be presented in a "purely *de facto*" system that had not had any state action but nevertheless had some "all black and all white schools," but he quickly acknowledged the difficulty in finding such a situation, stating that "there are remnants of *de jure* segregation in almost every school system in the nation, north and south."[107] The clerk agreed with many of the justices that the question was about a remedy for past discrimination, "not a substantive right to an education in a racially balanced school." Justice Brennan wrote a memo on *Swann* that indicated his view that "the evil of segregation was stigma," so the "goal and purpose of desegregation is the elimination of stigma."[108] In this reading of the focus on the psychological effects of segregation, even Brennan, generally regarded as one of the most liberal justices, was deferring to the definition set out by *Brown* for the kinds of harm that the court could acknowledge. Arguing that separation of people by groups in public facilities was not "per se unconstitutional," and pointing as an example to "separate but equal" schools for boys and girls, which did not seem to be constitutionally objectionable, Brennan said he did not read *Brown* as "establishing a general principle of equal educational opportunity" for school segregation cases.

In a draft dissent circulated by Stewart on *Swann* in February 1971, he argued for a more complex understanding of racial and economic structures of discrimination that sustained segregation. He stated that "racial discrimination in the society at large, combined with the play of social and economic forces, often creates divisions within the community and marked differences in the educational needs of children. A policy of deliberate 'blindness' to these social realities is not required by the Constitution."[109] Stewart rejected "colorblind neighborhood zoning" as a way for a school board to discharge its affirmative duty of dismantling a formerly dual-race school system, stating that school systems were still organized under the lingering effects of segregation:

> A public school system is not built in a day; it is not built in isolation from the community around it. As a school system takes shape through innumerable decisions by hundreds of educational and noneducational officials acting in many different capacities, it acquires a formidable stability and imperviousness to change. Practices, predispositions and attitudes build up in administrators, teachers, children, parents, and local noneducational officials, and come to be independent of particular administrative regulations or legal rules. At times, these may be strong enough to survive conscious decisions for change by those in positions of responsibility. For decades before Brown I, and for at least a decade after that decision, the school district involved in these cases subjected all of these choices to the test of race. Zone

lines, construction, capacity, grade structure, teacher assignment, extracurricular activities, transportation policy, even the naming of schools—all of these decisions and many more like them played their part in the construction of the dual system. When they are taken together with more general patterns of discrimination in the community, they constitute a structure which, as 16 years of litigation have shown, cannot be rendered "color blind" simply by the repeal of those local ordinances or regulations that made overt racial distinctions.[110]

Stewart argued that color-blind neighborhood zoning was in fact "closely analogous" to the "freedom of choice" plans presented by the *Green* cases.[111] As in the case of *Green*, he argued, the considerations that made color-blind zoning inadequate as a remedy were "considerations of *effectiveness*." The decisions by a school board to close schools "which appeared likely to become racially mixed" and to build new schools "in the areas of white suburban expansion furthest from black population centers" had ensured the maintenance of a separate school system. The choices of where to build schools and where to close schools, he argued, did not just have an impact on student population, but "may set the path of expansion of a metropolitan area and hasten or retard the transformation of inner-city neighborhoods." By building schools that "promote[d] segregated residential patterns" and then applying "neighborhood zoning," the board would "further lock the school system into the mold of separation of the races." Stewart was anxious to frame the decree so as to avoid "resegregation through the movement of white parents out of predominantly Negro attendance zones."[112]

Justice Douglas repeatedly articulated the need to eliminate the de jure/ de facto distinction as well in a 1970 memo arguing that the present state of segregation was based on elements of both public and private action that originally derived their "basic strength" from public law or governmental action, including racially restrictive covenants, zoning, city planning, urban renewal, the location of public housing, and the school boards' location of the schools. Ultimately, he argued, all the actions deriving from these policies were state actions.[113] Douglas also argued forcefully that "it is notorious, North and South, that white schools are better than black schools, not because they are white but because they have better libraries, better physical plants, better laboratory equipment, broader curricula. A neighborhood school that is all black is usually managed *not by the community* but by whites. History has shown that it is extremely difficult, if not impossible, in those circumstances to summon the resources necessary to upgrade the school of the blacks. The reason is that the school boards are white boards, not boards representing a cross-section of the community."[114]

The consequence of this, he argued, was that a high-quality white school, however distant, "may be irresistible" to the parents of a black student who sought a quality education for their child. Brennan wrote to Burger that whenever a decree created a disparity between schools "which invites the migration of white parents from one school zone to another, it does not adequately perform its function of dismantling the dual system."[115] Marshall was also displeased with Burger's draft, saying it would "inevitably result in the more affluent and educated Negro parents using the plan and leaving the poor Negroes stuck in the all-Negro school."[116]

In the final court opinion in *Swann*—the last unanimous school case— the compromises necessary to unify these obviously disparate opinions were apparent in the cautious language employed by Burger, who stated specifically that "segregation was the evil struck down by *Brown I*," that segregation was the violation remedied in *Brown II*, and that segregation was the basis of the duty placed on school districts in *Green*.[117] Though the court upheld the district court's busing order as within the bounds of traditionally broad forms of equitable remedy, the opinion emphasized that the concern of the court in the school cases was "with the elimination of the discrimination inherent in the dual school systems, not with myriad factors of human existence which can cause discrimination in a multitude of ways on racial, religious, or ethnic grounds." Notably, economic discrimination and inequality were left off the list. Stating that "one vehicle can carry only a limited amount of baggage," the court cautioned that it would not serve the "important objective" of *Brown I* to attempt to use school desegregation cases "for purposes beyond their scope."[118]

Conclusion

The poverty jurisprudence of the Supreme Court in the 1960s and early 1970s illustrates both a brief window of sympathy to the claims of the poor in certain cases and the unwillingness of the court to address simultaneous claims of race and class discrimination in a country that was rapidly transitioning from Jim Crow segregation to more oblique and opaque forms of racial discrimination, often through economic means. Even as they briefly recognized some protections for people based on poverty alone, the court refused to acknowledge the connections between race and poverty in cases like *Valtierra* and *Swann*. To those antiwelfare, pro-segregation "taxpaying citizens" who wrote to the court in this period, however, the connection between race and economic status was expressed clearly and without hesitation. These sources, as well as those examined in the previous chapter, illustrate the legal consciousness on the part of many whites that taxpayers were engaged in a market relationship of purchasing public services from the state, which led them to conclude that welfare recipients (who, they assumed, did not "pay taxes") were automatically excluded from full citizenship rights.

This perspective also illustrates the ease with which many nonlegal actors were able to describe the links between race and economic inequality in discussing education rights. In its decisions on school segregation, the court throughout the 1960s was torn between the "separate" and the "equal" rationales of *Plessy v. Ferguson* but was continually unable to combine an analysis of the two concepts—the racial and the economic components of segregation—into a single judgment or remedy. The next chapter will discuss how this inability to articulate intersecting forms of discrimination was made manifest in a case asserting simultaneous racial school segregation and poverty-based funding inequality.

CHAPTER SEVEN

The Rich Richer and the Poor Poorer
Intersectional Claims

In 1971 the *New York Times* reported that Andrew J. Spano, a taxpayer in Westchester, was suing his local school district, Lakeland Central, as well as the State of New York, claiming that the use of local property taxes to fund education was unconstitutional.[1] Spano brought the suit shortly after the California Supreme Court ruled in favor of a similar suit in *Serrano v. Priest*. Spano argued that his district, with its minimal tax base and modest homes, had a real estate value of only about a third of a wealthy neighboring district, Montrose, though Montrose's tax rate was half as much as Lakeland's. Montrose nonetheless was able to spend hundreds of dollars more per pupil because of its affluent property tax base. Spano also pointed out that the high tax rate in his district had also led voters to turn down the proposed school budget twice already that year, forcing the schools to run on austerity. In an interview with the *Times* reporter, Spano said, "our backs are to the wall" because "taxes have destroyed our sense of community." Since city services, particularly schooling, relied so heavily on property taxes, Spano said planning had become "entrenched in the concept of who comes in and who can bring us the most money." The trial court in Westchester County, however, ruled in favor of the school district and opined that "one scholar, one dollar" may become the "law of the land" one day, but it would require legislative action to do so.[2]

After *McDonald*, as discussed in the last chapter, many lower courts simply assumed that the Supreme Court had in fact made wealth a suspect class, particularly where education was involved, given the interpretation of *Brown* as a virtual declaration of education as a fundamental right. School funding schemes were the perfect test arena for this assumption, as in *Spano*. In 1971 and 1972, several state and lower federal courts agreed with claims that local property-tax-based school financing violated the equal protection clause by discriminating on the basis of wealth.[3] While property taxes accounted for only 14 percent of the taxes collected in the nation overall in 1968, they continued to supply more than half of school funding on average.[4] Federal aid, even after the Elementary and Secondary Education Act of 1965, amounted to only around eight cents out of every dollar spent on education.[5]

Serrano v. Priest, the California case challenging property-tax-based school financing laws, received a great deal of press coverage and comment and spurred many similar suits in the years after it was decided.[6] Though the plaintiff himself was Latino, *Serrano* did not make a claim of race discrimination, arguing only wealth status (poverty) as a suspect class and education as a fundamental right. This was a strategic choice made by public-interest attorneys who had brought the suit as a class action on behalf of all California public school students, or all public school students "except children in that school district, the identity of which is presently unknown, which school district affords the greatest educational opportunity of all school districts within California." The parent class in *Serrano* brought suit as parents and as property taxpayers, a group that undoubtedly did not fully overlap with all the parents of children in the schools of California. In the Los Angeles County examples used in the case, Baldwin Park citizens paid a school tax of $5.48 per $100 of valuation in 1968–69 but still had less than half as much to spend per child as did Beverly Hills residents, who were taxed only $2.38 per $100. Given the positive response of lower courts as shown by *Serrano*, the Supreme Court had clearly made an impression with its earlier language on wealth disparity as an invalid basis for unequal treatment by the government. In *Serrano*, the California Supreme Court critiqued the disparities between districts bluntly, saying that "affluent districts can have their cake and eat it too; they can provide a high quality education for their children while paying lower taxes. Poor districts, by contrast, have no cake at all."[7]

In a nearly identical Minnesota case decided shortly after *Serrano*, the court also overturned the school finance law, arguing that "the inexorable effect of educational financing system such as here maintained puts the state in the position of making the rich richer and the poor poorer."[8] And in 1972 New Jersey overturned its property-tax-based school financing law for similar reasons, in an opinion that dismissed the "artificial aristocracy" created by wealth and birth.[9] Aside from the Westchester County trial court in *Spano*, in fact, lower courts seemed consistently convinced that education had virtually been declared a fundamental right in *Brown* and that poverty had essentially been made a suspect class for constitutional scrutiny in the 1960s line of poverty cases. *San Antonio v. Rodriguez*, however, a case that dealt with wealth discrimination in combination with race discrimination and education as a right, reached the Supreme Court first and determined the fate of *Serrano* and all the other cases.

Taxpayer Rights to Segregated Schools

But before these taxpayer rights cases seeking equality were filed, white seg-regationists had attempted to slow or stop any movement toward desegre-gation in schools across the country. The autumn of 1964 was the moment of truth for segregated schools nationwide as numerous districts acknowl-edged the *Griffin* ruling out of Prince Edward County and made plans for various forms of integrated education for the first day of classes. Lawsuits from aggrieved white taxpayers flooded in. In Philadelphia, a suit was filed by the Parents and Taxpayers Association of Philadelphia to block the board of education from busing 2,900 black students. But taxpayer standing was an extremely limited basis for litigation by the 1960s. The Supreme Court had progressively narrowed the recognition of the "harms" incurred by one who solely made a claim as a taxpayer (as opposed to the more specific harm of a parent, for example) from its nineteenth-century equity court roots to emphasize that courtroom doors could not simply be open to anyone who disliked public spending projects. Though on the federal court level tax-payer status was virtually irrelevant to cases determining constitutional questions, die-hard segregationists, "as taxpayers and parents," pursued in-junctions against local school boards to prevent them from moving forward with desegregation plans. And briefly after *Brown*, segregationists who were *not* parents with children who would be directly affected by desegregation still tried to utilize their identity as taxpayers to push back against desegre-gation, despite courts' dismissal of their standing.

Though the Supreme Court was increasingly unwilling to wait for Southern cities to implement desegregation plans, taxpayer suits to prevent integra-tion began to stream through courts in the 1960s, only to hit the limits of the legal logic of the taxpayer identity claim. A suit on behalf of "12 persons described as Georgia taxpayers" successfully achieved a temporary injunc-tion in the Atlanta Superior Court in 1961 to bar allocation of state funds to the city's four integrated high schools.[10] On appeal, the Georgia Supreme Court issued a brief opinion in response to the taxpayer suit brought by a William K. Boggs and a group of white parents against ten members of the Georgia State Board of Education.[11] In their suit, Boggs and his associates claimed they could reach beyond the sovereign immunity typically enjoyed by governments (in this case, the state had given no statutory consent to be sued) and sue the board members as individuals as well as officials because they had acted beyond their authority by violating the provisions of the state constitution that required that separate schools be provided.

Specifically, their suit alleged that the disbursement of taxpayer funds to Atlanta public schools necessitated injunctive relief, since separate schools "were not being provided."[12] The court simply pointed to the fact that they were acting as state actors in both collecting and disbursing taxes for educational purposes and argued that therefore the suit could not continue.

The year before *Brown v. Board of Education*, the school leaders in Walton County, Georgia, had developed a joint plan to shuffle tax funds between systems to "get around" the mandatory integration they feared would result from the case. The board of education of Walton County agreed that it would enroll all the black students from the city public school system into the county schools, with provisions for transportation and financing the transfer per pupil, and the independent city public school system trustees (the Academy of Social Circle Board of Trustees) agreed that they would enroll the white students from designated areas in the rest of the county. The contract between county and city was a twenty-five-year agreement, but finally in 1968, after the Supreme Court's terse order in *Alexander*, the U.S. District Court ordered the school boards to operate unitary school systems starting with the 1968–69 school year. In 1970–71, a disagreement developed between the city and county boards over compensation to the city school for the cost of educating the county students who had been included in the new zone created by the court-mandated unitary school system, which the court ruled had to be repaid.[13]

North Carolina again had a long series of legal attempts to block desegregation.[14] A white taxpayer in Anson County, North Carolina, filed suit on behalf of all other county taxpayers for an injunction to stop the ongoing sale of school bonds for construction projects. The bonds had been voted on in 1952, authorizing $1.25 million in tax levies for school facilities, including two projects out of the nine facilities listed in the referendum that would be, in the words of the levy, "suitable for colored children." After *Brown v. Board of Education*, this white taxpayer charged that the levy and construction plans were discriminatory against white children because of this phrase and must be stopped completely. The Supreme Court of North Carolina dismissed his claim, yet it went to pains to suggest that there was no way to "reconcile" the intent of the framers of the U.S. Constitution with the implication of *Brown*, and that therefore the taxpayer's assumption that the *Brown* decision implied the desegregation of public schools in the state was premature.[15]

On November 3, 1964, a referendum vote was held on a group of state and local school taxes in North Carolina.[16] In 1966, after a large matching grant of federal funds to Southern states to build integrated schools, three North Carolina "taxpayers" brought a suit in Beaufort County to stop construction of an integrated high school, saying the original $1.4 million bond issue "would not have passed" if the voters had known it was to be used for integrated schools.[17] One of the school bonds was publicized before the election as an allocation for the new "Central High School on the north side of the river," which would be a consolidated high school for white students from the Pantego, Bath, and Wilkinson high schools. These three schools had only white students, while two other high schools in the district served only black students. The bond issues were all approved by a three-to-one majority of voters. In the wake of this vote, however, the school board of Beaufort County had to develop and adopt a plan for compliance with Title VI of the Civil Rights Act of 1964, which had become law four months prior to the North Carolina referendum. On April 20, 1965, the board adopted a plan that proposed to consolidate all five of the high schools in the district into one central high school for children of all races. A group of white "taxpayers" brought suit against the school board, seeking an injunction to prevent the expenditure of the funds from the tax bonds because they alleged that the referendum was invalid in light of the revised expenditure plan. The trial court judge dissolved their preliminary injunction and found the referendum valid, and the taxpayers appealed to the state supreme court. The North Carolina Supreme Court reversed the lower-court ruling and reinstated the injunction to stop the building of the desegregated school because the board of county commissioners had to also approve the reallocation of the funds and the school board did not have authority to approve the reallocation independently. The plan to build Central High School was abandoned.

After this ruling, Alton Boomer and a group of other parents filed suit for a permanent injunction against racial discrimination in the operation of Beaufort County public schools.[18] Following the ruling that ended the Central High School plan in 1966, the school board held a freedom-of-choice period during the 1966–67 school year, permitting students to request reassignment to previously all-white or all-black schools. In all, 119 African American students (out of approximately 2,500 in the school district) requested reassignment to white schools, while no white students requested reassignment to black schools. Therefore, plaintiffs argued, all-black schools would remain racially homogenous under the continuation of the freedom-of-choice model for the foreseeable future, which sparked the lawsuit by African American parents. In 1968, the federal district court issued a ruling ordering that school attendance zones be established geographically to include all students within pairs of formerly segregated schools.[19]

Louisiana had followed the example of Virginia and many other Southern states in seeking private, tuition grant programs to ensure segregation could continue for white children. In 1958 Louisiana created a grant-in-aid program, making tuition grants available to parents and private schools "where no racially segregated public school" was provided as an alternative. In 1961, the U.S. district court found this to be unconstitutional state action, in an opinion expressing exasperation that despite repeated instruction from the U.S. Supreme Court and the district court in prior cases, the Louisiana legislature continued to enact into law schemes to avoid desegregation.[20] The district court viewed the Louisiana law as directly contradicting the Supreme Court's ruling in *Cooper v. Aaron* (the ruling that followed the events surrounding the Little Rock Nine, in which nine African American students desegregated Little Rock Central High School in 1957, holding that states must abide by and enforce the Supreme Court's decisions even if they disagreed with them), but it also found a second ground for unconstitutionality—namely, that the law was only being put into practice in Saint Helena Parish, a very poor community with no private schools for black or white students. "It is dead certain, therefore, that absent active, extensive unconstitutional state support of private schools, closing of public schools in St. Helena under Act 2 will mean the end of school education for all children in the parish, white and Negro, except a handful of well-to-do white children. This then is the legislature's option: segregated schools contrary to the equal protection clause or no schools."[21]

The Orleans Parish School Board was finally ordered by the district court in 1960 to submit a plan of desegregation, after the Louisiana legislature had spent the years after the *Brown* decision passing law after law in an attempt to circumvent judicially mandated school desegregation. But as soon as attention focused on New Orleans, the state jumped into action yet again, and when the Orleans Parish School Board announced it would admit five first-grade black girls to two historically all-white schools, the Louisiana legislature responded.[22] After calling another special session, the legislature passed acts abolishing the Orleans Parish School Board, transferring administration of the New Orleans schools to the state legislature, and removing four school board members from office.

Louisiana House Concurrent Resolutions 2, 23, and 28 in the Second Extraordinary Session of 1960 specifically denied the school board control of its funds in local banks and warned banks not to honor the school board's checks. The banks blocked these accounts, and the school board was forced to ask the court to require banks in New Orleans to honor its checks and the City of New Orleans (as the board's official tax collector) to remit the taxes for schools that it had gathered. The court agreed with both injunctions, and it saved special wrath for the degree to which the legislature had both ignored the repeated rulings of federal courts and harassed the school board of the city when it attempted to comply with the federal court injunction requiring it to desegregate its schools. And, though the legislature had allowed itself, in act 5, to replace the counsel for the school board with its own attorney general, the district court described this as "one of the Legislature's less sophisticated attempts to preserve racial discrimination in the public schools of New Orleans."[23]

Following these cases, the state once again attempted to use tuition grants for private schools for white children. In 1966, a class-action case was brought by African American schoolchildren and parents in New Orleans.[24] Act 147 of 1962 was the law at issue in the case, another attempt to circumvent prior district court rulings. It created the Louisiana Financial Assistance Commission to distribute grants from state funds directly to children attending private schools or to their parents, as long as they could show they were admitted to a private, legally operating school. The state paid $360 yearly to each student attending private school but allocated only $257 per year for each public school student.

Circuit Judge John Minor Wisdom was unmoved by the claim of the defendants that the families were simply bringing a "taxpayer's suit" seeking to stop the unlawful expenditure of state funds, which, the defendants argued, would mean that they lacked sufficient standing to pursue a federal class-action case at all. Judge Wisdom pointed out that, in fact, the plaintiffs were concerned "only indirectly" with the improper disbursement of public funds; their primary claim was a federal constitutional one regarding the creation of a segregated school system by the State of Louisiana. Taxpayer status, in other words, was far less important than the harms created by constitutional violations. Though the district court found ample reason to approve the injunction against the state grant-in-aid system in the plaintiffs' equal-protection claim, the judges also highlighted that there was "a due process argument that public funds derived, at least in some part, from taxes paid by the plaintiff" should not be appropriated to create a segregated school system and deprive the plaintiff children of their right to integrated schools.[25]

But white resistance to desegregated schools was by no means centered in the South. At the same time that Louisiana was passing laws to ensure private all-white alternatives to integrated schools, a referendum in New Rochelle, New York, set the board of education against advocates for desegregation. Out of twelve neighborhood elementary school districts in New Rochelle, African American families were overwhelmingly located in a carefully drawn district served by Lincoln School, where 94 percent of students were black. After public protests in the fall of 1959 against the racial segregation of Lincoln School, which was also in poor repair and out of date, the school board put forth a referendum to replace the current Lincoln building with a new school on the same site to serve the same neighborhood. The board's own referendum committee prepared advertisements warning "taxpayers of New Rochelle" that there would be "harsh financial consequences" if the new Lincoln proposal were defeated, and branding opponents "extremists and propagandists." After African American parents and children brought suit, a district court judge found that the New Rochelle school board had in fact created and maintained segregated schools and was responsible for immediately taking action to desegregate them.[26]

Meanwhile, talks in New York City in the fall of 1964 among those attempting to avoid a public school boycott on the first day of classes collapsed, and the members of the Parents and Taxpayers Coordinating Council (PAT) and the Joint Council for Better Education began to prepare for the boycott in order to protest the board of education's integration plans.[27] PAT initially had brought a taxpayer lawsuit to block the board's plans to pair a predominantly white school and a predominantly black school in Long Island City in a join desegregation attempt, but their suit was denied by the New York State Supreme Court.[28] In the course of PAT's opposition to the non-neighborhood transfer policy, they had engaged in what the NAACP described as a "systemic program of intimidation of public officials" so severe that it demanded a government investigation.[29] In the wake of hundreds of white parents protesting desegregation plans in front of school board offices in Brooklyn that spring, Eugene T. Reed, president of the State Conference of the NAACP, called specifically for an investigation into whether the John Birch Society or Southern White Citizens' Councils had "gained control" of the parents and taxpayers movement in New York.[30]

At the same time, a "group of white taxpayers" in Englewood, New Jersey, appealed to the U.S. district court to have the school's desegregation plan declared unconstitutional, which led a group of additional white taxpayers to intervene and demand further limitations on school desegregation by the board, but their suit was dismissed by the district court.[31] Even then, Englewood's school board had failed to act to correct the racial segregation in its school districts until a prior series of complaints to the state commissioner of education by black parents had directed it to do so.

In Manhasset, New York, a group of African American plaintiffs successfully sued the school district and won a judgment in favor of desegregating the schools in the district after showing that 100 percent of black elementary school children attended Valley Elementary School, separate from 99.2 percent of white children, who attended other elementary schools. The court found that neighborhood school attendance lines, coupled with a strict no-transfer policy, were equivalent to government-imposed segregation. The court's decree simply directed the Manhasset school board to allow children in the Valley Elementary School attendance area to transfer to other schools in the district beginning with the September 1964 school year, and the defendant school board acted accordingly and chose not to appeal the ruling. Immediately after the decision, however, a group of six white "residents and taxpayers" in the neighborhood of one of the white schools and parents of children attending the white schools sought to intervene and take on the appeal as defendants (since the school district had chosen not to do so). To intervene in such a way is unusual, though legally permissible, but it requires that the intervenor would or may be legally bound by a judgment in the action, therefore necessitating their intervention. They claimed that they qualified as intervenors because they would be "bound in that the necessity of additional facilities and buses will be required, all at a cost to them as taxpayers." The district court dismissed their petition, ruling that even if they could show that the ruling would lead to higher taxes for them, that was not a sufficient basis to claim they would be "legally bound" by the court's decision.[32]

In 1964, another group of white self-proclaimed "taxpayers and parents" sued the board of education in Rochester to stop it from implementing an open enrollment plan adopted in November 1963.[33] Schools in Rochester were heavily imbalanced on the basis of race, and the board was attempting to address that with the transfer of a handful of African American students into overwhelmingly white neighborhood schools. The ruling in this case hinged much more explicitly than most on whether it was a taxpayers' case, and the lower court in Monroe County, New York, ultimately found that the suit could go forward and was not an untenable "taxpayer's action" against the district but rather did show alleged harms that could potentially occur, permitting injunctive relief. The court listed the harms as being that "receiving schools will become overcrowded[,] ... citizens in the neighborhood receiving school will be deprived of their rights as parents and taxpayers[,] ... the neighborhood school concept will be destroyed[,] ... taxes will be increased," and children would be forced to travel long distances and deprived of their formerly proper educational facilities. After a short tangent expressing the idea that racial balance was not constitutionally mandated and that "innocent children" should not be used in "weird sociological chess games," the court granted the white taxpayers' motion to stop the open enrollment plan.

Following this, Doyle Etter and other white parents in the West Irondequoit School District in Monroe County, New York, sued "as taxpayers" to stop the local school board from attempting to transfer first-grade students from "culturally and racially imbalanced" schools in Rochester to their district in 1965.[34] West Irondequoit was on a common boundary with the Rochester city school district but was outside the city itself. Rochester agreed to pay tuition fees so that there would be no cost to the receiving schools, and it was left to parents to choose to transfer or remain in the Rochester schools. Prior to this, out of 5,800 students in West Irondequoit schools, there were 4 nonwhite children. The agreement between the two school boards led to the transfer of 25 first-grade pupils upon their parents' request and prompted the lawsuit by the group of white parents, who argued that the plan was discriminatory and who sought a permanent injunction to stop any transfers. The Monroe County Supreme Court dismissed the lawsuit and granted the school district's motion for summary judgment.

Yet so-called white taxpayer revolts outside of court cases continued to defeat numerous school budgets in communities across the country throughout the late 1960s and early 1970s. In May 1968 alone, the *New York Times* calculated that at least two dozen school budgets were turned down by voters in Suffolk, Nassau, Rockland, and Westchester. According to the *Times*, in some cases "the possibility of busing Negro children into predominantly white school districts was linked to a defeat." Forty-six thousand students were shut out of classes in September 1970 in four suburban districts north of Saint Louis, Missouri (including Ferguson), by what was called "the biggest and most serious" taxpayer revolt of its kind to date—a revolt made easier by the rule in Missouri requiring a two-thirds majority to pass tax levies.[35] But describing these as taxpayer revolts erases the responsibility of demographic specificity. It is a phrase that carries the aura of populism, of anonymity, of democracy in action. If these are instead framed as white revolts, or as revolts by white property owners against black children, then the picture appears different. A very different kind of taxpayer activism—a communitarian vision of taxpaying rights—provided the foundation for the *Spano* and *Serrano* cases, as well as the case that ultimately split the Supreme Court after nineteen years of unanimous school rulings.

Intersectionality, Property Taxes, and the Constitution

Demetrio Rodriguez was a forty-two-year-old veteran who had worked for more than fifteen years at Kelly Air Force Base outside San Antonio before he signed on as the lead plaintiff in the 1968 complaint against San Antonio and Texas officials.[36] Three of his four sons attended Edgewood Elementary School in San Antonio, where the "building was crumbling, classrooms lacked basic supplies, and almost half the teachers were not certified and worked on emergency permits."[37] Over 90 percent of Edgewood students were Hispanic and 6 percent were African American.[38] Students in the Edgewood district had one-third as many library books, one-fourth as many guidance counselors, and classes that were 50 percent more crowded than those in neighboring white districts.[39]

Rodriguez and a handful of other concerned parents, all Mexican American, took their complaint to Arthur Gochman, a local graduate of the University of Texas Law School. Gochman was known for his record of defending civil rights and participating in local sit-ins for desegregation of facilities.[40] Rodriguez himself participated in numerous advocacy organizations for Mexican American rights, such as the League of United Latin American Citizens (LULAC) and the Mexican American Betterment Association.[41] Gochman told them the central legal issue was the state financing system, which enforced local caps on taxation.[42] If property values in an area were low, as they were in Edgewood, voters were simply barred from taxing themselves at a higher rate. So they could not even choose to fund schools at the same level as Alamo Heights, a wealthy, overwhelmingly white school district only six miles away that frequently served as a counterpoint to Edgewood in the litigation.[43] Consequently, despite their comparatively high tax rate, Edgewood schools raised only $26 per child, while Alamo Heights raised $333.[44]

Legal scholar Ian F. Haney-López argues that after *Brown*, the law moved away from using racial categories oppressively toward using those categories to ease race discrimination.[45] Thus, seemingly tangential legal processes or cases "may be far more central to the legal construction of race today—for instance ... race-neutral laws."[46] The property-tax school financing law at issue in the *Rodriguez* litigation is one such seemingly race-neutral law that points to the formalistic legal construction of race as a singularity unrelated to economic circumstances or any of the other historical effects of prejudice and discrimination. While *Rodriguez* produced a very different result from *Brown*, the formalistic construction of race and rights in *Rodriguez* in fact followed from the relentless categorizing process reified in *Brown* and fundamental to U.S. law in general. In *Rodriguez*, this formalistic notion of race allowed the court to erase the racial identity of the plaintiff children from consideration. The result was both a legitimation of seemingly "color-blind" racialized thinking and an example of another case in which "the poor people have lost again."[47]

José A. Cárdenas, superintendent of the Edgewood Independent School District, admitted that state funding did little to equalize resources. Texas required at least twenty-six Spanish-speaking students in a school in order to receive $150,000 for a bilingual education program. Alamo Heights had so few minority students that, as Cárdenas noted, it had to combine students with another district in order to reach the minimum of twenty-six. This meant that "less than 26 students are receiving a bilingual program of $150,000," while Edgewood had to share the same amount among twenty-two thousand Spanish-speaking students.[48] Though financing differences were repeatedly framed by opponents and, later, justices as matters of private choice and marketplace decision making, even without the taxation caps the choice of the local Edgewood community was largely illusory. As one of the co-counsels who worked with Gochman on the case later said, "Poor districts do not choose to spend less for education. It's like telling a man who makes $50 a week that he has the same right as a millionaire to send his son to Exeter."[49]

Gochman filed a class-action lawsuit against local and state officials on behalf of all low-income or racial minority children similarly situated in Texas, making three central legal claims. Gochman's first claim was that poverty was a suspect class, a status that, after the cases discussed in the previous chapter, was seen to possibly lead to heightened constitutional scrutiny and protection against discrimination. When courts encountered other suspect classes, for example race or national origin, they approached them with deep suspicion. Unless the government could provide a compelling justification, such as national security, for using these suspect categories, legislation containing them was invariably struck down.[50] The alternative and more commonly used standard was the rational-basis test, in which the government simply had to give a "rational" reason for a court to uphold a law.

The two-tiered framework would give way to a three-tiered framework by the mid-1970s, incorporating a middle tier of scrutiny for "semi-suspect classifications" such as gender. Unfortunately for the *Rodriguez* claimants, their case reached the court at a moment when it was unclear whether the binary construction of equal-protection analysis would be permanent or whether the levels of scrutiny would continue to expand.

The second argument Gochman put forth in the Edgewood plaintiffs' suit was that education was a fundamental interest that was implicated in the school financing system and implicitly guaranteed by the Constitution. Other fundamental rights considered by the court to be implicit in the Constitution included the right to interstate travel, the right to vote, the right to privacy (encompassing reproductive rights, the right to procreate, and the right to marry), and Miranda rights. The fundamental-rights strand of equal-protection jurisprudence had a fairly short constitutional pedigree, largely from the previous few decades, though it had been in play longer than the suspect class categorization. If a law impinged on a fundamental right, it could be overturned even if no suspect class was involved. The court had repeatedly held that such actions as forced sterilization, refusal to allow citizens to travel between states, or even the institution of prohibitively high filing fees for marriage or divorce imposed intolerable burdens on these fundamental rights, even if there was no relationship to a suspect category such as race or national origin.[51] In *Brown* there seemed to be strong precedent supporting the assumption that education was a fundamental right, especially given its importance for the exercise of other explicit constitutional rights, such as freedom of speech, or implied rights, such as the right to vote.

As his third and final argument, like the plaintiffs in *Valtierra*, discussed in the previous chapter, Gochman argued that the Mexican American plaintiffs in *Rodriguez* constituted a suspect class discriminated against on the basis of race as well as wealth status. Gochman in fact chose Rodriguez as the named plaintiff in part because he hoped his Latino surname would emphasize the racial aspects of the case.[52] *Hernandez v. Texas*, decided the same year as *Brown*, had made clear that the equal protection clause applied heightened scrutiny to legislation classifying Mexican Americans, just as it did for African Americans. Litigants faced difficulties, however, in pressing their claims on the basis of *Brown*, in part because many attorneys for Mexican American clients did not utilize the precedent of *Brown* in their claims.[53]

Texas had an especially convoluted legal trajectory. In a 1905 Texas statute, the state required all public school teachers to use only English in school and created separate schools for students with Spanish surnames.[54] David Montejano has argued that the identification of Mexican Americans as a distinct "race" became, "like the question of political representation and civil rights, an important issue to be settled locally."[55] Their complex legal position in the Jim Crow era had led Mexican American advocates in many areas to embrace an identity as "other whites," which created difficulties in constructing a unified legal argument encompassing the de jure segregation condemned in *Brown* and the ongoing de facto segregation of Mexican Americans prevalent in Texas.[56] Indeed, the "other white" argument was used by many school boards to avoid or delay the desegregation of all-white schools ordered by *Brown* and its progeny by assigning African American and Mexican American students to the same schools—an action simplified by the proximity of ghettos and barrios in many urban areas—and arguing that these schools were then "desegregated" under *Brown* because Mexican Americans were classified as "other whites."[57]

This type of segregation (or, rather, avoidance of desegregation) was not declared illegal until a Texas district court case from 1970 ruled that Mexican Americans in Corpus Christi were entitled to Fourteenth Amendment protections and the protection of the *Brown* line of case precedent.[58] Judge Woodrow Seals rejected any judicial construction of *Brown* or the equal protection clause that implied that "any other group which is similarly or perhaps equally, disadvantaged politically and economically, and which has been substantially segregated in public schools," should receive less constitutional protection than African Americans, stating that "it is clear . . . that these cases are not limited to race and color alone."[59] While this opinion indicated a willingness to extend equal-protection examination to categories outside of race, the Supreme Court would prove less open to an expansive construction of the Fourteenth Amendment.

The three-judge Texas district court panel that convened to hear Gochman's complaint needed to find only one of his three arguments valid in order to force the state to provide "compelling justification" for its school financing system. The panel held, however, that the state had failed to "even establish a reasonable basis" for its financing system, without even reaching the debate on poverty as a suspect class, education as a fundamental right, or race as an equal-protection trigger.[60] The district court failed Texas on a rational basis, the most deferential judicial standard, and the state appealed. The panel in fact mentioned "minority status" only briefly, when discussing evidence that the richest school districts had 8 percent minority pupils, while the poorest had 79 percent. The judges prefaced this reference with the words, "as might be expected," an offhand indication that the linkage of race and class and the problem of a huge racial wealth gap with a direct effect on education were not particularly surprising to the judges.[61] This is the only mention the district court made of race in their opinion and later clarifications, but, as amici later argued, it served as a finding of (apparently uncontroversial) fact that race and class discrimination were intimately tied in the case, "as might be expected."

In 1971, the U.S. Senate instituted a Select Committee on Equal Educational Opportunity, holding hearings that specifically addressed inequalities in school finance and discussed cases such as *Rodriguez*. Sarah Carey from the Lawyers' Committee for Civil Rights under Law, the group that served as the central resource for the many nationwide lawsuits against school financing schemes, testified before Senator Walter Mondale's committee about the *Rodriguez* case. Carey testified that the principle of *Serrano*, the equalization of financing resources in different districts, could potentially lead to a reaffirmation of "separate but equal" in public schools.[62] She argued that in school financing cases, much like desegregation cases, redistricting rather than simply reorganizing taxation models was necessary. The goal of *Rodriguez*, according to Carey, was in part to go further than *Serrano* and merge wealthy white districts with poor minority districts in order to desegregate racially segregated districts.[63] She pointed out that San Antonio's school district lines were "drawn with great care so that Chicanos are in one area and the whites are in another."[64] Mondale responded that the San Antonio city fathers had also put all the public housing in one district, Edgewood. The potential for political coalitions to form around issues of race, class, and education came into focus in the Senate hearings as well. In his testimony before the Senate committee, James A. Kelly of the Ford Foundation mentioned that if *Serrano* became law, "a closer political identity on this issue might be perceived between blue collar workers living in suburbs and blacks in cities. . . . Both groups are misserved by the system."[65]

Out of dozens of documents produced in the case, race came up only rarely and sometimes in surprising ways, providing important indications of the difficulty legal discourse had treating intersectionality, and offering hints of the deep roots of the idea that race was a formal category best treated with a "color-blind" philosophy. The justices' notes on the case also indicate a preoccupation with tax policy questions of resource distribution and—particularly for Justice Lewis F. Powell, who would author the opinion—a concern with local fiscal control and a belief that tax-based inequalities in a capitalist country were fundamentally consistent with, and indeed perhaps required by, a "marketplace" conception of both education and citizenship.

One of the most common argumentative techniques offered by those seeking to overturn the lower-court decision was either to appropriate language around race or to ignore it entirely as irrelevant. The other arguments repeated consistently throughout the documents were that the principle of federalism or local control (in some cases an explicitly anti-communist Cold War understanding of local control) required overturning the lower-court decision and that the principle of equality also demanded that communities have complete control over their school's funding policies. The idea of equality was the only rhetorical overlap between the plaintiffs and defendants in this case—interpreted by one party to support federalism and by the other to illustrate the need for federal judicial action to protect those who were put at a disadvantage through local policies of taxation and distribution.

The amicus briefs filed by urban interest groups, including the NAACP and La Raza, discussed race and class together as a major intersecting element of the case. The first of these was filed by the Council of Great City Schools, representing the twenty-three largest city school districts in the United States, along with various city mayors and councils, the American Federation of Labor and Congress of Industrial Organizations, the Urban League, and other interest groups. This brief claimed that the amicus briefs submitted by "certain suburban interests" that "purport great concern" for the effects of *Rodriguez* on large cities did not represent the actual interests of the large cities they purported to be defending, and in fact were advancing claims adverse to the interests of those cities.[66] The authors went on to say that "cities and other urban interests can and do speak for themselves."[67] The brief explicitly linked race and poverty in discussing the crises in inner cities, citing the high proportion of African Americans and minorities and high levels of poverty in the Detroit population versus the overwhelmingly white and affluent suburbs surrounding it.[68] The authors argued that property-tax school financing discriminated against central city school children, explicitly refuting the claim by the appellants and amici that *Rodriguez* would be harmful to cities and minorities. They analyzed the case of Detroit specifically, showing that 65 percent of students in Detroit public schools were black or another minority group, while outlying suburbs like Grosse Pointe had student bodies with only 0.3 percent minority students.[69] And while Grosse Pointe students scored in the 97th percentile on seventh-grade achievement tests, Detroit seventh-graders scored in the 1st percentile. Yet Detroit schools were able to spend only three-quarters per pupil (even with federal aid) of what the suburban schools could spend, despite the fact that the city taxed itself for education at double the state-wide average rate.[70]

The ACLU filed an amicus brief in conjunction with La Raza and numerous religious, particularly Catholic, organizations on behalf of the plaintiffs. The authors argued that the basic fact that the lowest-income school districts had the highest proportion of minorities, while the highest-income school districts had the lowest proportion, constituted a prima facie case of racial discrimination and violation of the equal protection clause.[71] Finally, they stated pointedly that the "racial discrimination issue is not an afterthought to the litigants here" or to those nationwide supporting them. Rather, it was "the very core of this case."[72]

The local control argument offered by the State of Texas in response to the lawsuit was ultimately a powerful device enabling the court's majority to deny equal protection to the *Rodriguez* plaintiffs. In fact, *Rodriguez* was one of the cases that signaled the judicial redemption of federalism as legal doctrine after what was seen by many as "judicial activism" in *Brown*. Part of this renewed emphasis on federalism emerged in the Cold War anticommunist rhetoric that can be seen in some of the briefs as a result. Political scientist Paul Sracic has argued that the *Rodriguez* decision was part of a shift from an emphasis on the importance of education for civic society and the collective good to a postwar understanding of education as primarily important as an engine of economic advancement for the individual.[73] These two views of the benefits of education overlap, but they have important differences in the conceptualization of who is receiving the ultimate benefits, society as a whole or the individual. In this case, the plaintiffs were seeking both a personal right to education and a community right to have their children educated equally, but the idea of local fiscal (community) control would prove more compelling to a majority of the court than the idea of a community right to equality.

Rodriguez and Anticommunism

One clear undercurrent in the *Rodriguez* case was the fear that any acknowledgment that inequalities on the basis of disparate wealth were unjust would lead to communism and the loss of the Cold War. While racial inequality was beginning to be identified—sometimes grudgingly—as unjustifiable under capitalism by the 1970s, income inequality and resource inequalities of all kinds were viewed by many parties to the case as the sine qua non of the free market. In this section, I locate *Rodriguez* within a broader Cold War context, in which certain kinds of racial equality—what Lani Guinier calls "racial liberalism"—were acceptable and even helpful in battling Soviet propaganda, while claims of discrimination or unequal treatment on the basis of poverty had to be defended as a logical by-product of capitalism and protected against lurking socialist impulses. As Guinier wrote on the fiftieth anniversary of the *Brown* decision, "While anticommunist fervor helped fuel the willingness of national elites to take on segregation, it also channeled dissent from the status quo into status-based legal challenges that focused on formal equality through the elimination of de jure segregation."[74] The coalition of intersecting race and class identities that the *Rodriguez* case put forward was precisely the antithesis of what Cold War–era judicial politics encouraged. As Mary Dudziak has argued, this presumption of the acceptability of wealth differences reflected the widespread perception that "class-based inequality did not threaten the nation's core principles."[75]

For the justice tasked with drafting the opinion of the court in *Rodriguez*, the case was not about a coalition of intersecting identities and the right of a child to an equal education but about the dangers of encroaching communism. Justice Powell, just prior to his nomination for the Supreme Court, had in fact written a memo entitled "Attack on American Free Enterprise System" (known as the "Powell Memo"), which was not leaked until long after his confirmation but usefully highlights his political views regarding corporate interests and the role of the judiciary.[76] On the fortieth anniversary of this memo in 2011, the *Richmond Times-Dispatch* celebrated it as having "achieved a near-iconic cachet in many conservative circles."[77] The memo was addressed to Eugene B. Sydnor Jr., the chairman of the education committee at the U.S. Chamber of Commerce, and the opening line starts bluntly: "No thoughtful person can question that the American economic system is under broad attack." In identifying the "sources of the attack," Powell listed "the Communists, New Leftists and other revolutionaries who would destroy the entire system" as obvious dangers, but even more troubling to him were those from "perfectly respectable elements of society" such as college campuses, religious organizations, media, arts and literature, and politics.[78]

Like many prominent members of his era, Powell's anticommunism was deeply ingrained. When Powell served on the Richmond Board of

Education earlier in his career, he had suggested that a course teaching that "communism requires totalitarian dictatorship" be added to the high school curriculum.[79] Sracic has characterized Powell's understanding of democracy as "filtered through the prism of anticommunism," a belief system made visible in the memo.[80] Powell's memo reflected his fears of left-wing attacks on the economic structure of the United States and specifically his fears that groups would attempt to institutionalize "socialism or some sort of statism (communism or fascism)" in its place.[81] Of particular interest to Powell, as a former chair of the Richmond School Board and the future "education justice" on the court, was the way in which the battle between the free-market system and "socialist" ideas would manifest in the realm of education.

In his deliberations on *Rodriguez*, these anticommunist worries were made explicit. In his notes preparing for the initial conference on the case with his fellow justices, he immediately began to try to draw a line differentiating *Rodriguez* from *Brown v. Board of Education* precisely because he viewed discrimination based on wealth as different from discrimination based on race, and, he wrote, "in a free enterprise society we could hardly hold that wealth is suspect. This is a communist doctrine but is not even accepted (except in a limited sense) in Soviet countries."[82]

In many of his memos and notes on the case, he returned to the idea that the ultimate effect of overturning the property-tax-based school financing law in Texas would be "national control of education."[83] He stated that he "would abhor such control for all the obvious reasons . . . the irresistible impulse of politicians to manipulate public education for their own power and ideology—e.g. Hitler, Mussolini, and all Communist dictators."[84] Powell was not the only one to see the connection. One amicus brief filed in support of the school district by attorneys general from thirty-one states claimed that "there is little stopping place in plaintiff's logic short of compulsory state-run boarding schools on the early Soviet model."[85] Powell was particularly taken with a brief filed by a group of state government representatives from thirty states (known as the "Maryland brief") that had effectively deployed the anticommunist rhetoric of conservative sociologist James Coleman.[86] Indeed, the Maryland brief was cited more than anything else in Powell's voluminous notes and instructions to his clerks on the case, always with deference and approval. The Maryland brief authors argued that the fundamental issue in the case was whether the court would "impose upon the states full state funding as a matter of constitutional compulsion" and whether such a decision would be "consistent with the maintenance of local or private initiative in a free country."[87] They indicated many times that they saw it as consistent instead with "totalitarian regimes."[88] They were also deeply concerned with the political implications of school funding equalization goals, stating that "the application of this principle to all areas of consumption would do away in effect with income differences, destroying the whole system of incentives on which every society is founded."[89]

Coleman was well known for his foreword to the book *Private Wealth and Public Education*, by John E. Coons, William H. Clune II, and Stephen D. Sugarman.[90] This book was in fact the blueprint for many of the school finance lawsuits filed in the 1970s, from *Serrano v. Priest* in California to the *Rodriguez* case, but Coleman had done a rapid about-face in his views on school financing and unequal education in the few years since its publication, and his later vehement rhetoric against both school finance reform and busing for desegregation proved useful to the opposition to the *Rodriguez* case. The Maryland brief cited heavily to Coleman's statements that school finance reform based on the *Rodriguez* case would be an equivalent exploitation of public schools as in "Hitler's Germany . . . Stalin's Russia . . . Mao's China and . . . Castro's Cuba."[91] In the representatives' argument, it would lead inexorably toward nationalization, centralization, and statist dictatorship, if not directly to communism or fascism. They quoted Coleman's argument that democratic regimes were similar to totalitarian regimes in that they were "more likely to see the schools as instruments of social change than . . . the local government."[92] Coleman argued that the conflicts over school integration in the post-*Brown* era were the perfect illustration of this "because the national government, pressed by organizations at the national level, attempt[ed] to use the schools to create racial integration which is absent in other aspects of life and thus to bring about a major transformation of the social structure."[93]

But the Maryland brief also reflected the way in which the anticommunist discourse deployed in the case could wrap itself in the language of color blindness and concern for racial minorities, even when they were otherwise signaling to opponents of *Brown* that they sympathized. The authors of the brief studiously avoided mention of race or the race discrimination claim for almost all of the 119 pages, but in their one mention of race they claimed that the ruling was "actually destructive of the interests of urban areas and the interests of minority children."[94] Predicting that school finance reform would lead to higher taxes in urban areas and lower school expenditures for inner-city school districts, they claimed that the *Rodriguez* model would in fact "harm" the high percentage of racial minorities in those districts by limiting their educational opportunities even further.[95] This claim, made by several other opposing parties as well as Justice Powell in his majority opinion, was largely derived from the Maryland brief and its purported concern for inner-city schools.

For many this argument proved quite compelling as a "slippery slope" vision. Attorney Gochman, perhaps sensing the importance of the free-enterprise logic in the arguments of his opponents, tried to link his clients' claim to the right to education to that idea in his oral argument, stating that "it's important to the free enterprise system, to the individual not to be poor." And Justice Byron White particularly pressed him on the question of alternative kinds of reforms or financing systems that would answer the objections of the claimants "other than simply state control."[96] During the deliberations, one of Harry Blackmun's clerks expressed concern with the implications of the decision that might lead from taxation inequality to income inequality, saying, "Is this unconstitutional? Must incomes, as well as tax bases, be equalized? Indeed, the ability of citizens to finance the purchase of a variety of important commodities in our society depends on their disposable income, which often bears no 'rational relation' to whether the citizen should be able to purchase the commodity."[97] The clerk's comments also reflect the connection between consumer ideas of citizenship and purchasing power, and illustrate the ongoing narrative of taxpayers' power to "purchase" services and school funding from the state.

In an early internal memorandum indicating the justices' first impressions of the case, the initial votes hewed closely to the final five-to-four split. Chief Justice Warren E. Burger cast a straw vote for reversal. Powell's notes on the discussion indicate that Burger agreed with Charles Alan Wright's brief for the state of Texas and felt that the "holding would result in restructuring our system of state and local gov[ernmen]t."[98] Justice Potter Stewart also cast an early vote for reversal, arguing that "money is some index, but the [equal protection] clause does not require egalitarianism." Stewart went on to state that "unless there is a specific, identifiable class of people that is being discriminated against, the [equal protection] clause does not apply." According to Stewart, "'rich' and 'poor' are not discrete, specific, and identifiable classes," a concern that would show up again later in Powell's majority opinion. Justice William Rehnquist also noted his agreement with Stewart's assessment of the case in his vote for reversal. Justice Blackmun's vote for reversal, according to Powell's notes, was based simply on his assessment that the "Texas system provides adequate basic aid."[99]

Powell advocated strongly for the "quasi-personhood" of school districts. He claimed from his own experience on a school board that the educational problem of school funding based in local property taxes in Virginia was in the rural counties rather than the "urban centers inhabited by the blacks and the poor whites."[100] As an example, Powell cited the case of Giles County, in which there was little or no high-value commercial development or real estate. In Giles County, according to Powell, "the county is poor and the people are poor, but they are not 'ghetto' residents and there are very few blacks." By citing a piece of evidence in which poor whites also suffered from the ill effects of poverty, then, Powell was able to quickly dismiss the question of whether a system that operated particularly harshly on the poor also had a disproportionate racial impact. If whites were present in the case, even in the minute percentage of white students in Edgewood schools, then race discrimination could not be examined as a legal claim, a sort of inverse one-drop rule.

Illustrating the pervasiveness of the rhetoric of "formal race" that *Brown* had set up and his desire to distinguish this case from it, at the bottom of one of the pages of handwritten notes for conference on *Rodriguez*, Powell wrote in large letters that "*Brown* was based on *racial discrimination*" (emphasis in original).[101] He remained convinced by the Maryland amicus brief that any form of funding equalization would hurt minorities the worst. In his notes on the question of "racial discrimination," he wrote that "as the briefs [and] authorities cited show, if the opinion below stands the persons who will be disadvantaged the most will be the citizens who live in the urbanized areas."[102] Powell viewed urbanization, race, and poverty through the frame of Northern educational segregation in the first half of the twentieth century, a lens through which Southern states, such as Virginia (which he relied on repeatedly as an example), were the only places considered by courts when segregation was under discussion.

As the "education justice" and a former education official, Powell also sought to defend the power and purview of school boards, saying that "the local school board is, I believe, a unique American institution" that has "played a vital role in the development of our public school system, and especially in helping to generate the community support necessary to finance it."[103] In a telling paragraph, Powell stated that if a layman stopped him on the street and "inquired whether I thought education is fundamental to our democracy, there could be only one answer." But, Powell continued, "if the same layman asked whether public housing and welfare are fundamental where indigents are concerned, I would unhesitatingly give the same answer." One of Blackmun's clerks was even more explicit that local school district authority was not the only property-tax-funded entity at issue, saying, "I believe that what is at stake here is not just financing schools through the local property tax, but the local property tax itself as a means of financing all services provided by local government."[104]

The final opinion in the case was issued on March 21, 1973, six months after oral arguments. A five-to-four vote decided the fate of low-income school districts and property taxation schemes nationwide. Powell's majority opinion was joined by Justices Stewart, Blackmun, Rehnquist, and Burger. Stewart filed a concurring opinion, and Justices Brennan, Thurgood Marshall, and White each wrote dissenting opinions, which Justice William O. Douglas joined. Powell claimed that the financing plan was "certainly not the product of purposeful discrimination against any group or class" and instead was "rooted in decades of experience in Texas and elsewhere, and in major part is the product of responsible studies by qualified people."[105]

Powell's opinion reflected his understanding that, under constitutional jurisprudence, if education were declared a fundamental right or interest, it would be virtually impossible to sustain the funding structure in Texas, since the state would not be able to meet the compelling interest standard required of infringement on a fundamental right. His solution, ultimately accepted by a slim majority of the justices, was to conclude that education was not a fundamental right recognized by the Constitution. At one point the opinion indicated that if children were being excluded from schools outright, they might have a claim of violation of a fundamental right and be entitled to Fourteenth Amendment protections (which even Wright had virtually conceded at oral arguments), a case that was in fact decided a decade later, as will be discussed in the concluding chapter.[106] The majority in that case argued that a Texas law that deprived the children of undocumented workers of education risked creating a permanent underclass and stated that "the Equal Protection Clause was intended to work nothing less than the abolition of all caste-based and invidious class-based legislation."[107] In the *Rodriguez* case, however, the disadvantaged students were still receiving some "minimal" level of education. Since the Edgewood schools were simply unequal and not completely nonexistent, the disparities were acceptable. If segregation was imposed by state or government edict with the racial language explicit, it was unconscionable, but if it was a result of historically racialized property taxation and income disparities, it was characterized by the court as tradition.

Powell mentioned the racial identification of the plaintiffs in the opening sentence of the opinion, buried in between his description of the nature of the lawsuit and his description of its place of origin.[108] Other than a brief mention of race in listing the statistical descriptions of the two school districts under comparison, the opinion went on for another fifty-three pages without bringing race up again. In the last two pages, however, Powell mentioned that these children were not just poor but also nonwhite, an issue he shrugged off by stating that there was no consensus whether "the poor, the racial minorities, or the children in overburdened core-city school districts would be benefited by abrogation of traditional modes of financing education."[109] He then cited one example of a school district with a majority of Mexican American students whose per-pupil taxable wealth level was above the local average, and used this to argue that it was no more than "a random chance that racial minorities are concentrated in property-poor districts."[110] He followed with the statement that "these practical considerations, of course, play no role in the adjudication of the constitutional issues presented here."[111]

The seeming blind spot of the court in *Rodriguez* to the racial identity of the plaintiffs—an identity raised at least by the appellees and several amici— seems to be a refraction from the formal race underpinnings of *Brown*, in which race, as nothing more than skin color, implied no "practical considerations" outside of its own irrationality, certainly not a historicized context of racial discrimination. Indeed, in a page of handwritten notes on an early draft, Powell wrote, "Don't admit or refer to 'discriminatory treatment of children'—it is not 'discriminatory'; there are inequalities resulting from [the] system."[112] Inequalities or injustices resulting from a disembodied system of taxation, tradition, and local market choices were defensible in a way that inequalities resulting from explicit discrimination were not.

Justice Marshall, in a passionate dissent joined by Justice Douglas, took apart the arguments of the majority point by point. He mentioned race, however, only twice in his sixty-four-page dissent, perhaps strategically. First, when discussing the majority's refusal to accept the finding of fact by the district court that poor and minority group members tended to live in property-poor districts, he asserted that such a finding suggested "discrimination on the basis of both personal wealth and race."[113] When arguing that wealth classifications should (and had in previous decisions) constitute a suspect class, he paused to note that there were reasons to consider wealth discrimination differently from discrimination based on race or ethnicity. He acknowledged that while poverty may entail a social stigma similar to that historically attached to racial and ethnic groups, "personal poverty is not a permanent disability; its shackles may be escaped."[114] Marshall thus went out of his way in the dissent to point out that class was malleable and "separate" from race, since race was not a component of his argument. Yet given that the actual victims of the law at issue in this case were children, it is questionable how much they could do to escape their class status. And given that most of those children were racial minorities, it seems unnecessary to mark the division between the two categories in this dissent, except for the fact that Marshall was himself bound by the strictures of a legal system that recognized only one category of identity at a time. In order to write a dissent defending the need for equal protection against wealth discrimination as a constitutionally protected category of analysis, Marshall had to treat race as inconsequential to the case, because intersections of identity and discrimination were constitutionally incomprehensible to the court.

Marshall's mention of the "irrelevance" of race or nationality in comparison with personal wealth is a particularly striking example of the formal race philosophy of *Brown* carried forward by the case's most famous advocate. He stated that, "most importantly," wealth did not share the "general irrelevance as a basis for legislative action" that race or nationality had— an example of the nonrecognition of race even in a scenario in which race had been asserted by the plaintiffs as a basis for their claim and in which Marshall himself was in agreement that class deserved protection.[115] Even in his *Valtierra* dissent, discussed in the last chapter, Marshall refused to discuss the racial aspect of the case in supporting the wealth discrimination claim. This affirmation of the "general irrelevance" of race also did not necessarily bode well for the long-term prospects of future affirmative action legislation under the color-blind model. The NAACP brief asserted that "*plaintiffs are all Mexican Americans. They claimed relief as and for Mexican Americans*" (emphasis in original).[116] Yet perhaps the most famous attorney from the NAACP's most famous race discrimination litigation did not discuss in his dissent that the plaintiffs had based one of their three legal claims for relief specifically on race discrimination.

From the standpoint of history, the inescapable discursive theme running through the case is that, in the law, the Edgewood children and families could be either poor or Mexican American but not both. Nearly everywhere in the texts that form the body of this narrative, the plaintiffs either were told to choose between their race and their class or, more often, had the choice made for them.[117] Rights accrued to only one of these identity categories—race—but it was only the category of wealth that had the evidence of intent and explicit classification behind it, so race was, in the language of color-blind constitutionalism, irrelevant.

In the end, the property-tax finance law at issue in *Rodriguez* was upheld, in part, by a subtle but significant disentangling of race and class. The *Brown* precedent provided an interpretive backdrop of formal race disconnected from social, historical, and economic context that enabled the *Rodriguez* court to render the plaintiffs' race invisible. After drawing parallels between race and class as formal categories while reinforcing their own process of categorization in the 1960s development of equal-protection jurisprudence, the Supreme Court in *Rodriguez* artificially conflated the race and class of these children, subsuming their racial identity and rendering it invisible, then decided that based on class alone, the children would lose. Simultaneously, the majority artificially *separated* the legal statuses of race and class groups in the abstract in order to reach the same result. The inability of the law in this case to view the narrative historically is particularly ironic in a discourse that prides itself on adherence to prior precedent. The historical narrative tells of a systemic racial wealth divide entrenched by decades of racially restrictive covenants, employment discrimination, school segregation, and unequal taxation and finance policies. This historicization could have also made sense of the statistics showing dramatic overrepresentation of black and Latino children in low-income households and school districts. But the legal discourse saw only one or the other—either race discrimination or wealth discrimination—and if wealth discrimination was claimed, race could not be a factor.

The problem with law from a critical race perspective is that, as a mode of discourse, it seems incapable of both comprehending the unreality or incompleteness of a particular category (for example, Homer Plessy arguing that race was an incoherent category because of his mixed-race status) *and* addressing the power of categorization to have real-life consequences (for example, segregation).[118] If law does the first but not the second, it is left with a smug sense of "category-blindness" that is often simply ahistorical blindness to the lived experience of race.[119] If it does only the second, the complexity of multiple webs of oppression is lost, and the metaphorical results, in Kimberle Crenshaw's argument, are events such as the Clarence Thomas/Anita Hill hearings. Because two narrative categories (race as pertaining to a black man's experience, gender as pertaining to a white woman's experience) came up against each other in that case, everything came to a standstill and Hill's "position could not be told."[120] Similarly, the *Rodriguez* children's position could not be told due to the tendency of the law to reify a strict narrative category—in this case, formal race.

As much as the legal system has demanded categorical definitions as preconditions for rights claims, individuals such as Rodriguez have attempted to push back against such disciplinary frameworks by repeatedly asserting the nature of identity, oppression, and community as multiple, complex, and incapable of being simplistically separated. Rodriguez and his fellow plaintiffs demanded equality—they received categories. The plaintiffs refused to subsume one identity to another in making their case, but the legal system mapped its own categorizing process onto their claims for complexity. As Mario Obledo, director of the Mexican American Legal Defense and Educational Fund for San Antonio, testified before the Senate, "To a school child, segregation is segregation, irrespective of how it is labeled by the courts."[121]

Conclusion

In 1975, the Supreme Court of New Mexico heard a case in which a group of property owners outside the Navajo reservation demanded that a school board election and school bond vote be set aside because "reservation residents had illegally cast votes," since lands inside the reservation were not subject to state property taxes.[122] The school district itself contained land both on and off the Navajo reservation, and two-thirds of the students in the district were Navajo children who lived on the reservation. The property owners' argument, according to the state supreme court, could be summed up as "no representation without taxation." Two methods were utilized to restrain the poor, non–property owners, and "lesser" taxpayers from voting in the twentieth century: the direct tax method and, when that came under judicial disfavor, the exclusionary method, which is still utilized today. In the first and most well-known, poll taxes were implemented in a number of states that affected the full spectrum of voting rights. In one example of the exclusionary method, several states and school districts limited the vote in a number of elections to local positions (particularly local school board elections and school tax levies) to those who owned (or sometimes leased) taxable real property. In another, insidious implementation of the exclusionary method, states passed laws changing city or municipality boundaries to perfectly exclude groups they did not want to access the vote or obtain public services. Alabama passed such a law in 1958 to redraw city boundaries, excluding 99 percent of black voters from the city of Tuskegee while managing not to exclude a single white voter.[123]

The New Mexico court examined several cases as precedent, particularly the 1969 U.S. Supreme Court case that held that statutes limiting the right to vote on particular issues only to property owners violated the equal protection clause, despite its "taxpayer rights" rationale.[124] Therefore, the state court found, the residents of the reservation had a clear interest in the issues of the school district regardless of property tax status, and the state itself had no compelling reason to exclude reservation residents from the election. But the New Mexico court went further and pointed out that the litigants' claim that they would be liable for the $6 million bond, despite the fact that many of the schools constructed by the bond would be on the reservation, was in fact untrue. Though individual reservation residents did not pay property taxes on land within those boundaries, 97 percent of the property in the district was corporate property. And most of the corporate property was located on reservation land, leased from the tribe. Though the land itself was not taxed, the corporate buildings and equipment on the corporate property were assessed and taxed, and they would in fact provide the majority of the funds to repay the bond debt for the schools.

Rodriguez is a case in which the status of taxpayer reached its pinnacle as a "neutral" category erasing race or identity. The disentangling of race and class in the law's discourse was influenced enormously by long-standing trends rooted in U.S. racism and capitalism. In particular, the legacy of taxpayer citizenship rights and educational equality discussed earlier, which had constructed a framework in which more taxes would theoretically equal more rights, was clearly reflected in Powell's concern for local control of property tax funds. If citizens happened to live in a poor neighborhood, through the marketplace of choice, they would simply have to accept the limited ability of that poor neighborhood to supply education. Despite Powell's description of this philosophy in broad terms as simply local control, it was local *fiscal* control—and particularly the local fiscal inequalities— maintained through property-tax-based financing that was the crux of the case. As many scholars have noted, the notion that control over funding implies substantial control over educational content and services themselves ignores the reality that levels of funding are in fact often themselves quite determinative of actual decision-making ability.[125]

However, anxieties about the implications of the case in relation to the *Brown* decision emerged at almost every point in the case. *Rodriguez* is notable for many reasons, but one less often discussed reason is that it was the first education case decided by the Supreme Court since *Brown* that was not unanimous. Though the end of the era of *Brown* consensus is often historically marked with *Milliken v. Bradley* in 1974 (with the last unanimous decision in *Swann v. Charlotte-Mecklenburg* in 1971), it can be argued that the *Rodriguez* case showed that unanimity had already ended by 1973 in education cases. *Rodriguez* presented the court with a dilemma of unequal and largely segregated education that asked for a kind of response that was different from that some of the other education cases (that is, the Rodriguez family was not asking to attend the Alamo Heights schools) but that implicated many of the same core concerns and dilemmas raised by *Brown*.

Rodriguez is also a case that highlights the deference the court has shown to school districts and school boards as "more than mere conveniences." In many ways the brief era of desegregation cases was an anomaly in the midst of a longer history of court deference to school district and school board decisions. One journalist at the time *Rodriguez* was filed argued that in fact both school finance cases and integration cases were targeting the same power source: local control of school boards. "One cannot reform school financing in ways that meet the tests courts have adopted without striking directly at the problem the integration cases approach obliquely: the power of local school boards. . . . Integrationists are attacking the district from the front as a fortress of power and privilege, and fiscal reformers from the rear, but both are headed for the same strong room."[126]

This chapter has argued that anticommunist sentiments explain some of the motivation in *Rodriguez* to avoid anything that smelled like "equalizing" in education. The idea that inequality is an ultimately necessary—if occasionally sorrowful—by-product of a capitalist economic system has remained prevalent in political discourse at varying volumes, and the concern that sharing resources more widely across school district or town lines would always be a communistic process of subtraction and mediocrity has spurred continuous segregation and insularity in the provision of public education resources. As long as tax funds were distributed unequally, the illusion that those who had the most resources had "bought" and "earned" them could remain in full effect, regardless of whether it was true or just.

Conclusion

Education, Inequality, and the Hidden Power of Taxes

> One of the paradoxes of education [i]s that precisely at the point
> when you begin to develop a conscience, you must find yourself
> at war with your society.
>
> —JAMES BALDWIN, *The Price of the Ticket*

> All profound changes in consciousness, by their very nature,
> bring with them characteristic amnesias.
>
> —BENEDICT ANDERSON, *Imagined Communities*

In 1959, the United Nations adopted the Declaration of the Rights of the
Child, which held that children were entitled to receive free and compulsory education to enable them "on the basis of equal opportunity" to develop their abilities and become "useful member[s] of society."[1] Over fifty
years later, children enjoyed a constitutional right to education in Mexico,
Canada, the United Kingdom, Ireland, India, Japan, Korea, Taiwan, Fin-
land, Switzerland, Sweden, China, and Russia, among others, though, as
with many human rights, this is not always enforced.[2] But the U.S. Supreme
Court had still denied "fundamental right" status to an education system
that was nonetheless mandatory for every school-age child.[3] The more troubling comparison, however, is not of the United States' lack of constitutional recognition of education rights in relation to other countries. It is in
the comparison of different states' recognition of education rights and funding methods (and amounts) to each other that public education begins to
appear not only unequal but almost indefensibly irrational. In virtually
every state, and in the thousands of school districts across the country, there
is a different formula for educational financing, a sometimes wildly different level of local taxation and funding, and a different definition of what
constitutes equality and whether, in the end, a schoolchild has a right to
an education at all.[4] And, since the 1980s, racial segregation has been rapidly increasing in many of the largest school systems, putting many back
on a level of racial separation comparable to the year *Brown* was decided.[5]
A Stanford University study measuring what happens in school districts

released from judicial oversight of desegregation found that resegregation began to increase once districts were released from court orders starting in the 1990s.[6]

Judicial Aftermath

One prominent U.S. historian of education in 1947 concluded his treatise on the history of public schooling with a call to make education the next great "nationalizing event," akin to the railroad, the telephone, or the highway.[7] Describing the dramatic inequalities between states at the time in their ability to fund adequate public schools, he argued that the overhaul of education funding and resources on a national basis was "one of the great tasks of the next quarter century."[8] Since *Rodriguez* closed the federal constitutional door, cases have been filed in almost every state challenging property-tax-based education financing on a state constitutional basis. In the late 1970s and 1980s, two-thirds of these cases were lost by the plaintiffs, with courts often claiming that they had no way of remedying the inequalities. But since 1989, two-thirds of the cases brought have been won by the plaintiffs. The main reason for this about-face is not a shift in judicial sympathies; it is a change in litigation strategy—earlier losing cases were brought on the basis of the right to equal education. But as of 1973, the year *Rodriguez* was handed down, only seventeen states explicitly required that education be "open to all" in their state constitutions, and only five mentioned equality or equal opportunity, while most required an "adequate" education.[9] Since 1989, plaintiffs' lawyers have largely switched to a strategy of challenging only the *adequacy* of the education provided—these are the cases, by and large, that have been won.[10]

Ultimately, these cases do not—and cannot, because they are limited by *Rodriguez* to state constitutional definitions of adequacy—address the most significant component of educational inequality across the nation today, which is not inequality *within* states but inequality *between* states. Indeed, economists have found that two-thirds of nationwide inequality in district spending is between states and only one-third is within states.[11] This is a lucky break for those who live in largely rural states with prominent natural resources or other tax boons, but it is a profound inequality for students in poorer states. Thus, the only way to address the deepest educational funding inequalities is likely through federal remedies or oversight.

A few years after *Rodriguez*, describing a very different tax revolt from the one discussed in chapter 7, the *Baltimore Afro-American* reported that African American "taxpayers everywhere are threatening to revolt and for good reasons."[12] In this case, the comparison was between schools in Beverly Hills, which taxed itself at $3.18 per $100, and Compton, which taxed itself at $4.86 per $100 of assessed valuation. Yet Compton spent only $1,115 per child each year, while Beverly Hills was able to spend $2,063, thanks to Beverly Hills' property values, which were seven times higher than Compton's. So a child in Compton "is penalized because of where he lives." The role of residential segregation on the basis of race and economic class is critical in perpetuating such dramatic inequalities in educational resources and access, particularly under the predominant property-tax financing structure.

Education researchers Gary Orfield and Chungmei Lee have found that the majority of middle-class and even low-income whites are able to send their children to schools with a low percentage of students living in poverty. In contrast, middle-class black and Latino families frequently still end up in overwhelmingly segregated schools with high poverty concentrations due to entrenched residential segregation patterns.[13] A majority of black students in the ten largest U.S. cities now attend what are described as "apartheid" schools with a population that is 99 percent students of color.[14] These are invariably also the schools with the lowest funding levels, and the poor resources of these schools, along with other forms of discrimination, have contributed to a dropout rate for black and Latino students of nearly 50 percent nationwide.[15] In just one example in the state of Pennsylvania, in the 2002–3 school year, Lower Merion County, with a 91 percent white school population and a 4 percent low-income population, spent $17,261 per pupil. In the city of Philadelphia—just a few footsteps away from Lower Merion County across a fictional boundary road dividing line—school spending was $9,299, despite its higher property tax rate. Philadelphia has a 79 percent black and Latino student population and a 71 percent low-income population.[16] In 2008, Lower Merion County even participated in a program to distribute free Mac laptops to its high school students.[17] Philadelphia students were not included in the statewide pilot program.

It has proved difficult after *Rodriguez* for legal advocates to pursue claims on the basis of class discrimination or tax inequality, whether in education or other areas. Most such legislation by the late 1970s would fall into the category of facially neutral classifications. The category "facially neutral" was created by the court a few years after *Rodriguez* was decided, but it was presaged by the court's unwillingness to identify *Rodriguez* as a case claiming both race and class discrimination. A facially neutral classification, by definition, avoids deploying race or any other suspect class as a category in the statutory language. "Facially neutral" indicates the awareness that there can still sometimes be a disparate impact on particular racial groups. The framework for examining such classifications was decided in 1976, in *Washington v. Davis*, when the court required plaintiffs contesting facially neutral laws to show invidious intent.[18] This demand for a "smoking gun" in facially neutral legislation effectively served to bar most claims, as intent is notoriously difficult to prove.

Indeed, had the plaintiffs in *Rodriguez* brought their suit after *Washington* and based it on the disparate racial impact of the "facially neutral" funding scheme, they would have most likely still lost because of the inherent difficulty in proving malicious intent. The principle was entrenched, in the 1971 dicta in *Valtierra* and the 1976 precedent set by *Washington*, that facially neutral classifications, even if they had disproportionate impact on a protected class, would not be treated with the same level of scrutiny as legislation explicitly naming that class. Even if the facially neutral classification caused more measurable harm to the protected class, it received less protection. Facially neutral laws have, in the analysis of many legal scholars, become the primary means of unequally distributing resources and access and, as such, are largely beyond the reach of legal remedy.[19] One legal scholar, Reva Siegel, has described facially neutral doctrine as yet another new way to uphold the discriminatory impact of status categories such as race.[20]

Before *Washington* was decided, however, the final nail in the Supreme Court's brief history of endorsing desegregation plans came a year after *Rodriguez*, in a case from Detroit that combined the dilemmas of Northern school segregation and interdistrict busing.[21] Though the district court had found that there would be no possible way to desegregate Detroit schools without busing between school districts, the Supreme Court overturned interdistrict busing as a remedy in *Milliken v. Bradley*, finding a lack of state action to segregate. In fact, because there had never been black students living in the newly developed wealthy white suburbs, they were outside the legal definition of de jure, *Brown*-style "state action" segregation and therefore, based on the court's decisions, beyond the reach of remedy.[22]

By the time of *Milliken*, urban school financing was "in desperate shape," according to one of Justice Lewis F. Powell's own former Supreme Court clerks, who acknowledged that with decisions like *Rodriguez*, "the Court had not helped much."[23] Constance Baker Motley of the NAACP Legal Defense and Educational Fund, by 1974, stated that the *Brown* decision was minimally relevant to African Americans in the inner city.[24] But for many advocates, *Milliken* posed a way the court could "soften the fiscal blow dealt the dispossessed in *Rodriguez*" by creating larger school districts for district-wide busing and, implicitly, requiring district-wide taxation that included wealthy white suburban areas.[25]

Though the court had been willing to change or alter lines that had a clear segregative impact in voting redistricting cases, the prospect of busing white children from an affluent Northern suburb to a poor inner-city school pushed several justices to staunchly defend the sovereignty of school district lines and local taxation structures.[26] One of Justice Powell's main concerns regarding an interdistrict remedy in *Milliken* was the way in which school districts were traditionally organized and funded locally. Once school districts were made to bus students from city to suburb, he asked, "Who, in particular, determines school budgets, the assessment and collection of school taxes, etc.?"[27] An interdistrict remedy, he argued, "really will require consolidation so that a single controlling entity can make the vital decisions." The majority repeatedly expressed worries about tax levies and financing disparities among fifty-four districts if they were made to equalize through consolidation.[28]

School districts would ultimately find more protection than schoolchildren in *Milliken*, much as they had in *Rodriguez*. One of Harry Blackmun's clerks described the district court's mistake as "the legal assumption that district lines are simply artificial creatures of the state that can be disregarded whenever necessary," citing *Rodriguez* for the notion that districts have recognizable rights as legal creations that are "more than just administrative conveniences."[29] Like the rights of corporations or other legal fictions of personhood, school districts' rights were placed on the scale of justice alongside the rights of children and families. Justice Thurgood Marshall argued that whether state action was "responsible for the growth of the core of all-Negro schools" was "quite irrelevant." When the decision in *Milliken* was announced overturning interdistrict busing in Detroit based on a lack of "state action," Marshall read a statement in court reflecting on the *Brown* decision, saying that "after 20 years of small, often difficult steps toward that great end, the Court today takes a giant step backwards."[30]

This step was not limited to the judiciary, however. Busing had become an unpopular tool by the late 1970s, which saw an increase in antibusing organizations adopting the language of color blindness to argue for "neutrality" and fiscal responsibility with "tax dollars."[31] Several amendments to the Elementary and Secondary Education Act were passed from 1976 through 1983 prohibiting the use of federal funds for busing, sponsored by Senators Robert Byrd and Joseph Biden, among others.[32] In a 1983 amendment cosponsored by Senator Jesse Helms, the Department of Justice was banned from instigating lawsuits pursuing busing as a remedy and the government was forbidden from ordering students to be bused more than five miles from their homes. This put the burden of litigation costs "back on those least able to support it."[33] But litigation was often unlikely to conclude favorably for those seeking desegregation through busing. After a series of decisions in the late 1970s ambivalently maintaining busing as a limited remedy in some locales but not others, the court in 1982 upheld a referendum limiting the use of busing in Los Angeles.[34]

According to historian Lisa McGirr, of the many issues, including opposition to busing, that united conservative residents of Orange County in the 1970s, "none was more important than taxes."[35] Taxpayer citizenship claims would continue to grow louder in the 1970s and beyond. McGirr's analysis of Orange County indicates that various organizations sprung up from the late 1960s onward in support of property tax limitation amendments, such as 1968's Proposition 9. Orange County was in fact the state headquarters for the direct-mail campaigns of both the antibusing and the antitax movements, which shared some of the same rhetoric.[36] A typical antibusing letter read, "Are you willing to pay *higher property taxes* to finance the forced busing of 100,000 Los Angeles schoolchildren?"[37] But it would take another decade for the state's voters to pass Proposition 13 in 1978, limiting property taxes to 1 percent of market value.[38] McGirr argues persuasively that by the time of the economic crisis in the late 1970s, suburban homeowners like those in Orange County were frustrated over steeply increasing property values, along with high taxes overall, thus spurring them to vote to limit their property taxes.[39] In this, her research offers a historical alternative to the hypothesis offered by William Fischel that "homevoters" voted for Proposition 13 directly in response to the California Supreme Court's decision in the 1976 relitigation of the *Serrano* case (after the *Rodriguez* decision) *Serrano II* that the state's school financing scheme was unconstitutional under the California state constitution.[40]

Texas continued to serve as the front line in battles over educational equality and access in school financing systems. The state of Texas passed a law two years after *Rodriguez* that withheld state funds for the education of the children of undocumented immigrants and permitted local districts to exclude them from enrollment.[41] When the case reached the Supreme Court, Powell remained committed to his decision in *Rodriguez*, yet he also seemed to feel concerned about where such a ruling had led by the time of *Plyler*. He pushed for a heightened level of equal-protection scrutiny based on the fact that the class at issue was composed of "innocent children," which he sought to define as a suspect class. He did not acknowledge that he had refused heightened scrutiny to the *Rodriguez* complainants, who were of course in the same category of "innocence."[42] In the end, Justice William Brennan wrote the majority opinion, tracing the historical importance of education while stopping short, again, of describing it as a right. The court found that the Texas rule would "create and perpetuate a subclass" and that children could not be completely excluded from education under equal protection. In this, they solidified the simultaneously important and precarious position of education in the constitutional framework.

The immediate response to the *Plyler* decision was once again framed in terms of taxpayers' rights to inequality and, in this case, outright exclusion of immigrants. A North Carolina man expressed anger at "the decision requiring taxpayers to educate the children of illegal aliens."[43] An Oregon woman wanted to know where the Constitution required "the American taxpayer" to pay for "an illegal alien's education."[44] One newspaper article noted that "those most traumatized" by the court's decision were poor Mexican Americans who saw themselves as "hardworking taxpayers" and viewed themselves as "paying for the education of illegal aliens' children" while seeing "their jobs being taken away by these illegal aliens." According to Texas state senator Hector Uribe, the issue was "less one of racism than of nationalism and economics," in which the decision meant "the poorest of the poor" would be "educating the even poorer."[45] A Houston man wrote to the court blaming it for placing the "financial burden" of the education of children who were the "responsibility of the federal government" on the "taxpayers of Texas."[46] The author interpreted this action to mean that the court now "sets the budget and fixes the tax rate of all school districts in Texas." Another Houston resident was angry at what he viewed as a decision sanctioning people being paid in "untaxable wages," while he had to continue paying school taxes as a U.S. citizen.[47] Despite the taxes unquestionably being paid by undocumented people, the rhetoric of taxpayer rights shifted easily to demonize them and justify excluding their children.

Few other cases made it to the Supreme Court in the years after *Plyler* advocating either discrimination based on poverty or the right to education. In a 1988 case, Sarita Kadrmas and her mother protested their North Dakota school district's policy of charging a fee for school busing from rural non-reorganized school districts and argued that it denied equal protection to the children of poor parents.[48] Justice Sandra Day O'Connor wrote for the majority in dismissing this claim, going "out of her way," in the words of one of Blackmun's law clerks, to distinguish *Plyler* as only per-taining to the unique situation of undocumented immigrant children.[49] Unfortunately, the clerk argued, the majority decision would make it dif-ficult for the court to apply heightened scrutiny to any statute that poten-tially compromised "a minimally adequate education."[50] Marshall wanted a strong dissent in the case on behalf of the poor family, but even the law clerk he assigned to write it, Elena Kagan, was sympathetic to the majority position that there was not any legal doctrine under which to find in favor of the Kadrmas family.[51] Cases that reached the court on segregated schools were similarly disfavored as the justices began to consistently hold that school districts could be released from their obligation to desegregate, even if "unitary status" under *Green* had never been reached.[52]

The plaintiffs in the poor communities of San Antonio also continued to challenge the inequality of school funding for decades. Litigation based in Edgewood earned victories in state court years after *Rodriguez* on the ba-sis of arguments for minimal adequacy—rather than equality—in educa-tional provision, only to confront the unwillingness of the state legislature to remedy the inequities.[53] After litigating four different cases in Texas state courts out of Edgewood, the Mexican American Legal Defense Fund filed its most recent challenge in 2011, *Edgewood Independent School District v. Scott*. In the wake of state cuts of $4 billion in public school funding in 2011, the plaintiffs alleged that the Texas legislature had retreated from its court-ordered obligation to provide a fair and efficient school finance system.[54] Instead, MALDEF contended that the current system had "increased the inequity for low-wealth school districts to pre-1993 levels, forcing those dis-tricts to tax higher but yield less revenue compared to higher-wealth school districts."[55] The powerful intransigence of property-tax-based school funding systems is illustrated by the fact that four decades after the first of numerous victorious lawsuits was filed in Texas challenging the educational finance system, local property taxes continued to provide over 55 percent of the school revenue in the state.[56] Ultimately, the Texas Constitution has created a conundrum for courts and legislatures in the pursuit of educa-tional equality—the state is required to fund public schools efficiently and adequately, and it is also prohibited from implementing a statewide prop-erty tax, which courts have interpreted to mean that local school districts must have power to set their own rates.[57]

In another recent case, *Chicago Urban League v. Illinois*, settled in 2017, the plaintiffs argued that the combination of a school funding system heavily reliant on local property taxes and a system of schools in which African

American and Latino students attended schools in "majority-minority districts" was discriminatory on the basis of race.[58] The suit argued that the state's share of revenue for education had declined from 48 percent in 1976 to 28 percent in 2007.[59] The Cook County Circuit Court ruled in 2009—coincidentally on tax day—that the plaintiffs had shown a "demonstrable, disparate and adverse impact based on the Illinois Civil Rights Act of 2003," citing, among other things, the fact that Illinois "ranks 49th in the nation in the size of per-pupil funding disparity between its lowest and highest poverty districts." The equalized assessed valuation (EAV) per pupil ranged from between $1.2 million and $1.8 million in the wealthiest five districts to between $7,000 and $24,000 in the poorest five districts. In addition, districts at the bottom of the EAV range were disproportionately majority-minority districts. As an example, the court cited the Brooklyn, Illinois, district, ranked 386th out of 395 consolidated school districts in EAV per pupil in 2007, with 97 percent of its student body drawn from low-income households and nearly 100 percent from ethnic minority groups.[60] The court also noted that the disparity existed even though low-property-wealth areas were typically paying significantly higher property tax rates than areas with higher property wealth. Later, however, the case was dismissed as a nonjusticiable "adequacy" claim based on a 1996 precedent from the Illinois Supreme Court articulating the separation of powers in the Illinois government and endorsing the importance of local control.[61]

In the wake of this loss, two taxpayers filed an equity case in 2010 challenging the Illinois educational finance system on the basis of state constitutional law. Similar to a key element of the *Rodriguez* litigation, the *Carr v. Koch* case argued that property-poor school district residents paid a tax rate 23 percent higher than the rate paid by taxpayers in property-rich districts, but that per-pupil spending was 28 percent lower in the property-poor districts. Ron Newell, a high school social studies teacher and Cairo, Illinois, resident, as well as one of the two plaintiffs, hoped the lawsuit would break legislative gridlock. Newell said, "they could double our property taxes, they could triple them, and there's no way that we could keep up with other districts," arguing that it was "just not fair" that his community's funds "simply were not providing the kind of education that people were getting in other communities."[62] *Carr* was appealed to the Illinois Supreme Court, where the complaint was dismissed with prejudice due to lack of standing and "failure to state a direct or threatened injury."[63]

In *McCleary v. State of Washington*, the Washington Supreme Court in 2012 upheld a lower-court decision that the legislature was in violation of its state constitutional duty to fund public education, and it has retained jurisdiction of the case and held the state legislature in contempt for continually failing to meet this obligation.[64] The court had the benefit of a state constitutional provision that used words like "paramount duty" (which the Supreme Court interpreted as meaning "funded before anything else") and "ample" (which they again interpreted as meaning "more than enough," not just budgetary remnants). Even so, there is an ongoing struggle for the court's ruling to actually be effectuated by the state legislature, despite a set of sanctions imposed on the legislature of $100,000 a day for failing to meet the court's order.[65] *McCleary* is still perhaps a best-case-scenario example, if we compare it to another state constitutional provision, in South Carolina, which simply states that the legislature will supply "maintenance and support" for schools "open to all children"—a provision interpreted by that state's supreme court to require the legislature to provide each child a "minimally adequate education."[66] And though the *McCleary* case highlights the willingness of the Washington Supreme Court to take action against unequally funded schools, another case from Seattle had a very different outcome at the Supreme Court just a few years prior. In *Parents Involved in Community Schools v. Seattle School District No. 1*, the majority of the court overturned voluntary school desegregation plans in Seattle and Louisville, Kentucky, as overly broad and, in so doing, affirmed what Michael J. Dumas describes as the "white accumulation" of educational advantage.[67] Despite the historical context of de jure segregation in both cities, the five-to-four majority found that the voluntary desegregation efforts were not narrowly tailored enough to address only "the harm that is traceable to segregation."[68]

Indeed, in education researcher Jonathan Kozol's 2005 work, he finds that attorneys for low-income school district residents in resegregated areas are now in the position of arguing that their clients should receive "separate, but equal" education packages. As a result of the legal and wider social discourse around them, plaintiffs' lawyers in these cases "rarely choose to speak at all of racial isolation."[69] Lizabeth Cohen has argued that *Brown* became increasingly meaningless due to growing residential segregation and deep-rooted localism.[70] The desegregation that was ostensibly supposed to occur after *Brown* didn't actually begin until 1969, and desegregation outside the South never happened in a meaningful way once *Milliken* ruled out busing and metropolitan desegregation remedies.[71] The high point of desegregated schools is usually placed by scholars around 1988, with increasing resegregation ever since.[72] Many parents and advocates continued to pursue the fight for equal financing in state courts, first attempting to locate their arguments in the equal protection clauses of state constitutions. These arguments typically failed and led to another wave of cases using the frequently vague education clauses of state constitutions, demanding adequacy, not equality, in education and seeking a "minimally adequate" floor of education funding for poorer school districts.[73]

Taxpayer Rights Movements and the Legacy of Exclusion

At the start of the recession of 2008, Kelley Williams-Bolar's daughters had been attending Copley-Fairlawn schools in suburban Ohio for two years already. Williams-Bolar worked as a classroom aide with Akron Public Schools and lived in Akron, but she had grown worried about her daughters' safety walking home from the Akron schools when she was at work. She listed her father's address on the enrollment forms for Copley-Fairlawn, which allowed them to attend Copley schools as residents without the out-of-district tuition fee. In 2008, Copley-Fairlawn hired private investigators to track parents' addresses and began offering a hundred-dollar bounty to anyone who turned in another family "illegally" obtaining education. By 2008, a private investigator hired by the district had been watching Williams-Bolar's home in Akron for months, keeping track of the time her family spent away from her father's home in Copley.[74]

Though the case was picked up by national media, defenders of the school district remained convinced that local taxes could, should, and did define the rights of citizenship not only for Williams-Bolar but also for her children. Copley resident and *Akron Beacon Journal* editorialist Bob Dyer argued that the case had nothing to do with race and blamed Williams-Bolar for her predicament, saying, "I pay a lot of money in property taxes, 53 percent of which go to the schools, and I want that money to go to the people who live in the district."[75] In January 2011, Williams-Bolar was found guilty of felony record tampering and sentenced to five years in prison (later reduced to ten days with time served). That felony conviction, falsifying records to attend a different school, was a first for Ohio.[76] Since that conviction, which endangered her special education career plans, Governor John Kasich has reduced such convictions to misdemeanors, stating that the original punishment was "too harsh."[77] Williams-Bolar has since organized an Ohio "parents union" as an intended counterweight to teachers' unions. In organizing this parents' union, Williams-Bolar now works with a self-described "free market think tank" to advocate for parental choice and school vouchers.[78]

Another African American mother, Tanya McDowell, was arrested and charged with first-degree larceny for the "theft" of educational services from the Norwalk, Connecticut, school district in April 2011. McDowell, who was homeless at the time of the arrest, was accused of living outside Norwalk since she rotated between a Norwalk homeless shelter and a friend's house in Bridgeport, Connecticut, where she could sometimes stay the night (but wasn't allowed to be during the day).[79] Though the city, rather than the school district, brought the charges against McDowell in the case, Norwalk school board president Jack Chiaramonte told a local newspaper that "there has to be a penalty for stealing our services."[80] McDowell was sentenced in March 2012 to five years in prison for felony larceny of $15,686 of "free" education services from Norwalk and four counts of sale of narcotics.[81] As the language of these cases indicates, the notion that some people are "taxpaying citizens" who have "paid" for the public schools and that some (poor, black, female) people are "stealing" services is not only still pervasive but perhaps better organized than ever.

In East Baton Rouge Parish, Louisiana, wealthy and middle-class residents have sought to create their own new city, school district, and property tax system in the name of local control. The reported impetus for this move is that the current East Baton Rouge school district of forty-two thousand students encompasses a number of high-poverty neighborhoods along with the wealthy, high-value-property neighborhoods pursuing separation. One mother of two students in the district, Tania Nyman, said that the plan would "devastate us," because "they're not only going to take the richer white kids out of the district, they are going to take their money out of it."[82]

Other cities, including Birmingham, Alabama, have pursued similar plans to split districts between wealthy and poor neighborhoods. But Alabama also has the distinction of the lowest per capita property taxes in the nation. In 2012, in *Lynch v. Alabama*, poor schoolchildren and their representatives brought suit against the state arguing a rare historical argument—they claimed that the property tax system created in the 1901 constitution was intended to protect wealthy landowners from high property taxes and prevent black schools from accessing funds and was therefore discriminatory.

Added to this, in the 1970s, state constitutional amendments ensured that certain types of land, specifically timberland and farmland, would be taxed at levels as low as possible. This left rural school districts in Alabama's Black Belt unable to raise enough funds for basic educational needs.[83] Plaintiff Stella Anderson, a mother of two who lives in rural Sumter County, stated that "if things continue the way they are with farmland and timberland not being taxed properly, then what we're going to see is more declining of educational resources within rural communities especially but the entire state. . . . This is not about trying to increase anyone's taxes. It's about doing the right thing."[84] In 2011 district court judge Lynwood Smith penned an 854-page opinion denouncing the history of racial discrimination in Alabama's education system but dismissing the claim that the property tax laws were enacted with racially discriminatory intent, and in early 2014 the ruling was upheld by a federal appeals court.[85]

While only a handful of such challenges to property-tax-based, racialized school finance systems have survived litigation, taxpayer rights agendas and tax politics have only grown more deafening in recent years. And the attention and anger of these movements is frequently focused on the poor, immigrants, or perceived recipients of government payments. A minor media outcry emerged in 2010 when it was claimed—through a partial use of statistical information—that nearly half of all households "do not pay" federal income tax.[86] By 2012 the notion that almost half of U.S. households were "shirking" their tax responsibilities had become a conservative standard. While Mitt Romney faced a great deal of criticism when he made remarks about the "47% of the people . . . who are dependent upon government, who believe that they are victims," it is perhaps most telling that he linked each of these negative stereotypes specifically with the notion that "these are people who pay no income tax."[87] The rhetorical connection between the amount and type of tax payments (since there does not seem to be any serious analysis that claims that these families pay no taxes of any kind) and the degree of citizenship and rights has never been more openly embraced than in the past two years. Simultaneously, movements explicitly centered on tax-based anger, like the Tea Party, have focused their ire on the Department of Education and tax-based public education funding in particular as "blatantly unconstitutional."[88] The secretary of education under the Donald J. Trump administration, Betsy DeVos, formerly ran a campaign in Detroit with the hashtag #endDPS (end Detroit Public Schools), and she is a vocal advocate of "school choice," even once describing historically black colleges and universities that emerged in part from the roots of segregation as "real pioneers" of school choice.[89]

At the same time, recipients of the earned income tax credit are often described in derogatory terms as welfare recipients or "takers," including by members of Congress, and they are among the groups most heavily targeted for audits.[90] In fact, comparative analysis of state tax systems illustrates that many states' taxation schemes force their lowest-income residents to pay up to six times more of their income in taxes than the wealthy pay.[91] Meanwhile, racialized economic disparities continue to seriously affect education funding. And there are calls for more progressive taxes to fund education—in California, Proposition 30 was passed in November 2012, temporarily raising the income tax rates on the wealthiest residents while increasing the sales tax by a quarter of a cent, while Proposition 38, which would have temporarily raised income taxes on all income over $50,000, failed.[92]

Exempting pure subsistence income from taxes is inherent in our graduated income tax structure—the Tax Policy Center has illustrated convincingly that for most households with no federal income tax liability, the "zeroing out" results from low levels of income rather than any particular tax breaks.[93] Ironically, it was the George W. Bush tax cuts, lowering marginal tax rates across the board and granting a huge windfall to the wealthiest Americans, that bumped millions of lower-income families into that "47%" by eliminating their modest federal income tax liabilities.[94] That signature Republican policy has now created a quite explicitly class-based argument that nearly half the nation is made up of half citizens, people who cannot be fully brought into conversation or consideration since their federal individual income tax liability zeroed out in one or more years. These half citizens, viewed as such due to an inextricable combination of their (tax-based) class and (class-imputed) race, are particularly vulnerable to attacks on basic common goods like public education.

The organization EdBuild developed a map in the summer of 2015 that illustrates the nature of the inequalities in school financing in spatial terms. This map exposes the way that the children of, for example, Camden, New Jersey, are "fenced off from their more affluent peers—in effect, sacrificed to keep the poverty of the city from dragging down the property wealth of its neighbors."[95] Kozol, in his discussion of economically and racially segregated school districts, points out that most citizens never have to acknowledge the denial of equal opportunities to other people's children because "inequality is mediated for us by a taxing system that most people do not fully understand and seldom scrutinize."[96] The quiet power of tax systems is their ability to hide in plain sight, even as they enact great injustices.

Conclusion

Popular U.S. history and legal mythology about public education understandably focus on the importance of *Brown v. Board of Education.* Backlashes, court battles, and Cold War cynicism aside, it represents what many Americans see as the best of the nation in the last fifty-plus years. *Brown*, however, cannot make sense of the ongoing racial and economic segregation that continues in U.S. schools. The problem of racially segregated, economically unequal school expenditures predates and has long outlasted formal Jim Crow segregation laws and their overturning in *Brown*. The techniques of separate taxation structures facilitating segregation and inequality may have been pioneered in the South in the nineteenth century, but they have since been perfected in the North and West. Hidden behind the seeming innocuousness (and impenetrability) of tax law and "local control," these racially separate property tax bases have created dramatic disparities in the funding of white and black schools since the Civil War that *Brown* did very little to change. In *Rodriguez* the court ruled that there was no constitutional right to education and that property-tax-based school financing did not discriminate on the basis of wealth, despite the 96 percent minority student population and the fraction of funding they received compared to overwhelmingly white, wealthy school districts. In doing so, the court reflected a legal consciousness of taxpayer citizenship rights that had briefly appeared a hundred years prior to offer equity and protection for poor families. But in *Rodriguez* they pushed it to its logical end to argue that those who were too poor to pay high enough taxes or live in a wealthy enough area to fund their schools adequately were simply enjoying the "equality" of the marketplace.

The story of racial segregation in public schools and the legal battle to overcome it has been told many times before as a battle over race and rights. This book argues, however, that that legal battle was also strongly connected to a racial consciousness of "taxpayer" rights that had an earlier legacy in aspirational equality litigation and that would have an important effect on later possibilities for demanding educational equality in the courtroom. Ultimately, though newly freed slaves, school board attorneys, segregationists, and NAACP activists would seem to have little in common as a group, they shared an emphasis on the perceived centrality of taxpayer status for claiming the right to education. Just as many African Americans who wrote to the NAACP identified their legal rights through the lens of broad "taxpayer citizenship," segregationists who wrote to the Supreme Court after *Brown* demanded the maintenance of their separate and unequal schools in a similar, but more exclusionary, language of "taxpayers' rights." The category of "taxpaying citizen" does not have a legally important meaning by itself that could win most of these cases—legal standing as parents or direct constitutional rights violations were virtually always the basis for judicial decisions—yet it was powerfully important in the legal consciousness of citizenship for people on each side of the racial divide. But because of its deep historical linkage to the idea of whiteness and exclusion, the identity of taxpayer bent toward inequality far more often than justice. This act of claiming citizenship and rights through a rubric that is so easily defined in terms of wealth, in terms of who pays "more" and who "doesn't pay," continues to haunt the struggle for equal education.

Education is the sine qua non of the democratic experiment. Without education, freedom of speech loses its function, the franchise loses its effectiveness, and the law loses its meaning. The fight for integrated and equal education continues, but it has also continued to be deflected by a legal system unwilling to see the connections between economic and racial inequality, local taxation, and widespread segregation. A wrong that was given shape and form in the law, nurtured and built up by precedent and legal classification, has yet to find a remedy, but it survives as a rhetoric. In part because of the opaqueness, almost mysteriousness, of the deep structure of tax codes and tax policy, the system of racialized school financing and the equally racialized language of taxpayer status have resisted virtually every other social movement transformation of the twentieth century. When we say government funds for schools or roads or parks belong to "the taxpayers," it has a different connotation than if we say the funds belong simply to "the people." Though an identity as a "taxpayer" may have inspired momentary coalitions and sometimes prompted bursts of pride and patriotism, ultimately the division between "taxpayers" and "taxeaters" grew from the roots of racial segregation, white entitlement, and unequal taxation, and its use continues to enable and facilitate those structures today.

Notes

Introduction

1. "Pages from Donald Trump's 1995 Income Tax Records," *New York Times*, October 1, 2016, https://www.nytimes.com/interactive/2016/10/01/us/politics/donald-trump-taxes.html?_r=0.

2. Nick Gass, "Trump: 'People Don't Care' about My Tax Returns," *Politico*, September 6, 2016, http://www.politico.com/story/2016/09/trump-taxes-people-dont-care-227763. See also David Wright, "Trump Says Public Doesn't Care 'at All' about His Taxes," *CNN*, January 11, 2017, http://www.cnn.com/2017/01/11/politics/trump-tax-returns-answer-news-conference/index.html.

3. Eric Bradner, "Trump: People Don't Care about My Tax Returns," *CNN*, January 22, 2017, http://www.cnn.com/2017/01/22/politics/kellyanne-conway-trump-tax-returns/index.html.

4. David Brooks, "Trump, Taxes and Citizenship," *New York Times*, October 4, 2016, https://www.nytimes.com/2016/10/04/opinion/trump-taxes-and-citizenship.html.

5. "What the 2012 Election Would Have Looked like without Universal Suffrage," *BuzzFeed*, November 9, 2012, https://www.buzzfeed.com/buzzfeedpolitics/what-the-2012-election-would-have-looked-like-with?utm_term=.ve3gLPbBk#.mbwrpO25g.

6. The map appeared first on right-wing website *The Burning Platform* on August 28, 2016: "What if Only Taxpayers Voted?" https://www.theburningplatform.com/2016/08/28/what-if-only-taxpayers-voted/. This use of data was debunked in "Data and Taxes," *Snopes*, September 1, 2016, http://www.snopes.com/what-if-taxpayers-only-voted-map/.

7. "What if Only Taxpayers (or White People) Could Vote?," *Daily Pepe*, August 29, 2016, http://www.dailypepe.com/2016/08/29/what-if-only-taxpayers-could-vote/. For more on how the Internet meme of Pepe the Frog became known as a hate symbol, see Emanuella Grinberg, "Pepe the Frog Designated a Hate Symbol by ADL," *CNN*, September 28, 2016, http://www.cnn.com/2016/09/28/us/pepe-the-frog-hate-symbol-trnd/index.html.

8. In this, I rely on the idea of "legal consciousness" put forth by Hendrik Hartog, Martha Minow, and William Forbath in their important work on legal histories "from below." As exemplified by the New York City pig-keeping law Hartog examines, the difference between the law on the books and the law as people understand, assert, and enforce it can be profound, and often illuminating. Similarly, the voices of individual "nonlegal" actors in my book belong to people who felt strongly enough about what they believed their legal rights to education to be that they wrote to

courts or legal advocacy organizations, usually identifying themselves as "taxpayers" when they did so. By relying on sources produced by nonlegal actors as well as Supreme Court justices, *Racial Taxation* attempts to illustrate the multiple perspectives on how rights are earned and how educational equality should be defined. Hartog, Minow, and Forbath, "Introduction."

9. See Quadagno, *Color of Welfare*; and Edsall and Edsall, *Chain Reaction*.

10. See Michelmore, *Tax and Spend*.

11. Margo, "Race Differences in Public School Expenditures," 213.

12. In fact, the modern notion of "standing" to bring suit was created by the Supreme Court in a case brought by a taxpayer. For the case commonly viewed as the origin of modern standing doctrine, see *Frothingham v. Mellon*, 262 U.S. 447 (1923). For a critical analysis of the mythology of standing, see Winter, "Metaphor of Standing." See also *Flast v. Cohen*, 392 U.S. 83 (1968); *Valley Forge Christian College v. Americans United for Separation of Church and State*, 454 U.S. 464 (1982); and *DaimlerChrysler Corp. v. Cuno*, 547 U.S. 332 (2006). For a spirited debate by legal scholars on who could possibly be excluded from taxpayer standing if it were extended, see Bittker, "Case of the Fictitious Taxpayer"; and Kenneth Culp Davis, "Case of the Real Taxpayer."

13. Vaughn, *Schools for All*, 99.

14. This sense of pay-in was crucial for many communities, given the position education holds in a broader national narrative of meritocracy and opportunity, a position exemplified in the language describing education in Earl Warren's opinion in *Brown*. See Perkinson, *Imperfect Panacea*; and Tyack and Cuban, *Tinkering toward Utopia*. For the seminal work that pierced the comfortably mythologized origin story of American education in the nineteenth century, see Katz, *Irony of Early School Reform*. For an account critical of the role of education in the creation of consumer-driven capitalism, see Spring, *Education*; and Bowles and Gintis, *Schooling in Capitalist America*. For a description of American faith in education for social advancement as "so strong as to appear at times almost pathetic," see Knight, *Fifty Years of American Education*, 296. When education is identified as a straightforward economic advantage, quantifiable and income directed, "an easy next step is to regard schooling as a consumer good rather than a common good." Tyack and Cuban, *Tinkering Toward Utopia*, 140–41. For further discussion of the pursuit of "excellence" in universities focused on students and parents as "customers," see Readings, *University in Ruins*. The current view of education as simply a consumer commodity has perhaps emerged, in part, in response to the question at the center of this book, whether tax expenditures entitle one's children to a certain level of educational rights.

15. Einhorn, *American Taxation, American Slavery*, 257.

16. Ibid., 259.

17. For more on the racial undertones of the backlash against welfare and the War on Poverty, see Quadagno, *Color of Welfare*. For an analysis that carries the racialization of welfare back to the nineteenth-century roots of the "welfare queen" idea, see SenGupta, *From Slavery to Poverty*.

18. For a discussion of how local government functions on a market basis with respect to the primacy of home property values and a defense of school finance policies

in local bodies, see Fischel, *Homevoter Hypothesis*, and my discussion of Fischel's argument with regard to school finance litigation in the conclusion to this book. For a discussion of the way in which a market economy focus on individualism and exclusion has proved destructive to social welfare programs, see Katz, *Price of Citizenship*.

19. Holmes and Sunstein, *Cost of Rights*, 30.

20. See Katz, *Price of Citizenship*; and Tyack and Cuban, *Tinkering toward Utopia*.

21. For this argument and more on the connections between emerging residential segregation and marketplace individualism ideas in the postwar era, see Freund, *Colored Property*.

22. Moreo, *Schools in the Great Depression*, 137.

23. Cohen, *Consumers' Republic*; Jacobs, *Pocketbook Politics*.

24. Shklar, *American Citizenship*.

25. For a discussion of the importance of considering obligations in citizenship, see Kerber, "Meanings of Citizenship."

26. Kerber, *No Constitutional Right to Be Ladies*, 81.

27. See Kessler-Harris, *In Pursuit of Equity*. For an analysis of the contractual origins of U.S. citizenship, see Kettner, *Development of American Citizenship*. For an overview of the racialized and gendered development of unequal citizenship for workers, see Glenn, *Unequal Freedom*. See also Margot Canaday, *Straight State*.

28. See Edsall and Edsall, *Chain Reaction*; Berman, *America's Right Turn*; Lowndes, *New Deal to the New Right*; Lassiter, *Silent Majority*; Kruse, *White Flight*; Sokol, *There Goes My Everything*; and McGirr, *Suburban Warriors*.

29. For discussion of the various elements of the *Brown* debate, see chapter 4.

30. Eaton and Orfield, "*Brown v. Board of Education*," 129. See also Kozol, *Shame of the Nation*.

31. For a history of the NAACP by a participant, see Jonas, *Freedom's Sword*. For a thorough history of the early NAACP, see Sullivan, *Lift Every Voice*. For a legal analysis of the early cases brought by the organization, see Tushnet, *NAACP's Legal Strategy*.

32. See Goluboff, *Lost Promise of Civil Rights*.

33. Mack, "Rethinking Civil Rights Lawyering"; Mack, "Law and Mass Politics."

34. See Horwitz, *Transformation of American Law, 1780–1860*; and Horwitz, *Transformation of American Law, 1870–1960*.

35. For recent works that call for more historical examinations of taxation and public finance, see Brownlee, *Funding the Modern American State*, 4; and Martin, Mehrotra, and Prasad, *New Fiscal Sociology*, 26–27.

36. For a general overview of the development of federal taxation systems in the twentieth century, see Brownlee, *Federal Taxation in America*. For a history of the federal income tax as a "state-building" exercise, see Zelizer, *Taxing America*. For an overview of the recent critical tax theory scholarship that focuses on present tax inequalities, see Infanti and Crawford, *Critical Tax Theory*.

37. See Fisher, *Worst Tax?*

38. See Lassiter, *Silent Majority*; Kruse, *White Flight*; Sokol, *There Goes My Everything*; McGirr, *Suburban Warriors*; Lowndes, *New Deal to the New Right*; Edsall and Edsall, *Chain Reaction*; and Berman, *America's Right Turn*.

39. For a defense of taxation and rights against antitax and antigovernment ide-
ologies that also suggests a quasi-market relationship between taxes paid and rights
or "public goods," see Holmes and Sunstein, *Cost of Rights*.

40. "5 Foster Children Barred from Class," *Baltimore Afro-American*, October 8,
1960.

Chapter 1

1. *Memphis Evening Scimitar*, June 4, 1892, quoted in Wells, *Southern Horrors*, 15.
2. Kousser, *Dead End*, 5.
3. Cubberley, *Public Education in the United States*, 177–78.
4. Ibid., 178.
5. Ibid., 179.
6. Ibid., 182.
7. Pitkin, *Public School Support*.
8. Ibid., 196–207.
9. Butchart, *Northern Schools*, 182.
10. Tyack, James, and Benavot, *Shaping of Public Education*, 142.
11. Vaughn, *Schools for All*, 126.
12. Liu, "Education, Equality and National Citizenship," 372–73.
13. Tyack, James, and Benavot, *Shaping of Public Education*, 150.
14. Butchart, *Northern Schools*, 207.
15. Vaughn, *Schools for All*, 99.
16. Meier, Stewart, and England, *Race, Class, and Education*, 42.
17. Ibid.
18. Margo, *Disfranchisement*, 9.
19. See Horace Mann Bond, *The Education of the Negro in the American Social Order*
(New York: Octagon Books, 1966); and Gunnar Myrdal, *An American Dilemma* (New
York: Harper Collins, 1944), cited in Margo, "Race Differences in Public School
Expenditures," 204.
20. Margo, "Race Differences in Public School Expenditures," 207.
21. Ibid., 213.
22. Bryan Lyman, "A Permanent Wound: How the Slave Tax Warped Alabama
Finances," *Montgomery Advertiser*, February 5, 2017. See also Thornton, *Politics and
Power*; and Einhorn, *American Taxation, American Slavery*.
23. Leslie Brown, *Upbuilding Black Durham*, 150–51.
24. Liu, "Education, Equality and National Citizenship," 370–71.
25. Butchart, *Northern Schools*, 169, 171. For more discussion of the importance of
education to freedmen, see Vaughn, *Schooling for All*, 10–15.
26. Liu, "Education, Equality and National Citizenship," 374; H.R. 1326, 41st Cong.
(2d Sess. 1870).
27. Liu, "Education, Equality and National Citizenship," 378.
28. Ibid., 385–87, 394.
29. Slaughter-House Cases, 83 U.S. 36 (1873); Liu, "Education, Equality and National Citizenship," 339–45.

30. Chase v. Stephenson, 71 Ill. 383 (January 1874).

31. Ibid., 384.

32. Ibid., 385–86.

33. Cory v. Carter, 48 Ind. 327 (November 1874).

34. Lewis v. Henley, 2 Ind. 332, 334 (1850).

35. Ibid.

36. Ibid., 334–35.

37. Cubberley, *Public Education in the United States*, 186–87.

38. Ibid.

39. 3 Ind. Stat. 472 (1869), § 1.

40. Douglas, *Jim Crow Moves North*, 65.

41. Lewis v. Henley, 2 Ind. 332, 362–63 (1850).

42. Ibid., 341–42.

43. Douglas, *Jim Crow Moves North*, 73.

44. *Lewis*, 2 Ind. at 342–43.

45. Slaughter-House Cases, 83 U.S. 36 (1873) (no right to pursue a particular calling); Bradwell v. Illinois, 83 U.S. 30 (1874) (no right to practice law for women as citizens).

46. Cory v. Carter, 48 Ind. 327 (November 1874), 354.

47. Ibid., 359.

48. Ibid., 362.

49. Douglas, *Jim Crow Moves North*, 74.

50. People ex rel. Joseph Workman v. Board of Education of Detroit, 18 Mich. 400 (S. Ct. May 1869).

51. Mich. Laws § 43 (1867).

52. *Workman*, 18 Mich. at 409–10.

53. Ibid., 415.

54. Clark v. Board of Directors, 24 Iowa 266 (June 1868).

55. Ibid., 267–68.

56. Ibid., 269.

57. Ibid., 275.

58. Ibid., 276.

59. Ibid., 277.

60. Ibid., 280–81.

61. People v. Gallagher, 93 N.Y. 438 (Ct. App. October 1883).

62. Ibid.

63. Ibid., 458.

64. Ibid., 460.

65. Ibid., 462.

66. Ibid., 465.

67. Williams v. School Directors, Wright Rep. 578–79 (Ohio 1833).

68. Ibid.

69. Enos van Camp v. Board of Education of Logan, 9 Ohio St. 406 (S. Ct. November 1859).

70. Ibid., 407.

71. Ibid., 409.

72. Ibid., 410.

73. Ohio ex rel. William Garnes v. John W. McCann, 21 Ohio St. 198, 203 (S. Ct. December 1871).

74. Ibid., 207–8.

75. Ibid., 207.

76. Ibid., 211.

77. Claybrook v. City of Owensboro, 16 F. 297 (Dist. Ct., D. Ky. 1883).

78. Ibid., 303.

79. Ibid., 304.

80. Claybrook v. Owensboro, 23 F. 634 (Circ. Ct., D. Ky. March 1884).

81. Maddox v. Neal, 45 Ark. 121 (S. Ct. May 1885).

82. J. C. Puitt v. Commissioners of Gaston County, Raleigh, 94 N.C. 709 (1886).

83. Chrisman v. City of Brookhaven, 70 Miss. 477 (S. Ct. October 1892).

84. Ibid., 460.

85. Davenport et al. v. Cloverport et al., 72 F. 689 (Dist. Ct., D. Ky. February 1896).

86. Ibid., 694–95.

87. Tyack, James, and Benavot, *Shaping of Public Education*, 152.

88. For more on the role of "customary law" in the interpretation of and noncompliance with court decisions, see Hartog, "Pigs and Positivism."

89. Heather Andrea Williams, *Self-Taught*, 30.

Chapter 2

1. Gong Lum v. Rice, 275 U.S. 78 (1927).

2. Petition for Writ of Error, October 16, 1925, 44, Box 7896, *Gong Lum v. Rice*, U.S. Supreme Court Appellate Case Files, SCR.

3. Petition for Writ of Mandamus in Circuit Court, Box 7896, *Gong Lum v. Rice*, U.S. Supreme Court Appellate Case Files, SCR.

4. Rice v. Gong Lum, 139 Miss. 760, 104 So. 105 (1925).

5. *Gong Lum*, 275 U.S. 78.

6. Cumming v. Board of Education of Richmond County, 175 U.S. 528 (1899).

7. Chirhart, *Torches of Light*.

8. James D. Anderson, *Education of Blacks in the South*, 192.

9. Ibid., 49.

10. Ibid., 50.

11. June O. Patton, "The Black Community of Augusta and the Struggle for Ware High School, 1880–1899," in Franklin and Anderson, *New Perspectives on Black Educational History*, 53.

12. Motion to Advance, George F. Edmunds, Box 2930, File 17-206, U.S. Supreme Court Appellate Case Files, SCR.

13. Cumming v. Board of Education of Richmond County, 175 U.S. 528 (1899).

14. Deposition of Charles S. Bohler, Tax Collector, October 11, 1897, and Mandate 164, December 18, 1899, Box 2930, File 17-206, U.S. Supreme Court Appellate Case Files, SCR.

15. Ibid.

16. Plessy v. Ferguson, 163 U.S. 537 (1896).

17. Ibid.

18. Siegel, "Why Equal Protection No Longer Protects," 1126.

19. Przybyszewski, *Republic According to John Marshall Harlan*, 86–87; Civil Rights Cases, 109 U.S. 3 (1883).

20. Sears, *Utopian Experiment in Kentucky*. See also Peck, *Berea's First 125 Years*.

21. Berea College v. Commonwealth of Kentucky, 211 U.S. 45 (1908).

22. Harlan's dissent in *Berea* illustrates his unwillingness to diminish the citizenship (particularly market- or economic-based citizenship) of corporations, despite his readiness in *Cumming* to discount the economic citizenship of the black parents.

23. Lochner v. New York, 198 U.S. 45 (1905).

24. See, for example, *Thomas et al. v. Field et al.*, 143 Md. 128 (1923); *Gong Lum v. Rice*, 275 U.S. 78 (1927); and *Williams v. Zimmerman*, 172 Md. 563 (1937).

25. Tucker v. Blease et al., 97 S.C. 303 (1914), 4 (internal pagination of testimony begins at 1).

26. Ibid., 7.

27. Ibid.

28. Ibid., 15.

29. Ibid., 18.

30. Ibid., 16.

31. Ibid., 18–20.

32. Ibid., 21–22.

33. Ibid., 26–27.

34. Ibid., 38, 326.

35. State v. Cantey, 20 S.C. L. 614 (1835).

36. *Tucker*, 97 S.C. at 46, 331.

37. See Pascoe, *What Comes Naturally*; and Ariela Gross, *What Blood Won't Tell*.

38. Wertheimer et al., "'Law Recognizes Racial Instinct,'" 471, 472.

39. Ibid., 477.

40. Blalock-Moore, "*Piper v. Big Pine School District*," 346, 354.

41. Piper v. Big Pine School District of Inyo County, 193 Cal. 664 (S. Ct. 1924).

42. School District No. 21 in Fremont County v. Board of County Commissioners of Fremont County et al., 15 Wyo. 73 (S. Ct. 1906). See also "Honoring the Past, Challenging the Future" at Wyoming Indian Schools home page, http://www.fremont14.k12.wy.us/.

43. O'Brien, *Politics of Race and Schooling*, 30.

44. Memorandum, Bulletin 37, 1916, Part I, Series C, Box 405, NAACPP.

Chapter 3

1. Bryant v. Barnes, Tax Collector, 144 Miss. 732 (S. Ct. 1925).

2. Ibid.

3. See Part I, Series C, Boxes 187, 188, 189, NAACPP.

4. Peterson, "Negro Separate School," 351.

5. See *Marshall v. Donovan*, 73 Ky. 681 (1874) (white taxpayer suit protesting unequal taxation and discrimination against black schools dismissed due to lack of standing or harm); *Hickman College v. Trustees Colored District*, 111 Ky. 944 (1901) (railroad tax should be divided proportionately between white and black schools); *Taylor v. Russell*, 117 Ky. 539 (1904) (school tax vote by white voters in which they voted out the possibility of a black school deemed unconstitutional and invalid); *Munfordville Mercantile Company v. Board of Trustees District No. 39*, 155 Ky. 382 (1913) (school tax vote in which only whites were allowed to vote held to be constitutional since it was for a white school); and *Miller v. Feather*, 176 Ky. 268 (1917) (school special election in which only white voters were allowed to participate was constitutional since there appeared to be no black children of school age in the community and therefore no need for a school).

6. Trustees of Graded Free Colored Common Schools of the City of Mayfield, Kentucky v. Trustees of the Graded Free White Common Schools of the City of Mayfield, Kentucky, 180 Ky. 574 (1918); Board of Trustees of the Graded Free Colored Common School of Mayfield, Kentucky v. Board of Trustees of the Graded White Common School of Mayfield, Kentucky, 181 Ky. 303 (1918); Moss v. City of Mayfield, 186 Ky. 330 (1919) (submission of school bond for black school was appropriately submitted to only black voters and taxpayers, but the amount of the bond could not exceed mandatory limits).

7. Shadrack v. Board of Trustees of the Madisonville Graded Common School District, 188 Ky. 335 (1920).

8. Raley v. County Board of Education of Woodford County, 224 Ky. 50 (1928). See also *State Board of Education v. Brown*, 232 Ky. 434 (1929).

9. County Board of Education of Meade County v. Bunger, 240 Ky. 155 (1931).

10. Knox County Board of Education v. Fultz, 241 Ky. 265 (1931).

11. Jones v. Board of Education of City of Muskogee, 90 Okla. 233 (1923).

12. Board of Education of City of Guthrie v. Excise Board of Logan County, 86 Okla. 24 (1922).

13. James D. Anderson, *Education of Blacks in the South*.

14. Ibid.

15. Amos Daniels to Arthur Spingarn, March 15, 1924, Part I, Series C, Box 405, NAACPP.

16. Carter Wesley to Walter White, April 16, 1924, Part I, Series C, Box 203, NAACPP.

17. S. A. McAshan and George McNemee to NAACP, March 11, 1928, Part I, Series C, Box 288, NAACPP.

18. New York (State). Supreme Court. NAACP Articles of Incorporation, June 6, 1911. W. E. B. DuBois Papers (MS 312). Special Collections and University Archives, University of Massachusetts Amherst Libraries.

19. R. T. Kerlin, "Chapter XII: The Educational Door of Opportunity," 1921, Part I, Series C, Box 287, NAACPP.

20. Secretary to Governor Henry Allen, February 18, 1919, Part I, Series C, Box 405, NAACPP.

21. "Outline—Address at Topeka, Kansas," February 22, 1919, Part I, Series C, Box 270, NAACPP.

22. Acting Secretary to Rockville Centre School Board, January 28, 1930, Part I, Series C, Box 405, NAACPP.

23. Press note, December 7, 1936, Part I, Series C, Box 198, NAACPP.

24. Editorial, "Where Are the Leaders?," *Baltimore Afro-American*, June 1, 1929.

25. Ibid.

26. S. D. Leaward, letter to the editor, *Commercial Appeal* (Memphis), November 2, 1921.

27. William Banister, letter to the editor, *Baltimore Evening Sun*, April 2, 1919.

28. NAACP Secretary to J. L. Bond, Department of Public Instruction, April 23, 1919, Part I, Series C, Box 270, NAACPP.

29. Ibid.

30. "Paying Their Bills," *Chicago Defender*, September 8, 1923, 12.

31. A. E. Monroe to National Office, November 6, 1936, Part I, Series C, Box 201, NAACPP.

32. Alice Timms to Arthur Spingarn, May 4, 1930, Part 1, Series C, Box 405, NAACPP.

33. Goluboff, *Lost Promise of Civil Rights*. See also Mack, "Rethinking Civil Rights Lawyering," and Mack, "Law and Mass Politics."

34. Unsigned letter to National Office, October 2, 1922, Part I, Series C, Box 287, NAACPP.

35. Alphonzo Lee to National Office, November 20, 1936, Part I, Series D, Box 88, NAACPP.

36. Raymond Pace Alexander, "Plea in Behalf of the Colored Citizens of Philadelphia Opposing the Contemplated Moving of the Central High School from Broad and Green Streets to the Olney-Ogontz Section of Philadelphia," letter, March 9, 1937, Part I, Series C, Box 198, NAACPP.

37. "Berwyn Case 90 Per Cent Solved, Says Alexander," *Baltimore Afro-American*, September 29, 1934.

38. Mary Scruggs to NAACP, October 2, 1927, Part I, Series D, Box 56, NAACPP.

39. Enoc P. Waters Jr., "How Negroes in One County Solved School Bus Problem," *Journal and Guide*, December 29, 1934, Part I, Series C, Box 435, NAACPP. See also James D. Anderson, *Education of Blacks in the South*.

40. Waters, "How Negroes in One County."

41. See Margo, "Race Differences in Public School Expenditures."

42. Beito, *Taxpayers in Revolt*, xii, 35.

43. Moreo, *Schools in the Great Depression*, 135. See also Pitkin, *Public School Support*.

44. Moreo, *Schools in the Great Depression*, 137.

45. Pauline Bush of Carnesville, GA, to Thomas, June 2, 1934, Part VI, Box A47, NAACPP.

46. See Leslie Brown, *Upbuilding Black Durham*.

47. Cubberley, *Public Education in the United States*, 734.

48. Homel, *Down from Equality*, 58–84.

49. Ibid., 82.

50. Douglas, *Jim Crow Moves North*, 3. See also Sugrue, *Sweet Land of Liberty*.

51. Douglas, *Jim Crow Moves North*, 6.

52. Ibid., 138–39.

53. Ibid., 191.

54. My discussion generally avoids using "de facto" terminology in favor of simply "segregation" or "legal segregation," in part due to ideas presented by Matthew Lassiter, who argues that language referencing "de facto" segregation tends to, in a sense, "let the North off the hook" for practices that should be recognized as effectively segregationist. I would also add that a dichotomy such as "de jure/de facto" tends to erase the accountability of law itself for practices that are ultimately, functionally legal, even if the statute books do not indicate as much. See Matthew D. Lassiter, "The Myth of Southern Exceptionalism," in Lassiter and Crespino, *Myth of Southern Exceptionalism.*

55. Mohraz, *Separate Problem*, 86. See also Butchart, *Northern Schools, Southern Blacks.*

56. Mohraz, *Separate Problem*, 86.

57. Ibid., 137.

58. State Teachers Association, "Negro Educational Progress in SC," March 1926, Part VI, Box A2, NULP, SRO.

59. Mrs. Annie Mae Hall of Newton, GA, letter, November 12, 1935, Part VI, Box A47, NULP, SRO.

60. Ibid.

61. Louis Campbell to Walter White, December 3, 1934, Part I, Series C, Box 203, NAACPP.

62. Charles Hamilton Houston to N. S. Bond, Chairman, Board of Supervisors, Wise County, December 31, 1935, Part I, Series C, Box 203, NAACPP.

63. Charles Hamilton Houston to J. J. Kelly, Superintendent, Wise County Schools, March 31, 1936, Part I, Series C, Box 203, NAACPP.

64. Louis Campbell to Walter White, March 29, 1938, Part I, Series C, Box 281, NAACPP.

65. Louis Campbell to *Opportunity*, "Shut Out," March 29, 1938.

66. Goluboff, *Lost Promise of Civil Rights*, 181.

67. Arthur William Martin to National Office, December 28, 1936, Part I, Series D, Box 88, NAACPP.

68. Leslie Brown, *Upbuilding Black Durham*, 177.

69. *Journal of Negro Education*, Fourth Yearbook Number, July 1935, 290, Part I, Series C, Box 198, NAACPP.

70. Sidney R. Redmond to Charles Hamilton Houston, August 27, 1935, Part I, Series D, Box 94, NAACPP.

71. W. B. Gibbs Jr. to National Office, December 12, 1936, Part I, Series D, Box 88, NAACPP.

72. "Atlanta Pastor Urges Teachers to Fight Cuts," *Baltimore Afro-American*, April 7, 1934.

73. Editorial, "Robbery," *Baltimore Afro-American*, January 30, 1920.

74. Editorial, "Guilty and Proud of It," *Baltimore Afro-American*, March 20, 1937.

75. "Long Island School Children Strike When Insulted by Wealthy Taxpayer," *Chicago Defender*, November 12, 1938, 10.

76. "300 Pupils Strike to Protest Insult," *New York Times*, November 1, 1938, 13.

77. McCulloch v. Maryland, 17 U.S. 327 (1819).

Chapter 4

1. "Higher Education Pattern Held Costly to Missouri," *Baltimore Afro-American*, June 29, 1946.

2. "Ducking the Blow," *Baltimore Afro-American*, February 22, 1936.

3. Ibid.

4. Tushnet, *NAACP's Legal Strategy*, 8–11.

5. Lloyd Imes to NAACP, June 11, 1934, Part I, Series C, Box 157, NAACPP.

6. Arthur Spingarn to Walter White, May 9, 1934, Part I, Series C, Box 157, NAACPP.

7. Murray v. Maryland (aka *Murray v. Pearson*), 169 Md. 478 (1936).

8. Leland Ware, "The Story of *Brown v. Board of Education*: The Long Road to Racial Equality," in Olivas and Schneider, *Education Law Stories*.

9. Chad Garrison, "The Mystery of Lloyd Gaines," *Riverfront Times*, April 4, 2007, http://www.riverfronttimes.com/2007-04-04/news/the-mystery-of-lloyd-gaines/.

10. Petition for Certiorari, October 1937, 38–39, File 56 C.T. 1938, Box 1350, *Missouri ex rel. Gaines*, U.S. Supreme Court Appellate Case Files, SCR.

11. Abstract of the Record for Appellant, October 1937, 2, File 56 C.T. 1938, Box 1350, *Missouri ex rel. Gaines*, U.S. Supreme Court Appellate Case Files, SCR.

12. Ibid., 3.

13. Alternative Writ of Mandamus, 22, October 1937, File 56 C.T. 1938, Box 1350, *Missouri ex rel. Gaines*, U.S. Supreme Court Appellate Case Files, SCR.

14. Respondents' Return to the Alternative Writ of Mandamus, 23, October 1937, File 56 C.T. 1938, Box 1350, *Missouri ex rel. Gaines*, U.S. Supreme Court Appellate Case Files, SCR.

15. Ibid., 26.

16. Relator's Evidence, 57, October 1937, File 56 C.T. 1938, Box 1350, *Missouri ex rel. Gaines*, U.S. Supreme Court Appellate Case Files, SCR.

17. Ibid., 54.

18. Ibid.

19. Appellant's Motion for a Rehearing and Suggestions in Support Thereof for the Missouri Supreme Court, 3–4, October 1937, File 56 C.T. 1938, Box 1350, *Missouri ex rel. Gaines*, U.S. Supreme Court Appellate Case Files, SCR.

20. *Gaines v. Missouri*, S. Ct. Mo., October 1937, File 56 C.T. 1938, Box 1350, *Missouri ex rel. Gaines*, U.S. Supreme Court Appellate Case Files, SCR.

21. Petition for Certiorari, October 1937, File 56 C.T. 1938, Box 1350, *Missouri ex rel. Gaines*, U.S. Supreme Court Appellate Case Files, SCR.

22. *U.S. v. Virginia*, 518 U.S. 515 (1996), was a case in which the court struck down the Virginia Military Institute's males-only admission policy on equal-protection grounds, asserting that the many intangible but important benefits accruing from a VMI education could not be matched by a recently constructed state institution for female students.

23. Missouri ex rel. Gaines v. Canada, 305 U.S. 337, 349 (1938).

24. Tushnet, *NAACP's Legal Strategy*, 74.

25. Rev. A. R. Vanlandingham of Danville, VA, to Black, December 28, 1938, Box 257, *Gaines v. Missouri* File, JHUBP.

26. Joseph McLemore to Senator Michael Kinney, March 20, 1939, Part I, Series D, Box 95, NAACPP.

27. Box 5183 E.21, 22, *Sipuel v. Oklahoma*, U.S. Supreme Court Appellate Case Files, SCR; Okla. Const., 1941, rev. stat. 1945, § 455.

28. Okla. Const., 1941, rev. stat. 1945, § 456.

29. Ibid., § 457.

30. Petition to Oklahoma Supreme Court for Writ of Certiorari, October 1947, 3, File 368 C.T. 1947, 372 C.T. 1947, Box 5183 E.21, *Sipuel v. Oklahoma*, U.S. Supreme Court Appellate Case Files, SCR.

31. Ibid., 80–81.

32. Ibid., 87–88.

33. Ibid.

34. Ibid., 90.

35. "A Lesson From Oklahoma," *Chicago Tribune*, March 26, 1965.

36. McLaurin v. Oklahoma Regents, 70 U.S. 851, 853 (1950).

37. Ibid., 642.

38. *Sweatt v. Painter*, 339 U.S. 629, 634 (1950).

39. Charles Hamilton Houston, "Along the Highway," *Baltimore Afro-American*, July 17, 1948.

40. Missouri ex rel. Gaines v. Canada, 305 U.S. 337, 351 (1938).

41. Ibid., 353.

42. Frymer, "Race's Reality," 180. See also Goluboff, *Lost Promise of Civil Rights*.

43. "Grade School Bias Attacked," *Baltimore Afro-American*, November 18, 1950.

44. Briggs v. Elliott, 342 U.S. 350 (1952).

45. "South Carolina's Educational Revolution," pamphlet, Box 322, JHUBP.

46. Mendez v. Westminster School District of Orange County, 64 F. Supp. 544 (D.C. Cal. 1946).

47. "School Suits Would End Segregation in Delaware," *Baltimore Afro-American*, June 16, 1951.

48. "All Eyes on U.S. Supreme Court," *Baltimore Afro-American*, December 13, 1952.

49. "Wasting Taxpayer's Money: Could Save $5,232,490 by Ending Dual Schools," *Baltimore Afro-American*, March 8, 1952.

50. See Gotanda, "Critique."

51. Bell, "*Brown v. Board of Education*," 518–21.

52. Dudziak, *Cold War Civil Rights*.

53. See Balkin, "*Brown v. Board of Education*." See also "Round Table: *Brown v. Board of Education*."

54. Guinier, "From Racial Liberalism to Racial Literacy," 95.

55. Ibid., 112.

56. "Nonrecognition is a *technique*, not a principle of traditional substantive common law or constitutional interpretation. It addresses the question of race, not by examining the social realities or legal categories of race, but by setting forth an analytical methodology. This technical approach permits a court to describe, to accommodate, and then to ignore issues of subordination. This deflection from the substantive to the methodological is significant. Because the technique appears purely procedural, its normative, substantive impact is hidden. Color-blind application of the technique is important because it suggests a seemingly neutral and objective method of decisionmaking that avoids any consideration of race." Gotanda, "Critique," 17, 18.

57. For additional discussion on all sides of the *Brown* debate, see Patterson, "*Brown v. Board of Education*" (arguing that, while *Brown* was not a step backward, the belabored implementation of *Brown* actually led to slippage back into segregation in many areas); Rosenberg, *Hollow Hope* (arguing that cases such as *Brown* actually did little to impact social movements and effect change); Peller, "Cultural Imperialism, White Anxiety" (pointing out the political appropriation of the color-blind race model by conservatives); Tushnet, *NAACP's Legal Strategy* (discussing the contingent nature of the NAACP's legal strategies leading up to *Brown*); and Klarman, *From Jim Crow to Civil Rights* (arguing that the backlash generated by *Brown* may have been more important in galvanizing civil rights supporters than the legal ramifications of the decision itself). See also Foley, "Black, White and *Brown*," and Webb, "Continuity of Conservatism."

58. Korematsu v. U.S., 323 U.S. 214 (1944).

59. Robert Jackson, memo on segregation cases, December 7, 1953, Box 181, Folder 5, Segregation File, JRJP.

60. Ibid., 8–9.

61. Ibid.

62. Ibid., 24.

63. Ibid., 13.

64. Ibid., 15.

65. Ibid., 21.

66. Ibid.

67. See Dudziak, *Cold War Civil Rights*.

68. "Oklahoma Association of Negro Teachers Committee on Integration," Part I, Series A, Box 50, NULP.

69. For more on the Urban League's role in pushing the desegregation of Northern urban cities such as New York, see Biondi, *To Stand and Fight*, 241–49.

70. Lester Granger to Harold S. Vincent, Superintendent of Milwaukee Public Schools, November 5, 1954, Part I, Series A, Box 50, NULP.

Chapter 5

1. Harry A. Johnston, Enterprise, AL, to Robert Jackson, February 25, 1954, Box 181, Folder 5, Segregation File, JRJP.

2. See Holmes and Sunstein, *Cost of Rights*. For a discussion of the recent anti-property-tax movement since the 1970s, particularly in California, see Martin, *Permanent Tax Revolt*.

3. See Kruse, *White Flight*; Sokol, *There Goes My Everything*; and Lassiter, *Silent Majority*.

4. Kruse, "Politics of Race and Public Space," 612–13.

5. Crespino, "Civil Rights and the Religious Right," 90–91.

6. Clerks, memo on segregation cases, March 12, 1954, 7, Box 181, Folder 5, Segregation File, JRJP.

7. Ibid., 9.

8. Aura Lee of South Carolina to Hugo Black, March 23, 1956, Box 328, Segregation Correspondence, October Term 1956, JHUBP.

9. John D. Fristoe Jr., Kansas City, MO, to Earl Warren, November 20, 1953, Box 181, Folder 5, Segregation File, JRJP.

10. Joseph I. Reece of Pickens, SC, to Hugo Black, 1954, Box 322, JHUBP.

11. George W. Waring of Hartsville, SC, to Earl Warren (copied to Hugo Black), December 31, 1954, Box 322, JHUBP.

12. E. M. Hall of Memphis, TN, to Hugo Black, March 15, 1956, Box 328, Segregation Correspondence, October Term 1956, JHUBP.

13. B. W. Middlebrook, Manager of Dixie Paper Shell Pecan Exchange, Barnesville, GA, to Hugo Black, June 21, 1957, Box 328, Segregation Correspondence, October Term 1956, JHUBP.

14. S. P. Holland of Virginia to Hugo Black, undated, Segregation File, Box 322, JHUBP.

15. Israel Pickens of Mobile, AL, to Hugo Black, October 11, 1954, Box 322, JHUBP.

16. "Beware of the Gruesome Harvest That We Caused in Germany," unsigned, undated letter, Segregation File, Box 322, JHUBP.

17. Mrs. H. N. Hannon of Alabama, to Hugo Black, March 25, 1956, Box 328, Segregation Correspondence, October Term 1956, JHUBP.

18. "Alabama Joe" of Chicago to Hugo Black, September 6, 1956, Box 328, Segregation Correspondence, October Term 1956, JHUBP.

19. Anonymous from Detroit to Justice B. K. Roberts of Florida Supreme Court, March 23, 1957, Box 328, Segregation Correspondence, October Term 1956, JHUBP.

20. "Integration, U.S.A.," unsigned, undated letter, Box 328, Segregation Correspondence, October Term 1956, JHUBP.

21. Ibid.

22. For more on whiteness as a property right, see Harris, "Whiteness as Property," 1710–12; Lipsitz, *Possessive Investment in Whiteness*; and Roediger, *Wages of Whiteness*.

23. Tulio Vasquez of Rio Piedras, PR, to Hugo Black, October 25, 1954, Box 322, JHUBP.

24. Ibid.

25. Carl B. White, Washington, DC, to Robert Jackson, September 30, 1953, Box 181, Folder 5, Segregation File, JRJP.

26. Excerpt from address of Robert Whitehead to the Cosmopolitan Club of Norfolk, VA, October 21, 1954, Box 322, JHUBP.

27. Ibid.

28. See *San Antonio v. Rodriguez*. See also Siegel, "'Rule of Love,'" 2184, for a discussion about how civil rights reform may alleviate some inequalities but simultaneously can deny reformers the capacity to challenge the residual inequalities that still remain. For further discussion of how this is reflected in the *Brown* decision, see Guinier, "From Racial Liberalism to Racial Literacy."

29. Payne, "'Whole United States Is Southern!'"; Klarman, *From Jim Crow to Civil Rights*.

30. See Branch, *Parting the Waters*.

31. Table 21, Valuations of School Property in Prince Edward County, VA, School Property Evaluation, Box 126, *Davis v. Prince Edward County*, Records of the U.S. District Court for the Eastern District of Virginia, USDCVA.

32. Vanessa Siddle Walker, *Their Highest Potential*, 61.

33. Brief on Behalf of Appellants, September 22, 1964, Box 126, *Davis v. Prince Edward County*, Records of the U.S. District Court for the Eastern District of Virginia, USDCVA.

34. Undated editorial from *Star* newspaper in "Universal Education Not a Dixie Tradition," Box 369, Segregation File, JHUBP.

35. Louis Lautier, "Virginia's Choices: Obey Law or Destroy Its School System," *Baltimore Afro-American*, December 24, 1955.

36. Louis Lautier, "Virginia War against Gray Plan Continues," *Baltimore Afro-American*, January 7, 1956.

37. "Virginians May Quit Paying State Taxes if Governor Persists in Jim Crow Plan," *Baltimore Afro-American*, September 8, 1956.

38. "Orders Integration: Board Told No Delays Are Possible," *Baltimore Afro-American*, October 25, 1958.

39. "Preserve Our Public School System, Speakers Tell Perrow Commission," *Baltimore Afro-American*, March 21, 1959.

40. "South Carolina Ends 'Race Tag' on Funds for Schools," *Baltimore Afro-American*, January 20, 1962.

41. Record on Appeal, filed January 19, 1959, Box 127, *Allen v. Prince Edward County*, 24 Records of the U.S. District Court for the Eastern District of Virginia, USDCVA.

42. Ibid., 25.

43. Ibid., 29–30.

44. Brief on Behalf of Appellants, September 22, 1964, Box 126, *Davis v. Prince Edward County*, Records of the U.S. District Court for the Eastern District of Virginia, USDCVA.

45. Ibid.

46. Ibid., 10–11.

47. Ibid. See also *Lee v. Macon County Board of Alabama*, 483 F.2d 242 (1964) (grant-in-aid statutes used to discriminate ruled unconstitutional).

48. Brief on Behalf of Appellants, September 22, 1964, Box 126, *Davis v. Prince Edward County*, 11.

49. Allen v. County School Board of Prince Edward County, 207 F. Supp. 349, 355 (D.C. E. D. Va. 1962).

50. Griffin et al. v. County School Board of Prince Edward County, et al., 377 U.S. 218, 233 (1964).

51. Ibid., 233–34.

52. Mrs. Nadine Casey White to Hugo Black, January 12, 1970, Box 369, JHUBP.

53. Mrs. J. A. Bridges of Shreveport, LA, to Hugo Black, September 16, 1967, Box 369, JHUBP.

54. "Why Are You Punishing White America?," unsigned, undated notecard, Box 428, *Alexander v. Holmes County* File, JHUBP.

55. Mrs. Matt. J. Schmidt of Madison, MS, to the President, published in the *Clarion-Ledger*, 1969, Box 428, *Alexander v. Holmes County* File, JHUBP.

56. Mrs. Evelyn B. Scruggs of Raleigh, NC, to Hugo Black, September 5, 1969, Box 428, *Alexander v. Holmes County* File, JHUBP.

57. Mrs. A. Fawke of La Plata, MD, to Hugo Black, November 29, 1969, Box 428, *Alexander v. Holmes County* File, JHUBP.

58. Mrs. Dorothy Nicholas of Greenville, AL, to Hugo Black, November 20, 1969, Box 428, *Alexander v. Holmes County* File, JHUBP.

59. John Perkins, Mississippi House of Representatives, Meridian, MS, to Hugo Black, October 30, 1969, Box 428, *Alexander v. Holmes County* File, JHUBP.

60. *Charlotte Observer*, May 19, 1969, quoted in Lassiter, *Silent Majority*, 140.

61. "The Confederate Yankee" to Hugo Black, January 4, 1970, Box 428, *Alexander v. Holmes County* File, JHUBP.

62. Fred J. Hurst of Jackson, MS, to Richard Nixon (copied to Hugo Black), January 27, 1970, Box 428, *Alexander v. Holmes County* File, JHUBP.

63. M. Kenneth Shutts, Fort Myers, FL, to William Brennan, August 29, 1969, Part I, Box 243, JWBP.

64. G. M. Pegg, Denver, to William Brennan, September 11, 1969, Part I, Box 243, JWBP.

65. Mary J. Egan of Oklahoma City, to Harry Blackmun, September 9, 1969, Part I, Box 243, JWBP.

66. Donna Mickle of Winston-Salem, NC, to Harry Blackmun, August 20, 1970, Box 127, Folder 4, JHABLP.

67. C. Courtland Rudolph of Florida to Fifth Circuit Court of Appeals (copied to Harry Blackmun), August 18, 1970, Box 127, Folder 4, JHABLP.

68. Les Sullivan of Coral Springs, FL, to Harry Blackmun, September 3, 1970, Box 127, Folder 4, JHABLP.

69. P. Card, Woonsocket, RI, to Harry Blackmun, December 4, 1970, Part I, Box 242, JWBP.

70. Ibid.

71. Lester Maddox, Atlanta, to Harry Blackmun, October 14, 1970, Part I, Box 243, JWBP.

72. Mrs. Charles H. White, Winston-Salem, NC, to Harry Blackmun, August 20, 1970, Box 127, Folder 4, JHABLP.

73. Beverly Webel of Fort Lauderdale, FL, to Harry Blackmun, September 3, 1970, Box 127, Folder 4, JHABLP.

74. Philip Gamble to Harry Blackmun, telegram, September 4, 1970, Box 127, Folder 4, JHABLP.

75. "An Angry Taxpayer and Mother" from Woodhaven, Queens, to Harry Blackmun, June 9, 1970, Box 127, Folder 4, JHABLP.

76. Caroline C. Goodwin of Winston-Salem, NC, to Harry Blackmun, August 21, 1970, Box 127, Folder 4, JHABLP.

77. Mrs. H. F. Veiner of Gulfport, FL, to Harry Blackmun, August 21, 1970, Box 127, Folder 4, JHABLP.

78. Carolyn Gaither of Secla, GA, to Hugo Black, September 11, 1969, Box 428, *Alexander v. Holmes County* File, JHUBP.

79. Anne F. Rutledge to Harry Blackmun, August 31, 1970, Box 127, Folder 4, JHABLP.

80. Davis Lee, "A Negro Editor's Views," *Telegram* (Newark, NJ), 1954, Box 322, JHUBP.

81. "N.Y. Congressman Attacks Government Appropriations for Jim-Crow Schools," *Baltimore Afro-American*, February 28, 1953.

82. "Powell Defends His School Amendment," *Baltimore Afro-American*, May 12, 1956.

83. Louis Lautier, "Capital Spotlight: NAACP Feels Let-Down by Powell Decision," *Baltimore Afro-American*, March 15, 1958.

84. Louis Lautier, "In the Nation's Capital: Scribe Urges Halt to Jim Crow Aid," *Baltimore Afro-American*, March 8, 1958.

85. "Fight Seen Over Private School Aid," *Baltimore Afro-American*, January 17, 1959.

86. "Key Clarendon County Verdict Reverses Judge," *Baltimore Afro-American*, December 15, 1962.

87. "Okay to Desegregate," *Baltimore Afro-American*, September 22, 1962.

88. "U.S. 'Fattens' Jimcrow with Billions," *Baltimore Afro-American*, September 23, 1961.

89. "The Willis Wagons," *Daily Defender* (Chicago), May 29, 1962, 11.

90. "The American Promise," March 15, 1965, Johnson, *Public Papers*, 1:107, 281, 287.

91. Ironically, the first reference to "taxeaters" I can locate seems to be a Depression-era critique of corporate greed and individualist culture and a defense of government regulation against private business, published in 1934. See Harding, *TNT (These National Taxeaters)*.

92. Pennsylvania v. Board of Trusts, 353 U.S. 230 (1957).

93. Complaint in *Pennsylvania v. Girard College Trustees*, December 16, 1965, Box 513, *Pennsylvania v. Girard College Trustees*, USDCPA.

94. Will of Stephen Girard (Exhibit A), February 16, 1830, Box 513, *Pennsylvania v. Girard College Trustees*, USDCPA.

95. Complaint in *Girard College*, December 16, 1965.

96. Ibid.

97. Countryman, *Up South*, 167–77.

98. Ibid.

99. Complaint in *Girard College*, December 16, 1965.

100. Ibid.

101. Ibid.

102. Ibid.

103. Pennsylvania v. Board of Trusts, 353 U.S. 230 (1957).

104. Ibid.

105. Ibid.

106. Pretrial examinations of Karl R. Friedmann and John A. Diemand, March 31, 1967, Box 515, *Pennsylvania v. Brown et al.*, USDCPA.

107. Commonwealth of Pennsylvania v. Brown, 392 F.2d 120 (3d. Cir. 1968), *cert. denied*. See also *Commonwealth of Pennsylvania v. Board of Directors of City Trusts of City of Philadelphia*, 353 U.S. 230, 77 S. Ct. 806, 1 L.Ed.2d 792 (1957).

108. Commonwealth of Pennsylvania v. Brown, 392 F.2d 120 (3d. Cir. 1968), *cert. denied*.

109. Mrs. John Fawcett Jr., "Disappearing School Control," *Baltimore Afro-American*, July 25, 1970.

110. Kruse, "Politics of Race and Public Space," 630.

Chapter 6

1. Transcript of questioning of Mr. Biggins before Walter E. Hoffman, District Judge, February 11, 1957, Box 45, Case 489, *Atkins v. Newport News*, Records of the U.S. District Court for the Eastern District of Virginia, USDCVA.

2. See Lassiter, *Silent Majority*; and Kruse, *White Flight*.

3. See Sokol, *There Goes My Everything*.

4. Kruse and Sugrue, *New Suburban History*.

5. Freund, *Colored Property*.

6. See Nadasen, *Welfare Warriors*; Kornbluh, *Battle for Welfare Rights*; and Rhonda F. Williams, *Politics of Public Housing*.

7. Kornbluh, *Battle for Welfare Rights*.

8. Cohen, *Consumers' Republic*.

9. Levy v. Louisiana, 391 U.S. 68 (1968).

10. For more discussion of the links between the court's new concern for poverty and the simultaneous revolution in criminal justice procedures, see Klarman, "Civil Rights and Civil Liberties Revolutions."

11. Michelman, "Supreme Court 1968 Term."

12. Griffin v. Illinois, 351 U.S. 12 (1956).

13. Jeffries v. State, 9 Okla. Cr. 573, 576 (1913).

14. *Griffin*, 351 U.S. at 17.

15. Ibid., 18.

16. *Griffin v. Illinois* draft opinion, undated, Box 326, JHUBP.

17. *Griffin*, 351 U.S. at 35.

18. Gideon v. Wainwright, 372 U.S. 335 (1963); Douglas v. California, 372 U.S. 353 (1963).

19. *Douglas*, 372 U.S. at 359.

20. Ibid., 361–62.

21. Brief for Appellants, 1965, Box 67, Folder 1, *Harper v. Virginia* File, JTMP.

22. Ibid., 16.

23. Ibid., 20.

24. U.S. Amicus Brief, 1965, 14, Box 67, Folder 1, *Harper v. Virginia* File, JTMP.

25. Brief for Appellees, Appendix A, Deposition of C. H. Morrissett, September 27, 1965, Box 67, Folder 1, *Harper v. Virginia* File, JTMP.

26. Harper v. Virginia State Board of Elections, 383 U.S. 663 (1966).

27. Ibid., 669.

28. Ibid., 672.

29. "Edward P. Morgan and the News," transcript, ABC Radio, March 24, 1966, Box 388, *Harper v. Virginia* File, JHUBP.

30. Ibid.

31. McDonald v. Board of Elections, 394 U.S. 802 (1969).

32. Gertsmann, *Constitutional Underclass*, 56.

33. Lochner v. New York, 198 U.S. 45 (1905) (striking down regulations on bakers' hours as inappropriate interference with the right to free contract). The New Deal Court and specifically *U.S. v. Carolene Products* were pivotal in marking the end of *Lochner*-era jurisprudence, to the point that it became virtually a dirty word among judges and legal scholars and remains so even to this day, despite the arguments of some legal scholars that its underlying premises remain judicially validated.

34. For more on the backlash against the War on Poverty, see Quadagno, *Color of Welfare*. For more on the gendered and racialized nature of welfare politics and welfare organizing in general, see Mink, *Whose Welfare?*; and Kornbluh, *Battle for Welfare Rights*.

35. Goldberg v. Kelly, 397 U.S. 254 (1970).

36. Levinson, "When (Some) Republican Justices." 21.

37. *Goldberg*, 397 U.S. at 265.

38. George W. Beggs of Spokane, WA, to William Brennan, March 24, 1970, Part I, Box 209, *Goldberg v. Kelly* File, JWBP.

39. Zelizer, *Taxing America*, 153.

40. Anonymous letter to Hugo Black attached to a letter of November 25, 1969, Box 415, *Goldberg v. Kelly* File, JHUBP.

41. Felipe Luciano to Department of Social Services of Long Island City, NY, September 7, 1970, Box 415, *Goldberg v. Kelly* File, JHUBP.

42. Mrs. Ethel Krancer of Brooklyn to Hugo Black, March 24, 1970, Box 415, *Goldberg v. Kelly* File, JHUBP.

43. Boddie v. Connecticut, 401 U.S. 371 (1971).

44. Jack C. Landau, "High Court Cool to Idea, but Will Get Cases of Injustice Cause by Poverty," *Jersey Journal*, December 5, 1970, 7.

45. John A. Cox of Wolcott, NY, to Hugo Black, March 5, 1971, Box 429, *Boddie v. Connecticut* File, JHUBP.

46. Lydia P. Hill of Sierra Madre, CA, to Hugo Black, March 15, 1971, Box 429, *Boddie v. Connecticut* File, JHUBP.

47. Martha V. Savage of Lacey, WA, to Hugo Black, March 7, 1971, Box 429, *Boddie v. Connecticut* File, JHUBP.

48. Jeane Bown, Jackson Heights, NY, to Hugo Black, March 1971, Box 429, *Boddie v. Connecticut* File, JHUBP.

49. Helen M. Mattice of Haddon Heights NJ, to Warren E. Burger (copied to Hugo Black), March 3, 1971, Box 429, *Boddie v. Connecticut* File, JHUBP.

50. Hugo Black, "Indigents Cases," memo, 2nd draft, March 30, 1971, Box 432, October Term 1970, Indigents Cases File, JHUBP.

51. Ibid.

52. Ibid.

53. See Glendon, *Rights Talk.*

54. For more on the race-based history of ballot measures in California's history, see HoSang, *Racial Propositions.*

55. James v. Valtierra, 402 U.S. 137 (1971).

56. Harry Blackmun, memo on case, March 2, 1971, Box 126, Folder 4, *James v. Valtierra, Shaffer v. Valtierra* Files, JHABLP.

57. Daniel B. Edelman, memo on *Valtierra,* March 26, 1971, Box 126, Folder 4, *James v. Valtierra, Shaffer v. Valtierra* Files, JHABLP.

58. Daniel B. Edelman, memo, November 1, 1970, Box 126, Folder 4, *James v. Valtierra, Shaffer v. Valtierra* Files, JHABLP.

59. Daniel B. Edelman, bench memo, March 2, 1971, Box 126, Folder 4, *James v. Valtierra, Shaffer v. Valtierra* Files, JHABLP.

60. Ibid.

61. Ibid.

62. Ibid.

63. Ibid.

64. James v. Valtierra, 402 U.S. 137 (1971).

65. Hunter v. Erickson, 393 U.S. 385 (1969).

66. *Valtierra,* 402 U.S. at 141.

67. Ibid. See also HoSang, *Racial Propositions.*

68. *Valtierra,* 402 U.S. at 145.

69. See *Shelley v. Kraemer,* 334 U.S. 1 (1948); and Fair Housing Act, Title VIII of the Civil Rights Act of 1968, 42 U.S.C. § 3601.

70. Unsigned and undated letter, Box 432, *James, Shaffer v. Valtierra* File, JHUBP.

71. Alan Schultz of Pittsburgh, to Hugo Black, undated, Box 432, *James, Shaffer v. Valtierra* File, JHUBP.

72. Mrs. E. J. King of Mesa, AZ, to Hugo Black, May 5, 1971, Box 432, *James, Shaffer v. Valtierra* File, JHUBP.

73. Wayne H. Sherwood to Hugo Black, April 27, 1971, Box 432, *James, Shaffer v. Valtierra* File, JHUBP. The Kerner Commission was created by President Johnson in 1967 to investigate the causes of civil unrest in major U.S. cities. The report ultimately released in 1968 warned that the nation was moving toward "two societies, one black, one white—separate and unequal."

74. The last hypothetical in this list was in fact brought to the court almost exactly as predicted in the case of *City of Cleburne v. Cleburne Living Center, Inc.,* 473 U.S. 432 (1985).

75. C. Salkin of Passaic, NJ, to Hugo Black, April 27, 1971, Box 432, *James, Shaffer v. Valtierra* File, JHUBP.

76. Editorial, "Devotion to Democracy," *Pittsburgh Press*, May 7, 1971, 22, Box 432, *James, Shaffer v. Valtierra* Files, JHUBP.

77. Cooper v. Aaron, 358 U.S. 1 (1958).

78. Green v. County School Board of New Kent County, 391 U.S. 430, 438 (1968).

79. Alexander v. Board of Education of Holmes County, 396 U.S. 19, 20 (1969).

80. Edsall and Edsall, *Chain Reaction*.

81. Editorial, "The Court, the Law, and the Administration," *Washington Post*, October 31, 1969, A22.

82. Editorial, "Integration Double Standard," *Jackson (MS) Daily News*, January 21, 1970, 12.

83. Ibid.

84. David Lawrence, "North Target in School Race Fight," Publishers-Hall Syndicate, 1969, Box 428, *Alexander v. Holmes County* File, JHUBP.

85. Ibid.

86. E. K. Cargill of Macon, GA, to Hugo Black and Warren Burger, November 1, 1969, Box 428, *Alexander v. Holmes County* File, JHUBP.

87. J. D. Henkel Jr. of Alabama to Hugo Black, December 24, 1960, Box 369, JHUBP.

88. Mrs. James W. Marley of Montgomery, AL, to Hugo Black, August 12, 1964, Box 369, JHUBP.

89. Opal Ridenour and Nell Farrow of Oklahoma City to William Brennan, September 1, 1969, Part I, Box 203, JWBP.

90. For a history of busing struggles in Boston that would come to national attention after the *Swann* decision, see Formisano, *Boston against Busing*.

91. "Supreme Court Sets the Stage for Definitive Mixing Ruling," *Richmond Times-Dispatch*, September 1, 1970.

92. Spencer Rich, "Children Bused for Many Miles to Maintain Segregation," *Washington Post*, March 9, 1970.

93. Ibid.

94. "School Cases—Conference of October 17, 1970 (to Be Destroyed)," Box 127, Folder 3, JHABLP.

95. Ibid.

96. Ibid.

97. Ibid.

98. Ibid.

99. Black, draft opinion, dissenting in part and concurring in part, Box 436, *Swann v. Charlotte-Mecklenburg* File, October Term 1970, JHUBP.

100. Hugo Black to Chief Justice Warren E. Burger, March 25, 1971, Box 436, *Swann v. Charlotte-Mecklenburg* File, October Term 1970, JHUBP.

101. Richard W. Skillman, Burger's law clerk, memo on draft memo, Box 436, *Swann v. Charlotte-Mecklenburg* File, October Term 1970, JHUBP.

102. Jeffries, *Justice Lewis F. Powell, Jr.*, 284.

103. Ibid., 285.

104. Ibid., 292, 304.

105. Harry Blackmun, memo on Charlotte school cases, October 12, 1970, Box 127, Folder 3, JHABLP.

106. Ibid.

107. Robert E. Gooding Jr., memo on *Swann*, October 14, 1970, Box 127, Folder 3, JHABLP.

108. William Brennan, memo on *Swann*, March 1970, Part I, Box 243, JWBP.

109. Potter Stewart, draft dissent in *Swann*, February 1971, 9, Part I, Box 243, JWBP.

110. Ibid.

111. Ibid.

112. Ibid.

113. William O. Douglas, memo on *Swann*, December 10, 1970, Part I, Box 243, JWBP.

114. William O. Douglas, memo on *Swann*, October 20, 1970, 6, Box 1514, JWODP.

115. William Brennan to Chief Justice Warren E. Burger, March 23, 1971, Box 127, Folder 1, *Swann v. Charlotte-Mecklenburg*, JHABLP.

116. Thurgood Marshall to Chief Justice Warren E. Burger, April 8, 1971, Box 127, Folder 1, *Swann v. Charlotte-Mecklenburg*, JHABLP.

117. Swann v. Charlotte-Mecklenburg Board of Education, 402 U.S. 1 (1971). For a reaffirmation of virtually the same idea in language that is not far removed, see the majority opinion in *Parents Involved in Community Schools v. Seattle School District No. 1*, 551 U.S. 701 (2007).

118. *Swann*, 402 U.S. at 22–23.

Chapter 7

1. "School-Tax Suit Names the State," *New York Times*, October 2, 1971, 55.

2. Spano v. Board of Education of Lakeland Central School District, 68 Misc. 2d 804 (1972).

3. Van Dusartz v. Hatfield, 334 F. Supp. 870 (D. Minn. 1971); Serrano v. Priest, 487 P.2d 1241 (Cal. 1971), *cert. denied*, 432 U.S. 907 (1977); Robinson v. Cahill, 287 A.2d 187 (N.J. 1972), *cert. denied*, 414 U.S. 976 (1973). In each of these cases, race was rendered invisible or subsumed completely under a discussion of wealth discrimination. In *Robinson* the only mention of race was in reference to what the *Brown* decision was based on, even though the NAACP was an amicus curiae in the *Robinson* case as well.

4. National School Boards Association, *State School Finance Laws Handbook*.

5. Ibid., 39; Elementary and Secondary Education Act, Pub. L. No. 89-10, 79 Stat. 27, 20 U.S.C. ch. 70 (1965).

6. Goldstein, "Interdistrict Inequalities in School Financing," 504.

7. Serrano v. Priest, 5 Cal. 3d 584 (1971).

8. Van Dusartz v. Hatfield, 334 F. Supp. 870, 876 (1971).

9. Robinson v. Cahill, 118 N.J. Super. 223 (1972).

10. "8 Prince Ed. Pupils in Mass. Schools," *Baltimore Afro-American*, September 30, 1961.

11. Peters v. Boggs, 217 Ga. 471 (1961).

12. The headnote in Lexis-Nexis appeared at the time of this writing to inaccurately switch the objective of the *Boggs* case by describing it as a suit against the board of education to *stop* them from using Georgia taxes for the operation of segregated schools for black and white students. As the opinion itself makes very clear, the claim was in fact that the board of education was failing to maintain the segregated schools it was required to maintain under the Georgia State Constitution, and the plaintiffs sought to stop them from disbursing taxpayer funds for *nonsegregated* public schools in Atlanta.

13. Walton County Board of Education v. Academy of Social Circle, 229 Ga. 114 (1972).

14. See *In Re Applications for Reassignment: Boyd et al.*, 247 N.C. 413 (1958) (attempt of white "taxpayers" and parents to block reassignment of black students to formerly all-white schools dismissed by court); and *Griffith v. Board of Education of Yancey County*, 186 F. Supp. 511 (1960) (court rules in favor of reassignment of black children after parent taxpayers appeal school board denial).

15. Constantian v. Anson County, 244 N.C. 221 (1956).

16. Dilday v. Beaufort County Board of Education, 267 N.C. 438 (1966).

17. "$5 Million Grant to 10 Southern Schools," *Baltimore Afro-American*, May 21, 1966.

18. Boomer v. Beaufort County Board of Education, 294 F. Supp. 179 (1968).

19. Ibid.

20. Hall v. St. Helena Parish School Board, 197 F. Supp. 649 (1961).

21. Ibid., 662.

22. Bush v. Orleans Parish School Board, 190 F. Supp. 861 (1960).

23. Ibid., 867.

24. Poindexter v. Louisiana Financial Assistance Commission, 258 F. Supp. 158 (1966).

25. Ibid., 163.

26. Taylor v. Board of Education of City School District of City of New Rochelle, 191 F. Supp. 181 (1961).

27. "It Was Inevitable: Miss. Schools Desegregate," *Baltimore Afro-American*, September 12, 1964.

28. "200 Pupils Kick Lid Off School Bar in 3 New Areas," *Baltimore Afro-American*, September 5, 1964.

29. "On the School Front," *Baltimore Afro-American*, March 28, 1964.

30. Leonard Buder, "Education Board to Meet N.A.A.C.P.," *New York Times*, March 19, 1964, 23.

31. "New Fall Crisis Ahead as 25 New School Districts Integrate," *Baltimore Afro-American*, June 13, 1964. For the case, see *Fuller v. Volk*, 230 F. Supp. 25 (1964).

32. Blocker v. Board of Education of Manhasset, 229 F. Supp. 714 (1964).

33. Di Sano v. Storandt, 43 Misc. 2d 272 (1964).

34. Etter v. Littwitz et al., 49 Misc. 2d 934 (1966). See also *Etter v. Littwitz*, 47 Misc. 2d 473 (1965) (plaintiffs' pursuit of preliminary injunction in the case denied).

35. William K. Stevens, "Tax Revolt: 46,000 Shut Out of School," *New York Times*, September 14, 1970.

36. Irons, *Courage of Their Convictions*, 283.

37. Ibid., 284.

38. San Antonio Independent School District v. Rodriguez, 411 U.S. 1, 12 (1973).

39. Amicus Curiae Brief of ACLU et al. in *San Antonio ISD v. Rodriguez*, filed September 7, 1972, (on file with author, available through Curiae Project at Yale Law School Library).

40. Schragger, "*San Antonio v. Rodriguez*," 91.

41. Valencia, *Chicano Students and the Courts*, 93.

42. Ibid., 285.

43. Schragger, "*San Antonio v. Rodriguez*," 86.

44. Affidavit of Dr. Jose A. Cardenas in *Rodriguez*, 1970 (on file with author, available through Curiae Project at Yale Law School Library).

45. Haney-López, *White by Law*, 113.

46. Ibid.

47. When asked for his reaction to the Supreme Court decision in his case, Demetrio Rodriguez said, "The poor people have lost again." Irons, *Courage of Their Convictions*, 292.

48. U.S. Senate Select Committee on Equal Educational Opportunity, Testimony of Dr. Jóse A. Cárdenas, in *Equal Educational Opportunity*, pt. 4, *Mexican American Education*, 2443.

49. Summary of remarks made at the National Council for the Advancement of Education Writing Seminar on School Finance, October 3, 1972, by Mark Yudof, cocounsel for the *Rodriguez* plaintiffs, *Rodriguez* backgrounder from National Council for the Advancement of Education Writing, January 1973, Part I, Box 297, JWBP.

50. Korematsu v. U.S., 323 U.S. 214 (1944).

51. See *Skinner v. Oklahoma*, 316 U.S. 535 (1942) (ruling forced sterilization of habitual criminals unconstitutional for impinging on fundamental right to procreate); *Edwards v. California*, 314 U.S. 160 (1941) (ruling state statute prohibiting bringing an indigent person into the state unconstitutional because interstate travel constituted a fundamental right); *Boddie v. Connecticut*, 401 U.S. 371 (1971) (ruling that filing fee for divorce imposed on a fundamental right of marriage for indigent people).

52. Schragger, "*San Antonio v. Rodriguez*," 92.

53. Hernandez v. Texas, 347 U.S. 475 (1954). See Steven H. Wilson, "*Brown* over 'Other White,'" 145.

54. Wilson, "*Brown* over 'Other White,'" 151.

55. Montejano, *Anglos and Mexicans*, 252. For more on the history of whiteness and race relations in Texas, see Foley, *White Scourge*.

56. Steven H. Wilson, "*Brown* over 'Other White,'" 175.

57. San Miguel, "*Let All of Them Take Heed*," 175.

58. Cisneros v. Corpus Christi Independent School District, 324 F. Supp. 599, 601 (S.D. Tex. 1970).

59. Ibid.

60. Rodriguez v. San Antonio Independent School District, 337 F. Supp. 280 (W.D. Tex. 1971), *rev'd*, 411 U.S. 1 (1973).

61. *Rodriguez*, 337 F. Supp. at 282.

62. U.S. Senate Select Committee on Equal Educational Opportunity, Testimony of Sarah Carey, in *Equal Educational Opportunity*, pt. 16B, *Inequality in School Finance, Sept. 29–Oct. 5, 1971*, 6872.

63. Ibid., 6870.

64. Ibid.

65. U.S. Senate Select Committee on Equal Educational Opportunity, Testimony of James A. Kelly, in *Equal Educational Opportunity*, pt. 16A, *Inequality in School Finance Sept. 21–23, 1971*, 6681.

66. Ramsey Clark et al., Amicus Curiae Brief by Council of Great City Schools, filed August 21, 1972, ii.

67. Ibid.

68. Ibid., 16–17.

69. Ibid., 16.

70. Ibid., 17.

71. Armando De Leon et al., Amicus Curiae Brief by La Raza/ACLU, filed September 7, 1972, 11.

72. Ibid., 22.

73. Sracic, "*Brown* Decision's Other Legacy," 216.

74. Guinier, "From Racial Liberalism to Racial Literacy," 101.

75. Dudziak, *Cold War Civil Rights*, 243.

76. Lewis F. Powell Jr., "Attack on American Free Enterprise System," memo to Eugene B. Sydnor Jr., August 23, 1971, Box 51-167, JLFPP, http://law.wlu.edu/deptimages/Powell%20Archives/PowellMemorandumTypescript.pdf.

77. Lyman Johnson, "Justice Powell and Free Enterprise," *Richmond Times-Dispatch*, August 24, 2011, http://www.timesdispatch.com/news/johnson-justice-powell-and-free-enterprise/article_81f16d98-369f-502a-b84c-55835324d612.html.

78. Powell, "Attack on American Free Enterprise," 2.

79. Jeffries, *Justice Lewis F. Powell, Jr.*, 166–67.

80. Sracic, "*Brown* Decision's Other Legacy," 217.

81. Powell, "Attack on American Free Enterprise," 2.

82. Sracic, "*Brown* Decision's Other Legacy," 217.

83. Lewis F. Powell Jr. to Larry Hammond, memo, October 9, 1972, 1–3, *San Antonio v. Rodriguez*, Series 10.6, Supreme Court Case Files, Box 8-153, JLFPP.

84. Ibid.

85. George W. Liebmann et al., Amicus Curiae Brief in Support of Jurisdiction, filed April 18, 1972, 6 (on file with author, available through Curiae Project at Yale Law School Library).

86. Shale C. Stiller et al., Amicus Curiae Brief of State Government Representatives, filed July 22, 1972, 68 (on file with author, available through Curiae Project at Yale Law School Library).

87. Ibid., 25, 44.

88. Ibid., 54.

89. Ibid., 53.

90. Coons, Clune, and Sugarman, *Private Wealth and Public Education*.

91. Stiller et al., Amicus Brief, 37.

92. Ibid., 47, citing Coleman, "The Struggle for Control of Education," in Bowers (ed.), *Education and Social Policy: Local Control of Education*, 64, at 77–78 (1970).

93. Ibid.

94. Stiller et al., Amicus Brief, 83.

95. Ibid., 83–88.

96. Oral arguments in *San Antonio v. Rodriguez*, presented October 12, 1972, *Oyez*, accessed January 2, 2014, http://www.oyez.org/cases/1972/71-1332.

97. James W. Ziglar to Harry Blackmun, bench memo on *Rodriguez*, October 4, 1972, Box 161, Folder 5, *Rodriguez* File, JHABLP.

98. Initial Vote Chart, Undated, *San Antonio v. Rodriguez*, Series 10.6, Supreme Court Case Files, Box 8-153, JLFPP.

99. Ibid.

100. Lewis F. Powell Jr. to J. Harvie Wilkinson III, memo, August 30, 1972, *San Antonio v. Rodriguez*, Series 10.6, Supreme Court Case Files, Box 8-153, JLFPP.

101. Undated conference notes, *San Antonio v. Rodriguez*, Series 10.6, Supreme Court Case Files, Box 8-153, JLFPP.

102. "Racial Discrimination" notes, Undated, *San Antonio v. Rodriguez*, Series 10.6, Supreme Court Case Files, Box 8-153, JLFPP.

103. Lewis F. Powell Jr. to Larry Hammond, memo, October 12, 1972, *San Antonio v. Rodriguez*, Series 10.6, Supreme Court Case Files, Box 8-153, JLFPP.

104. J. A. Weiss, "Try to Affirm," memo to Harry Blackmun, September 20, 1972, Box 161, Folder 5, *Rodriguez* File, JHABLP.

105. San Antonio Independent School District v. Rodriguez, 411 U.S. 1, 53 (1973).

106. Plyler v. Doe, 457 U.S. 202 (1982) (Powell joins Marshall, Blackmun, Brennan, and Stevens in a decision that a Texas statute completely denying school enrollment to children of undocumented aliens violated the equal protection clause).

107. Ibid., 213.

108. *Rodriguez*, 411 U.S. at 4.

109. Ibid., 56.

110. Ibid., 57.

111. Ibid., 57.

112. Undated revisions, *San Antonio v. Rodriguez*, Series 10.6, Supreme Court Case Files, Box 8-153, JLFPP.

113. *Rodriguez*, 411 U.S. at 94.

114. Ibid., 94–95.

115. Ibid., 95.

116. Jack Greenberg, et al, Brief for the NAACP Legal Defense Fund as Amicus Curiae Supporting Appellees, 7 (on file with author).

117. For a thoughtful examination of this trend in other legal cases, see Welke, "When All the Women Were White"; and Angela P. Harris, "Race and Essentialism" (particularly her analysis of *Santa Clara Pueblo v. Martinez*, 436 U.S. 49 (1978)).

118. Crenshaw, "Mapping the Margins," 1297–98.

119. See Gotanda, "Critique of 'Color-Blind Constitutionalism."

120. Crenshaw, "Mapping the Margins," 1298.

121. U.S. Senate Select Committee on Equal Educational Opportunity, Testimony of Mario Obledo, in *Equal Educational Opportunity*, pt. 4, *Mexican American Education*, 2522.

122. Prince v. Board of Education of Central Consolidated Independent School District No. 22, 88 N.M. 548 (1975).

123. Gomillion v. Lightfoot, 364 U.S. 339 (1960).

124. Kramer v. Union School District, 395 U.S. 621 (1969).

125. Millonzi, "Education as a Right," 1290–91.

126. Jerome Zukotsky, "Taxes and Schools," *New Republic*, June 17, 1972, 20–21.

Conclusion

1. United Nations Declaration of the Rights of the Child, G.A. res. 1386 (XIV), 14 U.N. GAOR Supp. (No. 16) at 19, U.N. Doc. A/4354 (1959).

2. For a database of educational rights by country and constitution, see http://www.unesco.org/new/en/education/themes/leading-the-international-agenda/right-to-education/database/, accessed July 4, 2017. For additional international context, see http://www.right-to-education.org/, accessed July 4, 2017.

3. See *San Antonio Independent School District v. Rodriguez*, 411 U.S. 1 (1973).

4. For a complete picture of the wide disparities in residential property taxes, see the 2013 report by the Brookings Institution: Benjamin H. Harris and Brian David Moore, *Residential Property Taxes in the United States*, Urban-Brookings Tax Policy Center, November 18, 2013, http://www.urban.org/research/publication/residential-property-taxes-united-states.

5. On deepening segregation for black and Latino students since the 1980s, see Orfield and Lee, *Brown at 50*.

6. Reardon et al., "'Brown Fades,'" 876.

7. Cubberley, *Public Education in the United States*, 743–46.

8. Ibid., 746.

9. U.S. Department of Health, Education and Welfare, *State Constitutional Provisions*, 6. The states requiring that education be "open to all" were Arizona, Arkansas, California, Colorado, Indiana, Iowa, New Mexico, New York, North Carolina, North Dakota, Oklahoma, South Dakota, Tennessee, Utah, Virginia, Washington, and Wyoming. Only Colorado, Indiana, North Carolina, South Dakota, and Tennessee mention equality or equal opportunity.

10. For information on the current status of school finance litigation and state-by-state details, see School Funding Info, Campaign for Educational Equity at Teachers College, Columbia University, accessed July 4, 2017, http://schoolfunding.info/.

11. Evans, Murray, and Schwab, "School Houses, Court Houses."

12. Yvonne Burke, "School Finance," *Baltimore Afro-American*, October 2, 1976.

13. Orfield and Lee, *Why Segregation Matters*, 15.

14. Orfield and Eaton, *Dismantling Desegregation*.

15. Orfield, *Dropouts in America*.

16. Kozol, *Shame of the Nation*, 322.

17. Richard Ilgenfritz, "Is Lower Merion Spying on Students within Their Home?," *Times Herald*, Norristown, PA, February 18, 2010.

18. Washington v. Davis, 426 U.S. 229, 240 (1976) (plaintiff class alleged that a written police department personnel test discriminated against African Americans because an unusually high number of African Americans were excluded based on the test; court demanded proof of invidious intent and held for police department since there was no regulation explicitly excluding applicants based on race).

19. Haney-López, *White by Law*, 113. See also Haney-López, *Racism on Trial*, 244, for the argument that the court since *Washington v. Davis* "seems to be developing an Equal Protection jurisprudence that defines racism both too narrowly (race must be openly considered) and too broadly (every explicit consideration of race constitutes racism)."

20. Siegel, "Equal Protection No Longer Protects," 1113. See also Boger, "Willful Colorblindness."

21. Milliken v. Bradley, 418 U.S. 717 (1974). For the first major decision on Northern school segregation, see *Keyes v. Denver School District No. 1*, 413 U.S. 189 (1973).

22. It is also interesting to note that in this case, as in many others, the only schools characterized as "segregated" are the all-black or mostly black schools, suggesting that all-white schools were not viewed as "segregated" despite their homogenous racial makeup.

23. Wilkinson, *From "Brown" to "Bakke,"* 220–21.

24. Constance Baker Motley, quoted from *New York Times*, May 13, 1974, in Patterson, *"Brown v. Board of Education,"* 168.

25. Wilkinson, *From "Brown" to "Bakke,"* 221.

26. See *Baker v. Carr*, 369 U.S. 186 (1962).

27. Lewis F. Powell Jr. to Chief Justice Warren Burger, memo, June 5, 1974, 9, Box 187, Folder 2, *Milliken* File, JHABLP.

28. Second draft of opinion, June 14, 1974, 24, Box 187, Folder 2, *Milliken* File, JHABLP.

29. Robert Richter to Harry Blackmun, memo on second draft of chief justice's opinion, June 12, 1974, Box 187, Folder 2, *Milliken* File, JHABLP. This definition of school districts as rights-bearing entities comes intriguingly close to the legal fiction of "corporate personhood." See *Citizens United v. FEC*, 588 U.S. 310 (2010).

30. "Read in Court by Justice Marshall," July 25, 1974, Box 131, Folder 4, *Milliken* File, JTMP.

31. See HoSang, "Triumph of Racial Liberalism."

32. Byrd Amendment, 20 U.S.C. S.1714(a); Eagleton-Biden Amendment, 20 U.S.C. S.1652 (Supp. 1984).

33. Salomone, *Equal Education under Law*, 63.

34. Crawford v. Board of Education, 458 U.S. 527 (1982). See also *Pasadena City Board of Education v. Spangler*, 427 U.S. 424 (1976); *Dayton Board of Education v. Brinkman*, 433 U.S. 406 (1977); and *Washington v. Seattle School District No. 1*, 458 U.S. 457 (1982).

35. McGirr, *Suburban Warriors*, 237.

36. HoSang, "Triumph of Racial Liberalism," 301–2.

37. Ibid.

38. See HoSang, *Racial Propositions*.

39. McGirr, *Suburban Warriors*, 238.

40. Serrano v. Priest II, 18 Cal. 3d 728 (1976). Fischel argues that these "homevoters" were motivated by the desire to protect their high property values from the loss of superior local school districts, whereas McGirr's evidence points to economic fears among many suburbanites that property values had in fact inflated so high as to create an untenable tax burden. Fischel, *Homevoter Hypothesis*, 109–27. For a response to Fischel that relies on evidence of voter attitudes and motivations that indicate voters did not vote on Proposition 13 in reaction to the *Serrano* chain of litigation, see Martin, "Taxpayer Revolt?," 525.

41. Plyler v. Doe, 457 U.S. 202 (1982).

42. Lewis Powell to William Brennan et al., memo on *Plyler*, January 30, 1982, Box 154, Folder 6, *Plyler* File, JHABLP.

43. Gerhard Lenski of Chapel Hill, NC, to Harry Blackmun, July 22, 1982, Box 154, Folder 6, *Plyler* File, JHABLP.

44. Jean S. Hale of Sweet Home, OR, to Harry Blackmun, July 21, 1982, Box 154, Folder 6, *Plyler* File, JHABLP.

45. Dan Belz, "Poor Alarmed by Ruling on Education of Aliens," *Washington Post*, Box 154, Folder 6, *Plyler* File, JHABLP.

46. Hugh M. Patterson of Houston to Lewis F. Powell Jr. et al., June 29, 1982, Box 154, Folder 6, *Plyler* File, JHABLP.

47. G. Ross Frazer of Houston to Harry Blackmun, July 21, 1982, Box 154, Folder 6, *Plyler* File, JHABLP.

48. Kadrmas v. Dickinson, 487 U.S. 450 (1988).

49. Emily Buss, memo on case, May 30, 1988, Box 503, Folder 86, *Kadrmas* File, JHABLP.

50. Ibid.

51. Charlie Savage, "Kagan's Link to Marshall Cuts 2 Ways," *New York Times*, May 12, 2010.

52. See *Board of Education of Oklahoma v. Dowell*, 489 U.S. 237 (1991); *Freeman v. Pitts*, 503 U.S. 467 (1992); and *Missouri v. Jenkins (Missouri II)*, 515 U.S. 70 (1995).

53. Edgewood Independent School District v. Kirby, 777 S.W.2d 391 (Tex. 1989).

54. Francisco Vara-Orta, "MALDEF Files School Finance Lawsuit against State," *My SA*, December 13, 2011, http://www.mysanantonio.com/news/education/article /MALDEF-files-school-finance-lawsuit-against-state-2400788.php.

55. Petitioner's Complaint, *Edgewood Independent School District v. Scott* (2011), http://www.maldef.org/assets/pdf/Original%20Petition.FINAL.12-13-11.pdf.

56. Ibid.

57. Morgan Smith, "An Updated Guide to Texas School Finance Lawsuits," *Texas Tribune*, July 3, 2012, http://www.texastribune.org/2012/07/03/an-updated-guide-to -texas-school-finance-lawsuits/.

58. Diane Rado, "Chicago Urban League settles lawsuit with state over school funding," *Chicago Tribune*, February 17, 2017.

59. Complaint, Chicago Urban League v. Illinois, August 19, 2008, 13, https://www
.thechicagourbanleague.org/cms/lib/IL07000264/Centricity/Domain/53/Complaint
.pdf, accessed July 5, 2017.

60. Chicago Urban League et al. v. Illinois State Board of Education (Cir. Ct.
Cook Cty., Ill., April 15, 2009).

61. See *Committee for Educational Rights v. Edgar*, 672 N.E.2d 1178 (1996).

62. Kristen Mack and Tara Malone, "Suit to Target School Funding," *Chicago Tribune,* March 23, 2010, http://articles.chicagotribune.com/2010-03-23/news/ct-met
-school-funding-lawsuit-20100323_1_education-funding-system-local-tax-property
-poor-districts.

63. Carr v. Koch, 2012 Ill. 113414 (S. Ct. November 29, 2012).

64. McCleary v. State, 84362-7 WA (2012).

65. Paige Cornwell, "Catch Up with the McCleary School-Funding Case," *Seattle
Times*, September 6, 2016, http://www.seattletimes.com/education-lab/qa-on-mccleary
-school-funding-case/.

66. Abbeville County Sch. Dist. v. State, 515 S.E.2d 535, 540 (1999).

67. Dumas, "Contesting White Accumulation"; Parents Involved in Community
Schools v. Seattle School District No. 1, 551 U.S. 701 (2007).

68. Parents Involved in Community Schools (2007), 721.

69. Kozol, *Shame of the Nation*, 259. Kozol goes on to argue, "Yet separate but equal
obviously has to have a place within these equity or adequacy cases. Given realities
of politics and precedent, there is no other argument attorneys plausibly can make.
Whether they ask for equal, adequate, high adequate, or basic minimal provision,
they are asking for post-modern versions of the promise *Plessy* made and the next
60 years of history betrayed." Ibid., 260. For more on resegregation of public schools
after *Brown*, see Orfield and Eaton, *Dismantling Desegregation*.

70. Cohen, *Consumers' Republic*, 251.

71. Milliken v. Bradley, 418 U.S. 717 (1974).

72. See Orfield and Eaton, *Dismantling Desegregation*.

73. James A. Gross, "Human Rights Perspective," 919.

74. Julianne Hing, "Kelley Williams-Bolar's Long, Winding Fight to Educate Her
Daughters," *Colorlines*, May 16, 2012, http://colorlines.com/archives/2012/05/kelley
_williams_bolar_school_choice.html.

75. Jeff St. Clair, "Ohio Case: The 'Rosa Parks Moment' for Education?," *NPR: All
Things Considered*, January 28, 2011, http://www.npr.org/2011/01/28/133307552/ohio
-case-the-rosa-parks-moment-for-education; Bob Dyer, "'Poor Mom' Reappears in
Connecticut," *Akron Beacon Journal*, May 3, 2011, http://www.ohio.com/news/dyer
/poor-mom-reappears-in-connecticut-1.208197.

76. St. Clair, "Ohio Case."

77. Timothy Williams, "Jailed for Switching Her Daughters' School District,"
New York Times, September 26, 2011, http://www.nytimes.com/2011/09/27/us/jailed
-for-switching-her-daughters-school-district.html.

78. John Higgins, "Williams-Bolar Becomes New Voice for School Choice," *Ohio
Beacon Journal*, February 22, 2012, http://www.ohio.com/news/local-news/williams
-bolar-becomes-new-voice-for-school-choice-1.266320.

79. David Gurliacci, "Tanya McDowell: 'When Does It Become a Crime to Seek a Better Education for Your Child?,'" *Norwalk (CT) Patch*, April 25, 2011, http://norwalk .patch.com/articles/tanya-mcdowell-when-does-it-become-a-crime-to-seek-a -better-education-for-your-child.

80. Moina Noor, "Mother Defends Enrolling Son in Norwalk School," *Norwalk (CT) Daily Voice*, April 22, 2011, http://norwalk.dailyvoice.com/news/mother -defends-enrolling-son-norwalk-school.

81. Graham Smith, "Homeless Mother Who Sent Six-Year-Old Son to Better School in the Wrong Town Jailed for Five Years," *Daily Mail*, March 1, 2012, http://www.dailymail.co.uk/news/article-2108733/Homeless-mother-Tanya -McDowell-sent-son-6-better-school-wrong-town-jailed-years.html.

82. Margaret Newkirk, "Baton Rouge's Rich Want New Town to Keep Poor Pupils Out: Taxes," *Bloomberg News*, February 5, 2014, http://www.bloomberg.com /news/2014-02-06/baton-rouge-s-rich-want-new-town-to-keep-poor-pupils-out -taxes.html.

83. Brian Lawson, "Appeals Court Takes Long Look at Alabama Property Tax Lawsuit That Alleges Racial Discrimination," *AL.com*, December 6, 2012, http://blog .al.com/breaking/2012/12/appeals_court_takes_long_look.html.

84. Dan Carsen, "Lynch v. Alabama," *WBHM.org*, May 11, 2011, http://www .wbhm.org/News/2011/LynchVsAlabama.html.

85. Brian Lawson, "Federal Appeals Court Rules Alabama Property Tax System Is Not Discriminatory, Rejects Lawsuit Filed by Poor Schoolchildren," *AL.com*, January 10, 2014, http://blog.al.com/breaking/2014/01/federal_appeals_court_rules_al.html.

86. David Leonhardt, "Yes, 47% of Households Owe No Taxes. Look Closer," *New York Times*, April 13, 2010.

87. Anne Lowrey, "Behind the 'People Who Pay No Income Tax,'" *New York Times*, September 17, 2012.

88. Julie Borowski, "Abolishing the Department of Education Is the Right Thing to Do," *Tea Party Tribune*, September 19, 2011, http://www.teapartytribune.com /2011/09/19/abolishing-the-department-of-education-is-the-right-thing-to-do/.

89. "News Hour: What Will Betsy DeVos' Focus on School Choice Mean for Public Education?," *PBS*, January 17, 2017, http://www.pbs.org/newshour/bb/will -betsy-devos-focus-school-choice-mean-public-education/; Yamichie Alcindor, "After Backlash, DeVos Backpedals on Remarks on Historically Black Colleges," *New York Times*, February 18, 2017.

90. Dorothy A. Brown, "Race and Class Matters," 147.

91. Carl Davis et al., *Who Pays?* The ten most regressive state tax systems in this analysis are Washington, Florida, South Dakota, Tennessee, Texas, Illinois, Arizona, Nevada, Pennsylvania, and Alabama.

92. "California Voters to Choose Which Tax Proposals Will Pay for Schools on November 6," *Citizens for Tax Justice*, October 11, 2012, http://www.ctj.org /taxjusticedigest/archive/2012/10/california_voters_to_choose_wh.php.

93. Robertson Williams, "Why Do People Pay No Federal Income Tax?," *Tax Policy Center*, July 27, 2011, http://taxvox.taxpolicycenter.org/2011/07/27/why-do -people-pay-no-federal-income-tax-2/.

94. Lowrey, "'People Who Pay No Income Tax.'"

95. "Dividing Lines: School District Borders in the United States," *EdBuild*, accessed July 24, 2015, http://maps.edbuild.org/DividingLines.html#.

96. Kozol, *Savage Inequalities*, 207. The taxing inequalities are reflective of a broad trend toward privatization and acceptance of educational inequalities. Schools in Washington, Colorado, Arizona, Indiana, Oregon, and elsewhere have introduced the practice of canceling full-day kindergarten—within public school systems—except for those whose parents can supply private funds to pay for it. See also Kozol, *Shame of the Nation*, 308.

Bibliography

Manuscripts and Archives

Harvard Law School, Langdell Library, Cambridge, MA
    Papers of Justice Felix Frankfurter (JFFP)
    Papers of Justice Louis Brandeis (JLBP)
Library of Congress, Manuscript Division, Washington, DC
    Papers of Justice Earl Warren (JEWP)
    Papers of Justice Harold Burton (JHBUP)
    Papers of Justice Harry Blackmun (JHABLP)
    Papers of Justice Hugo Black (JHUBP)
    Papers of Justice Melville Fuller (JMFP)
    Papers of Justice Robert Jackson (JRJP)
    Papers of Justice Thurgood Marshall (JTMP)
    Papers of Justice William Brennan (JWBP)
    Papers of Justice William O. Douglas (JWODP)
    Papers of the NAACP, Parts I, II and III (NAACPP)
    Papers of the National Urban League, Parts I, III and VI (NULP)
    Papers of the National Urban League, Southern Regional Office (NULP, SRO)
National Archives and Records Administration, Mid-Atlantic Region, Philadelphia, PA
    Records of the U.S. District and Other Courts in Delaware, 1790–1961, RG 21
    Records of the U.S. District and Other Courts in Virginia, 1793–1956, RG 21
      (USDCVA)
    Records of the U.S. District Court, Eastern District of Pennsylvania, 1938–1980,
      RG 21 (USDCPA)
National Archives and Records Administration, Washington, DC
    Records of District Courts of the United States, RG 21
    Supreme Court Records, RG 267 (SCR)
Temple University Urban Archives, Philadelphia, PA
    Urban League of Philadelphia Archives
Washington and Lee Law School Library, Lexington, VA
    Justice Lewis F. Powell, Jr. Papers (JLFPP)

Legal Cases

Abbeville County Sch. Dist. v. State, 515 S.E.2d 535, 540 (1999)
Alexander v. Board of Education of Holmes County, 396 U.S. 19, 20 (1969)
Allen v. County School Board of Prince Edward County, 207 F. Supp. 349, 355 (D.C. E. D. Va. 1962)

Baker v. Carr, 369 U.S. 186 (1962)

Berea College v. Commonwealth of Kentucky, 211 U.S. 45 (1908)

Blocker v. Board of Education of Manhasset, 229 F. Supp. 714 (1964)

Board of Education of City of Guthrie v. Excise Board of Logan County, 86 Okla. 24 (1922)

Board of Education of Oklahoma v. Dowell, 489 U.S. 237 (1991)

Board of Education of the City of Ottawa v. Leslie Tinnon, 26 Kan. 1 (1881)

Board of Trustees of the Graded Free Colored Common School of Mayfield, Kentucky v. Board of Trustees of the Graded White Common School of Mayfield, Kentucky, 181 Ky. 303 (1918)

Boddie v. Connecticut, 401 U.S. 371 (1971)

Boomer v. Beaufort County Board of Education, 294 F. Supp. 179 (1968)

Bradwell v. Illinois, 83 U.S. 130 (1873)

Briggs v. Elliott, 342 U.S. 350 (1952)

Brown v. Board of Education of Topeka, 347 U.S. 483 (1954)

Brown v. Board of Education of Topeka II, 349 U.S. 294 (1955)

Bryant v. Barnes, Tax Collector, 144 Miss. 732 (S. Ct. 1925)

Bush v. Orleans Parish School Board, 190 F. Supp. 861 (1960)

Carr v. Koch, 2012 Ill. 113414 (S. Ct. November 29, 2012)

Chase v. Stephenson, 71 Ill. 383 (January 1874)

Cheeks v. Wirt, 203 Ind. 121 (1931)

Chicago Urban League et al. v. Illinois State Board of Education (Cir. Ct. Cook Cty., Ill., April 15, 2009)

Chrisman v. City of Brookhaven, 70 Miss. 477 (S. Ct. October 1892)

Cisneros v. Corpus Christi Independent School District, 324 F. Supp. 599 (S.D. Tex. 1970)

City of Cleburne v. Cleburne Living Center, Inc., 473 U.S. 432 (1985)

Civil Rights Cases, 109 U.S. 3 (1883)

Clark v. Board of Directors, 24 Iowa 266 (June 1868)

Claybrook v. City of Owensboro, 16 F. 297 (Dist. Ct., D. Ky. 1883)

Claybrook v. Owensboro, 23 F. 634 (Circ. Ct., D. Ky. March 1884)

Committee for Educational Rights v. Edgar, 672 N.E.2d 1178 (1996)

Commonwealth of Pennsylvania v. Brown, 392 F.2d 120 (3d. Cir. 1968), *cert. denied*

Constantian v. Anson County, 244 N.C. 221 (1956)

Cooper v. Aaron, 358 U.S. 1 (1958)

Cory v. Carter, 48 Ind. 327 (November 1874)

County Board of Education of Meade County v. Bunger, 240 Ky. 155 (1931)

Craig v. Boren, 429 U.S. 190 (1976)

Crawford v. Board of Education, 458 U.S. 527 (1982)

Cumming v. Board of Education of Richmond County, 175 U.S. 528 (1899)

DaimlerChrysler Corp. v. Cuno, 547 U.S. 332 (2006)

Dallas v. Fosdick, 40 How. Pr. 249 (S. Ct. N.Y. February 1869)

Dandridge v. Williams, 397 U.S. 471 (1970)

Davenport et al. v. Cloverport et al., 72 F. 689 (Dist. Ct., D. Ky. February 1896)

Dayton Board of Education v. Brinkman, 433 U.S. 406 (1977)

Dilday v. Beaufort County Board of Education, 267 N.C. 438 (1966)

Di Sano v. Storandt, 43 Misc. 2d 272 (1964)

Douglas v. California, 372 U.S. 353 (1963)

Edgewood Independent School District v. Kirby, 777 S.W.2d 391 (Tex. 1989)

Edwards v. California, 314 U.S. 160 (1941)

Enos van Camp v. Board of Education of Logan, 9 Ohio St. 406 (S. Ct.
    November 1859)

Etter v. Littwitz, 47 Misc. 2d 473 (1965)

Etter v. Littwitz et al., 49 Misc. 2d 934 (1966)

Flast v. Cohen, 392 U.S. 83 (1968)

Freeman v. Pitts, 503 U.S. 467 (1992)

Frothingham v. Mellon, 262 U.S. 447 (1923)

Fuller v. Volk, 230 F. Supp. 25 (1964)

Gideon v. Wainwright, 372 U.S. 335 (1963)

Gleason v. University of Minnesota, 104 Minn. 359 (1928)

Gomillion v. Lightfoot, 364 U.S. 339 (1960)

Gong Lum v. Rice, 275 U.S. 78 (1927)

Green v. County School Board of New Kent County, 391 U.S. 430, 438 (1968)

Griffin et al. v. County School Board of Prince Edward County, et al., 377 U.S. 218
    (1964)

Griffin v. Illinois, 351 U.S. 12 (1956)

Griffith v. Board of Education of Yancey County, 186 F. Supp. 511 (1960)

Hall v. St. Helena Parish School Board, 197 F. Supp. 649 (1961)

Harper v. Virginia State Board of Elections, 383 U.S. 663 (1966)

Hernandez v. Texas, 347 U.S. 475 (1954)

Hickman College v. Trustees Colored District, 111 Ky. 944 (1901)

Hobson v. Hansen, 269 F. Supp. 401 (1967)

Hunter v. Erickson, 393 U.S. 385 (1969)

In Re Applications for Reassignment: Boyd et al., 247 N.C. 413 (1958)

James v. Valtierra, 402 U.S. 137 (1971)

J. C. Puitt v. Commissioners of Gaston County, Raleigh, 94 N.C. 709 (1886)

Jeffries v. State, 9 Okla. Cr. 573 (1913)

Jones v. Board of Education of City of Muskogee, 90 Okla. 233 (1923)

Kadrmas v. Dickinson, 487 U.S. 450 (1988)

Keyes v. Denver School District No. 1, 413 U.S. 189 (1973)

Knox County Board of Education v. Fultz, 241 Ky. 265 (1931)

Korematsu v. U.S., 323 U.S. 214 (1944)

Kramer v. Union School District, 395 U.S. 621 (1969)

Lee v. Macon County Board of Alabama, 483 F.2d 242 (1964)

Lehew v. Brummell, 103 Mo. 546 (S. Ct., Div. 1, October 1890)

Levy v. Louisiana, 391 U.S. 68 (1968)

Lewis v. Henley, 2 Ind. 332 (1850)

Lochner v. New York, 198 U.S. 45 (1905)

Loving v. Virginia, 388 U.S. 1 (1967)

Maddox v. Neal, 45 Ark. 121 (S. Ct. May 1885)

Marshall v. Donovan, 73 Ky. 681 (1874)

Martin v. Board of Education, Charleston, 42 W. Va. 514 (S. Ct. App. 1896)

McCleary v. State, 84362-7 WA (2012)

McCulloch v. Maryland, 17 U.S. 327 (1819)

McDonald v. Board of Elections, 394 U.S. 802 (1969)

McLaughlin v. Florida, 379 U.S. 184 (1964)

McLaurin v. Oklahoma State Regents for Higher Education, 339 U.S. 637 (1950)

Mendez v. Westminster School District of Orange County, 64 F. Supp. 544 (D.C. Cal.
    1946)

Miller v. Feather, 176 Ky. 268 (1917)

Milliken v. Bradley, 418 U.S. 717 (1974)

Milliken v. Green, 389 Mich. 1, 203 N.W.2d 457 (1972)

Missouri ex rel. Gaines v. Canada, 305 U.S. 337 (1938)

Missouri v. Jenkins (Missouri II), 515 U.S. 70 (1995)

Moss v. City of Mayfield, 186 Ky. 330 (1919)

Munfordville Mercantile Company v. Board of Trustees District No. 39, 155 Ky. 382
    (1913)

Murray v. Maryland (aka Murray v. Pearson), 169 Md. 478 (1936)

Nevada ex rel. Stoutmeyer v. Duffy, 7. Nev. 342 (S. Ct. January 1872)

Ohio ex rel. William Garnes v. John W. McCann, 21 Ohio St. 198, 203 (S. Ct.
    December 1871)

Ohio v. John Blain, 36 Ohio St. 429 (Ohio 1881)

Parents Involved in Community Schools v. Seattle School District No. 1, 127 S. Ct. 2738
    (2007)

Pasadena City Board of Education v. Spangler, 427 U.S. 424 (1976)

Pennsylvania v. Board of Trusts, 353 U.S. 230 (1957)

People ex rel. Joseph Workman v. Board of Education of Detroit, 18 Mich. 400
    (S. Ct. May 1869)

People v. Gallagher, 93 N.Y. 438 (Ct. App. October 1883)

Peters v. Boggs, 217 Ga. 471 (1961)

Pierce v. Society of Sisters, 268 U.S. 510 (1925)

Piper v. Big Pine School District of Inyo County, 193 Cal. 664 (S. Ct. 1924)

Plessy v. Ferguson, 163 U.S. 537 (1896)

Plyler v. Doe, 457 U.S. 202 (1982)

Poindexter v. Louisiana Financial Assistance Commission, 258 F. Supp. 158 (1966)

Prince v. Board of Education of Central Consolidated Independent School District No. 22,
    88 N.M. 548 (1975)

Raley v. County Board of Education of Woodford County, 224 Ky. 50 (1928)

Roberts v. City of Boston, 59 Mass. 198 (1849)

Robinson v. Cahill, 287 A.2d 187 (N.J. 1972), cert. denied, 414 U.S. 976 (1973)

Rodriguez v. San Antonio Independent School District, 337 F. Supp. 280 (W.D. Tex.
    1971)

San Antonio Independent School District v. Rodriguez, 411 U.S. 1 (1973)

Santa Clara Pueblo v. Martinez, 436 U.S. 49 (1978)

School District No. 21 in Fremont County v. Board of County Commissioners of Fremont County et al., 15 Wyo. 73 (S. Ct. 1906)

Serrano v. Priest, 487 P.2d 1241 (Cal. 1971), *cert. denied*, 432 U.S. 907 (1977)

Serrano v. Priest II, 18 Cal. 3d 728 (Cal. 1976)

Shadrack v. Board of Trustees of the Madisonville Graded Common School District, 188 Ky. 335 (1920)

Shelley v. Kraemer, 334 U.S. 1 (1948)

Sipuel v. Oklahoma State Board of Regents, 332 U.S. 631 (1948)

Skinner v. Oklahoma, 316 U.S. 535 (1942)

Slaughter-House Cases, 83 U.S. 36 (1873)

Spano v. Board of Education of Lakeland Central School District, 68 Misc. 2d 804 (1972)

State Board of Education v. Brown, 232 Ky. 434 (1929)

State v. Cantey, 20 S.C. L. 614 (1835)

Swann v. Charlotte-Mecklenburg Board of Education, 402 U.S. 1 (1971)

Sweatt v. Painter, 339 U.S. 629 (1950)

Taylor v. Board of Education of City School District of City of New Rochelle, 191 F. Supp. 181 (1961)

Taylor v. Russell, 117 Ky. 539 (1904)

Thomas et al. v. Field et al., 143 Md. 128 (1923)

Trustees of Graded Free Colored Common Schools of the City of Mayfield, Kentucky v. Trustees of the Graded Free White Common Schools of the City of Mayfield, Kentucky, 180 Ky. 574 (1918)

Tucker v. Blease et al., 97 S.C. 303 (1914)

U.S. v. Carolene Products, 304 U.S. 144 (1938)

U.S. v. Virginia, 518 U.S. 515 (1996)

Valley Forge Christian College v. Americans United for Separation of Church and State, 454 U.S. 464 (1982)

Van Dusartz v. Hatfield, 334 F. Supp. 870 (D. Minn. 1971)

Walton County Board of Education v. Academy of Social Circle, 229 Ga. 114 (1972)

Ward v. Flood, 48 Cal. 36 (1874)

Washington v. Davis, 426 U.S. 229 (1976)

Washington v. Seattle School District No. 1, 458 U.S. 457 (1982)

Williams v. School Directors, Wright Rep. 578–79 (Ohio 1833)

Williams v. Zimmerman, 172 Md. 563 (1937)

Wisconsin v. Yoder, 406 U.S. 25 (1972)

Wysinger v. Crookshank, 82 Cal. 588 (S. Ct., Dept. 1, January 1890)

Books and Articles

Ackerman, Bruce, "Beyond Carolene Products." *Harvard Law Review* 98 (1985): 713.

Aggarwal, Ujju. "The Ideological Architecture of Whiteness as Property in Educational Policy." *Educational Policy* 30, no. 1 (2016): 128–52.

Anderson, Benedict. *Imagined Communities: Reflections on the Origin and Spread of Nationalism.* New York: Verso, 1991.

Anderson, James D. *The Education of Blacks in the South, 1860–1935.* Chapel Hill: University of North Carolina Press, 1988.

Ansley, Frances Lee. "Stirring the Ashes: Race, Class and the Future of Civil Rights Scholarship." *Cornell Law Review* 74 (1989): 993–1077.

Auerbach, Jerold. *Unequal Justice: Lawyers and Social Change.* New York: Oxford University Press, 1976.

Baer, Judith A. *Equality under the Constitution: Reclaiming the Fourteenth Amendment.* Ithaca, NY: Cornell University Press, 1983.

Baldwin, James. *The Fire Next Time.* New York: Vintage International, 1963.

———. *The Price of the Ticket: Collected Nonfiction, 1948–1985.* New York: St. Martin's, 1985.

Balkin, Jack M., ed. *What* Brown v. Board of Education *Should Have Said: The Nation's Top Legal Experts Rewrite America's Landmark Civil Rights Decision.* New York: New York University Press, 2001.

Beadie, Nancy. *Education and the Creation of Capital in the Early American Republic.* Cambridge: Cambridge University Press, 2010.

Beito, David T. *Taxpayers in Revolt: Tax Resistance during the Great Depression.* Chapel Hill: University of North Carolina Press, 1989.

Bell, Derrick A., Jr. "*Brown v. Board of Education* and the Interest-Convergence Dilemma." *Harvard Law Review* 93 (1980): 518–33.

———. *Silent Covenants:* Brown v. Board of Education *and the Unfulfilled Hopes for Racial Reform.* Oxford: Oxford University Press, 2004.

Berger, Michele Tracy, and Kathleen Guidroz, eds. *The Intersectional Approach: Transforming the Academy through Race, Class, and Gender.* Chapel Hill: University of North Carolina Press, 2009.

Berke, Joel S. *Answers to Inequity: An Analysis of the New School Finance.* Berkeley: McCutchan, 1974.

Berman, William. *America's Right Turn: From Nixon to Clinton.* Baltimore: Johns Hopkins University Press, 1998.

Berry, Mary Frances. *And Justice for All: The United States Commission on Civil Rights and the Continuing Struggle for Freedom in America.* New York: Knopf, 2009.

Biondi, Martha. *To Stand and Fight: The Struggle for Civil Rights in Postwar New York City.* Cambridge: Cambridge University Press, 2003.

Bittker, Boris I. "The Case of the Fictitious Taxpayer: The Federal Taxpayer's Suit Twenty Years after *Flast v. Cohen.*" *University of Chicago Law Review* 36 (1968–69): 364–74.

Blalock-Moore, Nicole. "*Piper v. Big Pine School District of Inyo County*: Indigenous Schooling and Resistance in the Early Twentieth Century." *Southern California Quarterly* 94, no. 3 (Fall 2012): 346–77.

Boger, John Charles. "Willful Colorblindness: The New Racial Piety and the Resegregation of Public Schools." *North Carolina Law Review* 78 (September 2000): 1719–96.

Bowers, C.A., Doris Dyke, and Ian Housego. *Education and Social Policy: Local Control of Education*. New York: Random House, 1970.

Bowles, Samuel, and Herbert Gintis. *Schooling in Capitalist America: Educational Reform and the Contradictions of Economic Life*. Chicago: Haymarket Books, 1977.

———. "Schooling in Capitalist America Revisited." *Sociology of Education* 75, no. 1 (January 2002): 1–18.

Bowles, Samuel, Herbert Gintis, and Melissa Osborne Groves, eds. *Unequal Chances: Family Background and Economic Success*. Princeton, NJ: Princeton University Press, 2005.

Braeman, John. *Before the Civil Rights Revolution: The Old Court and Individual Rights*. Westport, CT: Greenwood, 1988.

Branch, Taylor. *Parting the Waters: America in the King Years, 1954–63*. New York: Simon and Schuster, 1988.

Brinkley, Alan. *The End of Reform: New Deal Liberalism in Recession and War*. New York: Vintage, 1995.

Brown, Dorothy A. "Race and Class Matters in Tax Policy." 107 *Columbia Law Review* (2007) 794–832.

———. "Racial Equality in the Twenty-First Century: What's Tax Policy Got to Do with It?" In *Critical Tax Theory: An Introduction*, ed. Anthony C. Infanti and Bridget J. Crawford, 42–45. Cambridge: Cambridge University Press, 2009.

Brown, Leslie. *Upbuilding Black Durham: Gender, Class, and Black Community Development in the Jim Crow South*. Chapel Hill: University of North Carolina Press, 2008.

Brownlee, W. Elliot. *Federal Taxation in America*. 2nd ed. Cambridge: Cambridge University Press, 2004.

———, ed. *Funding the Modern American State, 1941–1995: The Rise and Fall of the Era of Easy Finance*. Cambridge: Cambridge University Press, 1996.

Brown-Nagin, Tomiko. *Courage to Dissent: Atlanta and the Long History of the Civil Rights Movement*. Oxford: Oxford University Press, 2012.

Butchart, Ronald E. *Northern Schools, Southern Blacks, and Reconstruction: Freedmen's Education, 1862–1875*. Westport, CT: Greenwood, 1980.

Canaday, Margot. *The Straight State: Sexuality and Citizenship in Twentieth Century America*. Princeton, NJ: Princeton University Press, 2009.

Carr, Robert K. *Federal Protection of Civil Rights: Quest for a Sword*. Ithaca, NY: Cornell University Press, 1947.

Carrington, Paul D., and Trina Jones, eds. *Law and Class in America: Trends since the Cold War*. New York: New York University Press, 2006.

Cashin, Sheryll. *The Failures of Integration: How Race and Class Are Undermining the American Dream*. New York: Public Affairs, 2004.

Cecelski, David S. *Along Freedom Road: Hyde County, North Carolina, and the Fate of Black Schools in the South*. Chapel Hill: University of North Carolina Press, 1994.

Chafe, William H., ed. *The Achievement of American Liberalism: The New Deal and Its Legacies*. New York: Columbia University Press, 2003.

Chemerinsky, Erwin. "The Values of Federalism." *Florida Law Review* 47 (1995): 499–540.

Chirhart, Ann Short. *Torches of Light: Georgia Teachers and the Coming of the Modern South*. Atlanta: University of Georgia Press, 2005.

Cohen, Lizabeth. *A Consumers' Republic: The Politics of Mass Consumption in Postwar America*. New York: Vintage Books, 2003.

Coons, John E., William H. Clune III, and Stephen D. Sugarman. *Private Wealth and Public Education*. Cambridge, MA: Belknap Press of Harvard University Press, 1970.

Countryman, Matthew. *Up South: Civil Rights and Black Power in Philadelphia*. Philadelphia: University of Pennsylvania Press, 2005.

Cover, Robert. "Violence and the Word." *Yale Law Journal* 95 (1985–86): 1601–30.

Crenshaw, Kimberle. "Mapping the Margins: Intersectionality, Identity, Politics and Violence against Women of Color." *Stanford Law Review* 43 (1991): 1241–1300.

Crespino, Joseph. "Civil Rights and the Religious Right." In *Rightward Bound: Making America Conservative in the 1970s*, ed. Bruce J. Schulman and Julian E. Zelizer, 90–105. Cambridge, MA: Harvard University Press, 2008.

Cubberley, Ellwood P. *Public Education in the United States: A Study and Interpretation of American Educational History*. Cambridge, MA: Riverside, 1947.

Cushman, Barry. *Rethinking the New Deal Court: The Structure of a Constitutional Revolution*. New York: Oxford University Press, 1998.

———. "Some Varieties and Vicissitudes of Lochnerism." *Boston University Law Review* 85 (2005): 881–1000.

Dauber, Michele Landis. *The Sympathetic State: Disaster Relief and the Origins of the American Welfare State*. Chicago: University of Chicago Press, 2012.

Davis, Carl, Kelly Davis, Matthew Gardner, Robert S. McIntyre, Jeff McLynch, and Alla Sapozhnikova. *Who Pays? A Distributional Analysis of the Tax Systems in All Fifty States*. 3rd ed. Washington, DC: Institute on Taxation and Economic Policy, November 2009. http://www.itepnet.org/whopays3.pdf.

Davis, Kenneth Culp. "The Case of the Real Taxpayer: A Reply to Professor Bittker." *University of Chicago Law Review* 36 (1968–69): 375–77.

Davis, Martha. *Brutal Need: Lawyers and the Welfare Rights Movement, 1960–1973*. New Haven, CT: Yale University Press, 1993.

Delaney, David. *Race, Place and the Law, 1836–1948*. Austin: University of Texas Press, 1998.

Delgado, Richard, and Jean Stefancic. *Failed Revolutions: Social Reform and the Limits of Legal Imagination*. San Francisco: Westview, 1994.

de Schweinitz, Rebecca. *If We Could Change the World: Young People and America's Long Struggle for Racial Equality*. Chapel Hill: University of North Carolina Press, 2009.

Dittmer, John. *Local People: The Struggle for Civil Rights in Mississippi*. Urbana: University of Illinois Press, 1994.

Douglas, Davison M. *Jim Crow Moves North: Battle over Northern School Segregation, 1865–1954*. Cambridge: Cambridge University Press, 2005.

DuBois, W. E. B. *Darkwater: Voices from within the Veil*. 1920. New York: Dover, 1999.

———. *The Souls of Black Folk*. 1903. New York: Dover, 1994.

Dudziak, Mary. *Cold War Civil Rights: Race and the Image of American Democracy*. Princeton, NJ: Princeton University Press, 2000.

Dumas, Michael J. "Contesting White Accumulation in Seattle: Toward a Materialist Antiracist Analysis of School Desegregation." In *The Pursuit of Racial and Ethnic Equality in American Public Schools: Mendez, Brown and Beyond*, ed. Kristi L. Bowman, 291–314. East Lansing: Michigan State University Press, 2015.

Dworkin, Ronald. *Taking Rights Seriously*. Cambridge, MA: Harvard University Press, 1977.

Dyer, Richard. *White: Essays on Race and Culture*. New York: Routledge, 1997.

Eaton, Susan E., and Gary A. Orfield. *Dismantling Desegregation: The Quiet Reversal of Brown v. Board of Education*. New York: New Press (1997).

Edsall, Thomas B., and Mary Edsall. *Chain Reaction: The Impact of Race, Rights and Taxes on American Politics*. New York: W. W. Norton, 1992.

Einhorn, Robin L. *American Taxation, American Slavery*. Chicago: University of Chicago Press, 2002.

———. *Property Rules: Political Economy in Chicago, 1833–1872*. Chicago: University of Chicago Press, 1991.

Ely, John Hart. *Democracy and Distrust: A Theory of Judicial Review*. Cambridge, MA: Harvard University Press, 1980.

Entin, Jonathan L. "*Sweatt v. Painter*, the End of Segregation, and the Transformation of Education Law." *Review of Litigation* 5 (1986): 3–72.

Evans, William N., Sheila E. Murray, and Robert M. Schwab. "School Houses, Court Houses and State Houses after *Serrano*." *Journal of Policy Analysis and Management* 16, no. 1 (1997): 10–31.

Fairclough, Adam. *Better Day Coming: Blacks and Equality, 1890–2000*. New York: Viking, 2001.

———. *Teaching Equality: Black Schools in the Age of Jim Crow*. Athens: University of Georgia Press, 2001.

Fineman, Martha. "The Vulnerable Subject: Anchoring Equality in the Human Condition." *Yale Journal of Law and Feminism* 20, no. 1 (2008): 1–24.

———. "The Vulnerable Subject and the Responsive State." *Emory Law Journal* 60, no. 2 (2010), 251–76.

Fischel, William A. *The Homevoter Hypothesis: How Home Values Influence Local Government Taxation, School Finance, and Land-Use Policies*. Cambridge, MA: Harvard University Press, 2001.

Fisher, Glenn. *The Worst Tax? A History of the Property Tax in America*. Lawrence: University Press of Kansas, 1996.

Fiss, Owen M. "Groups and the Equal Protection Clause." *Philosophy and Public Affairs* 5 (1976): 107–77.

Flicker, Barbara, ed. *Justice and School Systems: The Role of Courts in Education Litigation*. Philadelphia: Temple University Press, 1990.

Foley, Neil. "Black, White and *Brown*." *Journal of Southern History* 70 (2004): 343–50.

———. *The White Scourge: Mexicans, Blacks, and Poor Whites in Texas Cotton Culture*. Berkeley: University of California Press, 1997.

Forbath, William E. "Caste, Class and Equal Citizenship." *Michigan Law Review* 98, no. 1 (October 1999): 1–91.

———. "Constitutional Welfare Rights: A History, Critique and Reconstruction." *Fordham Law Review* 69 (2001): 1821–92.

———. "The New Deal Constitution in Exile." *Duke Law Journal* 51 (2001): 165–222.

Formisano, Ronald P. *Boston against Busing: Race, Class, and Ethnicity in the 1960s and 1970s.* Chapel Hill: University of North Carolina Press, 1991.

"Forum: Whiteness and Others: Mexican Americans and American Law." *Law and History Review* 21 (2003): vii–213.

Franklin, Vincent P., and James D. Anderson, eds. *New Perspectives on Black Educational History.* Boston: G. K. Hall, 1978.

Fraser, Steven, and Gary Gerstle, eds. *The Rise and Fall of the New Deal Order, 1930–1980.* Princeton, NJ: Princeton University Press, 1989.

Freund, David M. P. *Colored Property: State Policy and White Racial Politics in Suburban America.* Chicago: University of Chicago Press, 2007.

Frymer, Paul. "Race's Reality: The NAACP Confronts Racism and Inequality in the Labor Movement, 1940–1965." In *Race and American Political Development*, ed. Joseph Lowndes, Julie Novkov, and Dorian T. Warren, 292–340. New York: Routledge, 2008.

Galanter, Marc. "Why the 'Haves' Come Out Ahead: Speculations on the Limits of Legal Change." *Law and Society Review* 9 (1975): 95–160.

Gardbaum, Stephen. "New Deal Constitutionalism and the Unshackling of the States." *University of Chicago Law Review* 64 (1997): 483–566.

Gertsmann, Evan. *The Constitutional Underclass: Gays, Lesbians, and the Failure of Class-Based Equal Protection.* Chicago: University of Chicago Press, 1999.

Gillman, Howard. *The Constitution Besieged: The Rise and Demise of "Lochner" Era Police Powers Jurisprudence.* Durham, NC: Duke University Press, 1993.

Gilmore, Glenda Elizabeth. *Defying Dixie: The Radical Roots of Civil Rights, 1919–1950.* New York: W. W. Norton, 2008.

Glendon, Mary Ann. *Rights Talk: The Impoverishment of Political Discourse.* New York: Simon and Schuster, 1991.

Glenn, Evelyn Nakano. *Unequal Freedom: How Race and Gender Shaped American Citizenship and Labor.* Cambridge, MA: Harvard University Press, 2002.

Goldstein, Stephen R. "Interdistrict Inequalities in School Financing: A Critical Analysis of *Serrano v. Priest* and Its Progeny." *University of Pennsylvania Law Review* 120 (1972): 504–44.

Goluboff, Risa L. *The Lost Promise of Civil Rights.* Cambridge, MA: Harvard University Press, 2007.

Gordon, Robert. "Critical Legal Histories." *Stanford Law Review* 36 (1984): 57–126.

Gotanda, Neil. "A Critique of 'Our Constitution Is Color-Blind.'" *Stanford Law Review* 44 (1991): 1–68.

Graber, Mark A. *Dred Scott and the Problem of Constitutional Evil.* Cambridge: Cambridge University Press, 2006.

Graetz, Michael J., and Linda Greenhouse. *The Burger Court and the Rise of the Judicial Right.* New York: Simon and Schuster, 2016.

Gross, Ariela. *What Blood Won't Tell: A History of Race on Trial in America.* Cambridge, MA: Harvard University Press, 2008.

Gross, James A. "A Human Rights Perspective on U.S. Education: Only Some Children Matter." *Catholic University Law Review* 50 (2001): 919–56.

Guinier, Lani. "From Racial Liberalism to Racial Literacy: *Brown v. Board of Education* and the Interest-Divergence Dilemma." In "Round Table: *Brown v. Board of Education*, Fifty Years After," *Journal of American History* 91 (2004): 92–118.

Hahn, Steven. *A Nation under Our Feet: Black Political Struggles in the Rural South from Slavery to the Great Migration.* Cambridge, MA: Harvard University Press, 2003.

Hale, Grace Elizabeth. *Making Whiteness: The Culture of Segregation in the South, 1890–1940.* New York: Vintage, 1999.

Hall, Jacqueline Dowd. "The Long Civil Rights Movement and the Political Uses of the Past." *Journal of American History* 91, no. 4 (March 2005).

Hamilton, Dona Cooper, and Charles V. Hamilton. *The Dual Agenda: The African American Struggle for Civil and Economic Equality.* New York: Columbia University Press, 1997.

Haney-López, Ian F. "Race, Ethnicity, Erasure: The Salience of Race to LatCrit Theory." *University of California Law Review* 85 (1997): 1143–1211.

———. *Racism on Trial: The Chicano Fight for Justice.* Cambridge, MA: Belknap Press of Harvard University Press, 2003.

———. *White by Law: The Legal Construction of Race.* New York: New York University Press, 1996.

Harding, T. Swann. *TNT (These National Taxeaters).* New York: Ray Long and Richard R. Smith, 1934.

Harris, Angela P. "Equality Trouble: Sameness and Difference in Twentieth-Century Race Law." *California Law Review* 88 (2000): 1923–2016.

———. "Race and Essentialism in Feminist Legal Theory." *Stanford Law Review* 42 (1990): 581–616.

Harris, Cheryl I. "Symposium: Race Jurisprudence and the Supreme Court: Where Do We Go From Here? In the Shadow of *Plessy*." *University of Pennsylvania Journal of Constitutional Law* 7 (February 2005): 867–902.

———. "Whiteness as Property." *Harvard Law Review* 106 (1993): 1707–91.

Hartog, Hendrik. "Pigs and Positivism." *Wisconsin Law Review* 1985, no. 4 (1985): 899–936.

Hartog, Hendrik, Martha Minow, and William Forbath. "Introduction: Legal Histories from Below." *Wisconsin Law Review* 1985 (1985): 759–66.

Higginbotham, Evelyn Brooks. "African-American Women's History and the Metalanguage of Race." *Signs* 17, no. 2 (Winter 1992): 251–74.

Hirsch, Arnold R. *Making the Second Ghetto: Race and Housing in Chicago, 1940–1960.* Cambridge, MA: Harvard University Press, 1983.

Hochschild, Jennifer. *Facing Up to the American Dream: Race, Class and the Soul of the Nation.* Princeton, NJ: Princeton University Press, 1995.

Hoffer, Peter Charles, Williamjames Hull Hoffer, and N. E. H. Hull. *The Supreme Court: An Essential History.* Lawrence: University Press of Kansas, 2007.

Holmes, Stephen, and Cass Sunstein. *The Cost of Rights: Why Liberty Depends on Taxes.* New York: W. W. Norton, 2000.

Homel, Michael W. *Down from Equality: Black Chicagoans and the Public Schools, 1920–1941.* Urbana: University of Illinois Press, 1984.

Horwitz, Morton J. *The Transformation of American Law, 1780–1860.* Cambridge, MA: Harvard University Press, 1977.

———. *The Transformation of American Law, 1870–1960.* New York: Oxford University Press, 1992.

———. *The Warren Court and the Pursuit of Justice.* New York: Hill and Wang, 1998.

HoSang, Daniel Martinez. *Racial Propositions: Ballot Initiatives and the Making of Postwar California.* Berkeley: University of California Press, 2010.

———. "The Triumph of Racial Liberalism, the Demise of Racial Justice." In *Race and American Political Development*, ed. Joseph Lowndes, Julie Novkov, and Dorian T. Warren, 482–519. New York: Routledge, 2008.

Huret, Romain D. *American Tax Resisters.* Cambridge, MA: Harvard University Press, 2014.

Infanti, Anthony C., and Bridget J. Crawford, eds. *Critical Tax Theory: An Introduction.* Cambridge: Cambridge University Press, 2009.

Irons, Peter. *The Courage of Their Convictions: Sixteen Americans Who Fought Their Way to the Supreme Court.* New York: Penguin, 1988.

———. *Jim Crow's Children: The Broken Promise of the* Brown *Decision.* New York: Penguin, 2002.

Irons, Peter, and Stephanie Guitton, eds. *May It Please the Court: The Most Significant Oral Arguments Made before the Supreme Court since 1955.* New York: New Press, 1993.

Jacobs, Meg. *Pocketbook Politics: Economic Citizenship in Twentieth Century America.* Princeton, NJ: Princeton University Press, 2005.

Jeffries, John C., Jr. *Justice Lewis F. Powell, Jr.: A Biography.* New York: Fordham University Press, 2001.

Johnson, Lyndon B. *Public Papers of the Presidents of the United States: Lyndon B. Johnson, 1965.* Washington, DC: Government Printing Office, 1966.

Jonas, Gilbert. *Freedom's Sword: The NAACP and the Struggle against Racism in America, 1909–1969.* New York: Routledge, 2007.

Jones, Jacqueline. *The Dispossessed: America's Underclasses from the Civil War to the Present.* New York: Basic Books, 1993.

Kaestle, Carl. *Pillars of the Republic: Common Schools and American Society, 1780–1860.* New York: Hill and Wang, 1983.

Kalodner, Howard I., and James J. Fishman, eds. *Limits of Justice: The Courts' Role in School Desegregation.* Cambridge, MA: Ballinger, 1978.

Karst, Kenneth L. "Why Equality Matters." *Georgia Law Review* 17 (1983): 245–90.

Katz, Michael B. *The Irony of Early School Reform: Educational Innovation in Mid-Nineteenth Century Massachusetts.* Cambridge, MA: Harvard University Press, 1968.

———. *The Price of Citizenship: Redefining the American Welfare State.* Philadelphia: University of Pennsylvania Press, 2008.

———. *Reconstructing American Education.* Cambridge, MA: Harvard University Press, 1987.

———, ed. *The "Underclass" Debate: Views from History.* Princeton, NJ: Princeton University Press, 1993.

———. *The Undeserving Poor: From the War on Poverty to the War on Welfare.* New York: Pantheon Books, 1989.

Katz, Michael B., Mark J. Stern, and Jamie J. Fader. "The New African American Inequality." *Journal of American History* 92, no. 1 (June 2005): 75–108.

Katznelson, Ira. *When Affirmative Action Was White: An Untold History of Racial Inequality in Twentieth-Century America.* New York: W. W. Norton, 2005.

Katznelson, Ira, and Margaret Weir. *Schooling for All: Class, Race, and the Decline of the Democratic Ideal.* Berkeley: University of California Press, 1988.

Kellogg, Charles Flint. *NAACP: A History of the National Association for the Advancement of Colored People 1909–1920.* Vol. 1. Baltimore: Johns Hopkins University Press, 1967.

Kelso, William A. *Poverty and the Underclass: Changing Perceptions of the Poor in America.* New York: New York University Press, 1994.

Kerber, Linda. "The Meanings of Citizenship." *Journal of American History* 84, no. 3 (December 1997): 833–54.

———. *No Constitutional Right to Be Ladies: Women and the Obligations of Citizenship.* New York: Hill and Wang, 1998.

Kessler-Harris, Alice. *In Pursuit of Equity: Women, Men and the Quest for Economic Citizenship in 20th Century America.* New York: Oxford University Press, 2003.

Kettner, James. *The Development of American Citizenship, 1608–1870.* Chapel Hill: University of North Carolina Press, 1978.

Klare, Karl E. "Judicial Deradicalization of the Wagner Act and the Origins of Modern Legal Consciousness, 1937–1941." *Minnesota Law Review* 65 (1978): 265–340.

Klarman, Michael J. *From Jim Crow to Civil Rights: The Supreme Court and the Struggle for Racial Equality.* Oxford: Oxford University Press, 2005.

———. "An Interpretive History of Modern Equal Protection." *Michigan Law Review* 90 (September 1991): 213–318.

———. "Rethinking the Civil Rights and Civil Liberties Revolutions." *Virginia Law Review* 82 (1996): 1–68.

———. *Unfinished Business: Racial Equality in American History.* New York: Oxford University Press, 2007.

Klein, Jennifer. *For All These Rights: Business, Labor, and the Shaping of America's Public-Private Welfare State.* Princeton, NJ: Princeton University Press, 2003.

Kluger, Richard. *Simple Justice: The History of* Brown v. Board of Education *and Black America's Struggle for Equality.* New York: Vintage, 1976.

Knight, Edgar W. *Fifty Years of American Education, 1900–1950.* New York: Ronald Press, 1952.

Kornbluh, Felicia. *The Battle for Welfare Rights: Politics and Poverty in Modern America.* Philadelphia: University of Pennsylvania Press, 2007.

Kousser, J. Morgan. *Dead End: The Development of Nineteenth-Century Litigation on Racial Discrimination in Schools.* Oxford: Clarendon, 1986.

———. "The Supremacy of Equal Rights: The Struggle against Racial Discrimination in Antebellum Massachusetts." *Northwestern University Law Review* 82 (1988): 941–1010.

Kozol, Jonathan. *Savage Inequalities: Children in America's Schools.* New York: Crown, 1991.

———. *The Shame of the Nation: The Restoration of Apartheid Schooling in America.* New York: Crown, 2005.

Kruse, Kevin. "The Politics of Race and Public Space: Desegregation, Privatization, and the Tax Revolt in Atlanta." *Journal of Urban History* 31 (2005): 610–33.

———. *White Flight: Atlanta and the Making of Modern Conservatism.* Princeton, NJ: Princeton University Press, 2007.

Kruse, Kevin, and Thomas Sugrue, eds. *The New Suburban History.* Chicago: University of Chicago Press, 2006.

Lassiter, Matthew D. *The Silent Majority: Suburban Politics in the Sunbelt South.* Princeton, NJ: Princeton University Press, 2007.

Lassiter, Matthew D., and Joseph Crespino, eds. *The Myth of Southern Exceptionalism.* New York: Oxford University Press, 2009.

Lassiter, Matthew D., and Andrew B. Lewis, eds. *The Moderates' Dilemma: Massive Resistance to School Desegregation in Virginia.* Charlottesville: University of Virginia Press, 1998.

Lawrence, Susan E. *The Poor in Court: The Legal Services Program and Supreme Court Decision Making.* Princeton, NJ: Princeton University Press, 1990.

Levinson, Sanford. "When (Some) Republican Justices Exhibited Concern for the Plight of the Poor: An Essay in Historical Retrieval." In *Law and Class in America: Trends since the Cold War*, ed. Paul D. Carrington and Trina Jones, 31–58. New York: New York University Press, 2006.

Lipsitz, George. *The Possessive Investment in Whiteness: How White People Profit from Identity Politics.* Philadelphia: Temple University Press, 1998.

Liu, Goodwin. "Education, Equality and National Citizenship." *Yale Law Journal* 330 (2006): 331–411.

Lofgren, Charles A. *The Plessy Case: A Legal-Historical Interpretation.* New York: Oxford University Press, 1987.

Lovell, George I. *This Is Not Civil Rights: Discovering Rights Talk in 1939 America.* Chicago: University of Chicago Press, 2012.

Lowndes, Joseph. *From the New Deal to the New Right: Race and the Southern Origins of Modern Conservatism.* New Haven, CT: Yale University Press, 2008.

Lowndes, Joseph, Julie Novkov, and Dorian T. Warren, eds. *Race and American Political Development.* New York: Routledge, 2008.

Mabee, Carleton. *Black Education in New York State: From Colonial to Modern Times.* Syracuse, NY: Syracuse University Press, 1979.

Mack, Kenneth. "Bringing the Law Back into the History of the Civil Rights Movement." *Law and History Review* 27 (2009): 657–70.

———. "Law and Mass Politics in the Making of the Civil Rights Lawyer, 1931–1941." *Journal of American History* 93 (2006): 37–62.

———. *Representing the Race: The Creation of the Civil Rights Lawyer*. Cambridge, MA: Harvard University Press, 2014.

———. "Rethinking Civil Rights Lawyering and Politics in the Era before *Brown*." *Yale Law Journal* 115 (2005): 256–355.

Margo, Robert A. *Disfranchisement, School Finance, and the Economics of Segregated Schools in the United States South, 1890–1910*. New York: Garland, 1985.

———. "Race Differences in Public School Expenditures: Disfranchisement and School Finance in Louisiana, 1890–1910." *Social Science History* 6, no. 1 (1982), 9–33.

Marshall, T. H. *Citizenship and Social Class and Other Essays*. Cambridge: Cambridge University Press, 1950.

Martin, Isaac William. "Does School Finance Litigation Cause Taxpayer Revolt? *Serrano* and Proposition 13." *Law and Society Review* 40, no. 3 (2006): 525–58.

———. *The Permanent Tax Revolt: How the Property Tax Transformed American Politics*. Palo Alto, CA: Stanford University Press, 2008.

Martin, Isaac William, Ajay K. Mehrotra, and Monica Prasad, eds. *The New Fiscal Sociology: Taxation in Comparative and Historical Perspective*. Cambridge: Cambridge University Press, 2009.

Martinez, George A. "The Legal Construction of Race: Mexican-Americans and Whiteness." *Harvard Latino Law Review* 2 (1997): 321–48.

Massey, Douglas S., and Nancy A. Denton. *American Apartheid: Segregation and the Making of the Underclass*. Cambridge, MA: Harvard University Press, 1993.

Mayeri, Serena. *Reasoning from Race: Feminism, Law, and the Civil Rights Revolution*. Cambridge, MA: Harvard University Press, 2014.

———. "The Strange Career of Jane Crow: Sex Segregation and the Transformation of Anti-Discrimination Discourse." *Yale Journal of Law and the Humanities* 18 (2006): 187.

McClellan, B. Edward, and William J. Reese, eds. *The Social History of American Education*. Chicago: University of Chicago Press, 1988.

McGirr, Lisa. *Suburban Warriors: The Origins of the New American Right*. Princeton, NJ: Princeton University Press, 2001.

Mehrotra, Ajay K. *Making the Modern American Fiscal State: Law, Politics, and the Rise of Progressive Taxation, 1877–1929*. Cambridge: Cambridge University Press, 2014.

———. "Reviving Fiscal Citizenship." *Michigan Law Review* 113, no. 6 (2015): 943–72.

Meier, Kenneth J., Joseph Stewart Jr., and Robert E. England. *Race, Class, and Education: The Politics of Second-Generation Discrimination*. Madison: University of Wisconsin Press, 1989.

Mettler, Suzanne. *The Submerged State: How Invisible Government Policies Undermine American Democracy*. Chicago: University of Chicago Press, 2011.

Michelman, Frank I. "The Supreme Court 1968 Term: Foreword: On Protecting the Poor through the Fourteenth Amendment." *Harvard Law Review* 83 (1969): 7–59.

Michelmore, Molly. *Tax and Spend: The Welfare State, Tax Politics, and the Limits of American Liberalism*. Philadelphia: University of Pennsylvania Press, 2012.

Millonzi, Kara A. "Education as a Right of National Citizenship under the Privileges or Immunities Clause of the Fourteenth Amendment." *North Carolina Law Review* 81 (March 2003): 1286–1311.

Mink, Gwendolyn. *The Wages of Motherhood: Inequality in the Welfare State, 1917–1942*. Ithaca, NY: Cornell University Press, 1995.

———, ed. *Whose Welfare?* Ithaca, NY: Cornell University Press, 1999.

Mohraz, Judy Jolley. *The Separate Problem: Case Studies of Black Education in the North, 1900–1910*. Westport, CT: Greenwood, 1979.

Montejano, David. *Anglos and Mexicans in the Making of Texas, 1836–1986*. Austin: University of Texas Press, 1987.

Moore, Jesse Thomas, Jr. *A Search for Equality: The National Urban League, 1910–1961*. University Park, PA: Pennsylvania State University Press, 1981.

Moreo, Dominic W. *Schools in the Great Depression*. New York: Garland, 1996.

Morrison, Toni. *Playing in the Dark: Whiteness in the Literary Imagination*. Cambridge, MA: Harvard University Press, 1992.

Nadasen, Premilla. *Welfare Warriors: The Welfare Rights Movement in the United States*. New York: Routledge, 2004.

National School Boards Association. *State School Finance Laws Handbook: Proceedings of the 1968 Workshop Sponsored by the National School Boards Association, Detroit, MI, March 28, 31, 1968*. Evanston, IL: National School Boards Association, 1968.

Nieman, Donald G., ed. *African Americans and Education in the South*. New York: Garland, 1994.

O'Brien, Thomas V. *The Politics of Race and Schooling: Public Education in Georgia, 1900–1961*. Lanham, MD: Lexington Books, 1999.

Olivas, Michael A., and Ronna Greff Schneider, eds. *Education Law Stories*. New York: Foundation, 2008.

Orfield, Gary, ed. *Dropouts in America: Confronting the Graduation Rate Crisis*. Cambridge, MA: Harvard Education Press, 2004.

Orfield, Gary, and Susan Eaton. *Dismantling Desegregation: The Quiet Reversal of Brown v. Board of Education*. New York: New Press, 1996.

Orfield, Gary, and Chungmei Lee. *Brown at 50: King's Dream or Plessy's Nightmare?* Cambridge, MA: Civil Rights Project at Harvard University, 2004.

———. *Why Segregation Matters: Poverty and Educational Inequality*. Cambridge, MA: Civil Rights Project at Harvard University, 2005.

Orren, Karen. *Belated Feudalism: Labor, the Law, and Liberal Development in the United States*. New York: Cambridge University Press, 1991.

Pascoe, Peggy. *What Comes Naturally: Miscegenation Law and the Making of Race in America*. New York: Oxford University Press, 2009.

Passow, A. Harry, ed. *Education in Depressed Areas*. New York: Teachers College, 1963.

Patterson, James T. *America's Struggle against Poverty, 1900–1985*. Cambridge, MA: Harvard University Press, 1986.

———. Brown v. Board of Education: *A Civil Rights Milestone and Its Troubled Legacy*. Oxford: Oxford University Press, 2002.

Pattillo, Mary. *Black on the Block: The Politics of Race and Class in the City*. Chicago: University of Chicago Press, 2007.

Payne, Charles M. *Getting What We Ask For: The Ambiguity of Success and Failure in Urban Education*. Westport, CT: Greenwood, 1984.

———. *I've Got the Light of Freedom: The Organizing Tradition and the Mississippi Freedom Struggle*. Berkeley: University of California Press, 1995.

———. "'The Whole United States Is Southern!': *Brown v. Board* and the Mystification of Race." In "Round Table: *Brown v. Board of Education*, Fifty Years After." *Journal of American History* 91 (2004): 83–91.

Peck, Elizabeth S. *Berea's First 125 Years, 1855–1980*. Lexington: University Press of Kentucky, 1982.

Peller, Gary. "Cultural Imperialism, White Anxiety, and the Ideological Realignment of *Brown*." In *Race, Law and Culture: Reflections on* Brown v. Board of Education, ed. Austin Sarat, 190–220. Oxford: Oxford University Press, 1997.

Perea, Juan F. "Why Integration and Equal Protection Fail to Protect Latinos." *Harvard Law Review* 117 (2004): 1420–69.

Perkinson, Henry J. *The Imperfect Panacea: American Faith in Education, 1865–1990*. 3rd ed. New York: McGraw-Hill, 1991.

Peterson, Gladys Tignor. "The Present Status of the Negro Separate School as Defined by Court Decisions." *Journal of Negro Education* 4, no. 3 (1935): 351–74.

Pitkin, Royce Stanley. *Public School Support in the United States during Periods of Economic Depression*. Brattleboro, VT: Stephen Daye, 1933.

Piven, Frances Fox, and Richard Cloward. *Poor People's Movements: Why They Succeed, How They Fail*. New York: Vintage, 1978.

———. *Regulating the Poor: The Functions of Public Welfare*. New York: Vintage, 1971.

Pole, J. R. *The Pursuit of Equality in American History*. 2nd ed. Berkeley: University of California Press, 1993.

Preer, Jean L. *Lawyers v. Educators: Black Colleges and Desegregation in Public Higher Education*. Westport, CT: Greenwood, 1982.

Przybyszewski, Linda. *The Republic According to John Marshall Harlan*. Chapel Hill: University of North Carolina Press, 1999.

Quadagno, Jill. *The Color of Welfare: How Racism Undermined the War on Poverty*. Oxford: Oxford University Press, 1994.

Readings, Bill. *The University in Ruins*. Cambridge, MA: Harvard University Press, 1997.

Reardon, Sean F., Elena Grewal, Demetra Kalogrides, and Erica Greenberg. "'Brown' Fades: The End of Court-Ordered School Desegregation and the Resegregation of American Public Schools." *Journal of Policy Analysis and Management* 31, no. 4 (Fall 2012): 876–904.

Robinson, Kimberly J. "Disrupting Education Federalism." *Washington University Law Review* 92 (2015): 959–1018.

Rodgers, Daniel T. *Age of Fracture*. Cambridge, MA: Belknap Press of Harvard University Press, 2011.

Roediger, David. *Wages of Whiteness: Race and the Making of the American Working Class*. New York: Verso, 1999.

Rosenberg, Gerald N. *The Hollow Hope: Can Courts Bring About Social Change?* Chicago: University of Chicago, 1991.

"Round Table: *Brown v. Board of Education*, Fifty Years After." *Journal of American History* 91 (2004): 19–173.

Rubin, Edward L., and Malcolm Feeley. "Federalism: Some Notes on a National Neurosis." *UCLA Law Review* 41 (1994): 903–52.

Salomone, Rosemary C. *Equal Education under Law: Legal Rights and Federal Policy in the Post-Brown Era*. New York: St. Martin's, 1986.

San Juan, E. "From Race to Class Struggle: Re-problematizing Critical Race Theory." *Michigan Journal of Race and Law* 11 (Fall 2005): 75–98.

San Miguel, Guadalupe. *"Let All of Them Take Heed": Mexican Americans and the Campaign for Educational Equality in Texas, 1910–1981*. Austin: University of Texas Press, 1987.

Schneider, Mark Robert. *We Return Fighting: The Civil Rights Movement in the Jazz Age*. Boston: Northeastern University Press, 2002.

Schragger, Richard. *"San Antonio v. Rodriguez and the Legal Geography of School Finance Reform."* In *Civil Rights Stories*, ed. Myriam E. Gilles and Risa L. Goluboff, 85–110. New York: Foundation, 2008.

Schwartz, Bernard, ed. *The Burger Court: Counter-revolution or Confirmation?* New York: Oxford University Press, 1998.

Scott, James C. *Seeing like a State: How Certain Schemes to Improve the Human Condition Have Failed*. New Haven, CT: Yale University Press, 1998.

Scott, Janny, and David Leonhardt. "Class Matters: Shadowy Lines That Still Divide." *New York Times*, May 15, 2005.

Sears, Richard. *A Utopian Experiment in Kentucky: Integration and Social Equality at Berea, 1866–1904*. Westport, CT: Greenwood, 1996.

Segal, Jeffrey A., and Harold J. Spaeth. *The Supreme Court and the Attitudinal Model Revisited*. New York: Cambridge University Press, 2002.

SenGupta, Gunja. *From Slavery to Poverty: The Racial Origins of Welfare in New York, 1840–1918*. New York: New York University Press, 2009.

Shaman, Jeffrey M. *Equality and Liberty in the Golden Age of State Constitutional Law*. New York: Oxford University Press, 2008.

Shklar, Judith. *American Citizenship: The Quest for Inclusion*. Cambridge, MA: Harvard University Press, 1998.

Siegel, Reva B. " 'The Rule of Love': Wife Beating as Prerogative and Privacy." *Yale Law Journal* 105 (June 1996): 2117–2208.

———. "Why Equal Protection No Longer Protects: The Evolving Forms of Status-Enforcing State Action." *Stanford Law Review* 49 (1997): 1111–48.

Sitkoff, Harvard. *A New Deal for Blacks: Emergence of Civil Rights as a National Issue*. Vol. 1, *The Depression Decade*. New York: Oxford University Press, 1978.

———. *The Struggle for Black Equality*. New York: Hill and Wang, 1981.

Sokol, Jason. *There Goes My Everything: White Southerners in the Age of Civil Rights, 1945–1975*. New York: Vintage Books, 2006.

Spann, Girardeau A. *Race against the Court: The Supreme Court and Minorities in Contemporary America*. New York: New York University Press, 1993.

Spring, Joel H. *Education and the Rise of the Corporate State*. Boston: Beacon, 1972.

Spurlock, Clark. *Education and the Supreme Court*. Urbana: University of Illinois Press, 1955.

Sracic, Paul A. "The *Brown* Decision's Other Legacy: Civic Education and the *Rodriguez* Case." *PS: Political Science and Politics* 31 (April 2004): 215–18.

——. *"San Antonio v. Rodriguez" and the Pursuit of Equal Education: The Debate over Discrimination and School Funding*. Lawrence: University Press of Kansas, 2006.

Subrin, Stephen N. "How Equity Conquered Common Law: The Federal Rules of Civil Procedure in Historical Perspective." *University of Pennsylvania Law Review* 135 (1987): 909–1002.

Sugrue, Thomas. *Origins of the Urban Crisis: Race and Inequality in Postwar Detroit*. Princeton, NJ: Princeton University Press, 1998.

——. *Sweet Land of Liberty: The Forgotten Struggle for Civil Rights in the North*. New York: Random House, 2008.

Sullivan, Patricia. *Lift Every Voice: The NAACP and the Making of the Civil Rights Movement*. New York: New Press, 2009.

Tanenhaus, David S. "Between Dependency and Liberty: The Conundrum of Children's Rights in the Gilded Age." *Law and History Review* 23, no. 2 (Summer 2005): 351–86.

Tani, Karen M. *States of Dependency: Welfare, Rights, and American Governance, 1935–1972*. Cambridge: Cambridge University Press, 2016.

Teaford, Jon C. *The Rise of the States: Evolution of American State Government*. Baltimore: Johns Hopkins University Press, 2002.

Theoharis, Jeanne, and Komozi Woodard, eds. *Freedom North: Black Freedom Struggles outside the South, 1940–1980*. New York: Palgrave MacMillan, 2003.

Thornton, J. Mills. *Dividing Lines: Municipal Politics and the Struggle for Civil Rights in Montgomery, Birmingham, and Selma*. Tuscaloosa: University of Alabama Press, 2002.

——. *Politics and Power in a Slave Society: Alabama, 1800–1860*. Baton Rouge: Louisiana State University Press, 1981.

Tushnet, Mark. *Making Civil Rights Law: Thurgood Marshall and the Supreme Court, 1936–1961*. Oxford: Oxford University Press, 1994.

——. *The NAACP's Legal Strategy against Segregated Education, 1925–1950*. Chapel Hill: University of North Carolina Press, 1987.

——, ed. *The Warren Court in Historical and Political Perspective*. Charlottesville: University of Virginia Press, 1993.

Tyack, David, and Larry Cuban. *Tinkering toward Utopia: A Century of Public School Reform*. Cambridge, MA: Harvard University Press, 1995.

Tyack, David, Thomas James, and Aaron Benavot. *Law and the Shaping of Public Education, 1785–1954*. Madison: University of Wisconsin Press, 1987.

U.S. Department of Health, Education and Welfare. *State Constitutional Provisions and Selected Legal Materials Relating to Public School Finance*. Washington, DC: Government Printing Office, 1973.

U.S. Senate Select Committee on Equal Educational Opportunity. *Equal Educational Opportunity: Hearings before the Select Committee on Equal Educational*

Opportunity. Pt. 4, *Mexican American Education*. Washington, DC: Government Printing Office, 1970.

———. *Equal Educational Opportunity: Hearings before the Select Committee on Equal Educational Opportunity*. Pt. 16A, *Inequality in School Finance, Sept. 21–23, 1971*. Washington, DC: Government Printing Office, 1971.

———. *Equal Educational Opportunity: Hearings before the Select Committee on Equal Educational Opportunity*. Pt. 16B, *Inequality in School Finance, Sept. 29–Oct. 5, 1971*. Washington, DC: Government Printing Office, 1971.

Vacca, Richard S., and H. C. Hudgins Jr. *The Legacy of the Burger Court and the Schools, 1969–1986*. Topeka, KS: National Organization on Legal Problems of Education, 1991.

Valencia, Richard R. *Chicano Students and the Courts: The Mexican American Legal Struggle for Educational Equality*. New York: New York University Press, 2008.

van Geel, Tyll. *The Courts and American Education Law*. Buffalo, NY: Prometheus Books, 1987.

Vaughn, William Preston. *Schools for All: The Blacks and Public Education in the South, 1865–1877*. Lexington: University Press of Kentucky, 1974.

Walker, Samuel. *The Rights Revolution: Rights and Community in Modern America*. Oxford: Oxford University Press, 1998.

Walker, Vanessa Siddle. *Their Highest Potential: An African American School Community in the Segregated South*. Chapel Hill: University of North Carolina Press, 1996.

Wallace, David. *Education for Extinction: American Indians and the Boarding School Experience, 1875–1928*. Topeka: University of Kansas Press, 1995.

Walsh, Camille. "Erasing Race, Dismissing Class: San Antonio Independent School District v. Rodriguez." *Berkeley La Raza Law Journal* 21 (April 2011): 133–72.

———. "*Rodriguez* in the Court: The Context of Judicial Decisionmaking." In *The Enduring Legacy of Rodriguez: Creating New Pathways to Equal Educational Opportunity*, ed. Kimberly Robinson and Charles Ogletree, 45–64. Cambridge, MA: Harvard Education Press, 2015.

———. "*San Antonio Independent School District v. Rodriguez*: 'The Poor People Have Lost Again.'" In *Poverty Law Canon*, ed. Marie Failinger and Ezra Rosser, 198–218. Ann Arbor: University of Michigan Press, 2016.

———. "White Backlash, the 'Taxpaying' Public, and Educational Citizenship." *Critical Sociology* 43, no. 2 (2017): 237–47.

Watkins, William H. *The White Architects of Black Education: Ideology and Power in America, 1865–1954*. New York: Teachers College Press, 2001.

Webb, Clive. "A Continuity of Conservatism: The Limitations of *Brown v. Board of Education*." *Journal of Southern History* 70 (2004): 327–36.

Wechsler, Herbert. "Toward Neutral Principles of Constitutional Law." *Harvard Law Review* 73, no. 1 (1959): 1–35.

Welke, Barbara Young. "Glimmers of Life: A Conversation with Hendrik Hartog." *Law and History Review* 27, no. 3 (Fall 2009): 629–56.

———. "When All the Women Were White and All the Blacks Were Men: Race, Class, Gender and the Road to *Plessy*." *Law and History Review* 13 (1995): 261–316.

Wells, Ida B. *Southern Horrors: Lynch Law in All Its Phases*. 1892. Lexington, KY: CreateSpace, 2014.

Wertheimer, John W., Jessica Bradshaw, Allyson Cobb, Harper Addison, E. Dudley Colhoun, Samuel Diamant, Andrew Gilbert, Jeffrey Higgs, and Nicholas Skipper. "'The Law Recognizes Racial Instinct': *Tucker v. Blease* and the Black-White Paradigm in the Jim Crow South." *Law and History Review* 29, no. 2 (May 2011): 471–95.

West, Robin. *Progressive Constitutionalism: Reconstructing the Fourteenth Amendment*. Durham, NC: Duke University Press, 1995.

White, G. Edward. *The Constitution and the New Deal*. Cambridge, MA: Harvard University Press, 2000.

Wilkinson, J. Harvie, III. *From* Brown *to* Bakke: *The Supreme Court and School Integration, 1954–1978*. New York: Oxford University Press, 1979.

Williams, Heather Andrea. *Self-Taught: African American Education in Slavery and Freedom*. Chapel Hill: University of North Carolina Press, 2005.

Williams, Juan. *Thurgood Marshall: American Revolutionary*. New York: Three Rivers, 1998.

Williams, Rhonda F. *The Politics of Public Housing: Black Women's Struggles against Urban Inequality*. New York: Oxford University Press, 2004.

Williamson, Vanessa, and Theda Skocpol. *The Tea Party and the Remaking of Republican Conservatism*. Oxford: Oxford University Press, 2013.

Wilson, Steven H. "*Brown* over 'Other White': Mexican Americans' Legal Arguments and Litigation Strategy in School Desegregation Lawsuits." In "Forum: Whiteness and Others: Mexican Americans and American Law," *Law and History Review* 21 (2003): 145–94.

Wilson, William Julius. *The Truly Disadvantaged: The Inner City, the Underclass, and Public Policy*. Chicago: University of Chicago Press, 1987.

Winter, Stephen L. "The Metaphor of Standing and the Problem of Self-Governance." *Stanford Law Review* 40 (July 1988): 1371–1516.

Woodson, Carter G. *The Education of the Negro Prior to 1861: A History of the Education of the Colored People of the United States from the Beginning of Slavery to the Civil War*. 1915. Lexington, KY: CreateSpace, 2014.

———. *The Mis-education of the Negro*. 1933. New York: Tribeca Books, 2013.

Zelizer, Julian. *Taxing America: Wilbur D. Mills, Congress, and the State, 1945–1975*. Cambridge: Cambridge University Press, 1998.

Index

Johns, Barbara Rose, 91
Johnson, Lyndon B., 103, 106, 109, 116
Judicial pronouncements, power of, 4

Kagan, Elena, 168
Kasich, John, 171
Kennedy, John F., 102
Kentucky, 16–17, 30, 39, 50, 51–53, 68, 102, 170; legislature, 52
Korematsu v. U.S., 81
Kozol, Jonathan, 170

La Raza, 147–48
Lautier, Louis, 92, 102
Legal consciousness, 18; of citizenship, 176; of "right to education," 8; of taxpayer, 4, 5, 7, 9, 10, 85, 86, 108; white, 11, 107, 175
Lewis v. Henley, 22
Louisiana, 5, 16, 67, 96, 137–38; legislature, 137–38
Lynch v. Alabama, 172

Majority-minority, 169
Margold Report, 70
Marketplace of citizenship, 5, 11, 86, 110
Marshall, Thurgood, 73, 76, 121–23, 130, 154–56, 165, 168
Maryland, 12, 16, 17, 19, 61, 66–68, 70–71, 77, 97, 101, 150–53; Court of Appeals, 70–71
McCleary v. State of Washington, 169–70
McCulloch v. Maryland, 68
McDowell, Tanya, 172
McGirr, Lisa, 166
McLaurin v. Oklahoma, 76
McReynolds, James, 77
Mendez v. Westminster School District, 79
Mexican American: students, 79, 145, 155–56; Legal Defense Fund, 158, 168; rights, 142; schools, 103
Michigan, 10, 16, 25, 27, 90
Middle class, 3; African American, 63, 121; white, 7, 100

Milliken v. Bradley, 160–65, 170
Mississippi, 16, 19, 32, 35, 49–51, 59, 68, 97–98, 106, 113, 123–25; Supreme Court, 32, 35, 49–51
Missouri, 10, 12, 69, 71–73, 88, 141; Supreme Court, 72; University of, 71
Missouri ex rel. Gaines, 12, 70–77
Motley, Constance Baker, 164
Moton High School, 91–92
Murray, Donald, 70–71
Murray v. Maryland, 12, 71

NAACP, 47, 50, 84, 102, 104, 139, 175; briefs, 119, 147, 156; educational litigation, 57–79; Legal Defense Fund, 10, 11, 164; letters to, 56, 60, 62, 66, 70, 175
Navajo reservation, 158
New Deal, 5, 6, 8
New Jersey, 10, 101, 117, 133, 139
New Mexico, 158–59
New York, 10, 16, 27, 57, 70, 101, 117, 120, 139–41; Supreme Court, 139
New York Times, 1, 132, 141
Nixon, Richard, 9, 115, 123
North Carolina, 16–17, 19, 31, 44, 50, 60, 66, 97, 99–100, 125, 135–36, 167; Supreme Court, 135–36

O'Connor, Sandra Day, 167
Ohio, 28–29, 63, 124, 171; Supreme Court, 28
Oklahoma, 50–51, 53–56, 68, 74–76, 83, 99, 111, 125; Constitution, 74; Criminal Court of Appeals, 111; Legislature, 76; Supreme Court, 54–55; University of, 74
One drop rule, 29, 42–43, 153
Oregon, 60, 167

Paiute Shoshone, 45–46
Perce Bill, 19
Peterson, Gladys Tignor, 51
Piper v. Big Pine, 45–47